SHORT COURSE SERIES

WORLD TRADE PRESS®

Professional Books for International Trade

International Trade Documentation

The documents of exporting, importing, transportation and banking

Edward G. Hinkelman

with contributions by:

Gilbert Mansergh

(50 country document requirements)

World Trade Press
1450 Grant Avenue, Suite 204
Novato, California 94945 USA
Tel: (415) 898-1124
Fax: (415) 898-1080
USA Order Line: 800-833-8586
Email: sales@worldpress.com
http://www.worldtradepress.com
http://www.globalroadwarrior.com

A Short Course in International Trade Documentation
By Edward G. Hinkelman
Cover Design: Ronald A. Blodgett
Text Design: Seventeenth Street Studios, Oakland, California USA

Copyright Notice
© Copyright 2002 by Edward G. Hinkelman. All Rights Reserved.
All rights reserved under International and Pan-American Copyright Conventions. No part of this book may be reproduced in any form or by any means, electronic or mechanical, including photocopying, without the express written permission of the publisher. All inquiries should be addressed to World Trade Press at the address above.

Disclaimer
This publication is designed to provide general information concerning aspects of international trade. It is sold with the understanding that the publisher is not engaged in rendering legal or any other professional services. If legal advice or other expert assistance is required, the services of a competent professional person or organization should be sought.

Library of Congress Cataloging-in-Publication Data
Hinkelman, Edward G., 1947–
A short course in international trade documentation: the key documents of exporting, importing, transportation and banking / Edward G. Hinkelman with Gilbert Mansergh.
p. cm. -- (Short Course in International Trade Series)
Includes bibliographic references.
ISBN 1-885073-59-3 (alk. paper)
1. International trade. 2. Banks and banking, International.
I. Title: International trade documentation. II. Mansergh, Gilbert.
III. Title. IV. Series.
HF1379 .H56 2001
382'.068--dc21

2001046653
Printed in the United States of America

INTRODUCTION

International trade documents are nearly as old as civilization itself. Scientists excavating the ruins of the ancient Sumerian city of Ur discovered that traders from this prosperous center of the fertile Tigris and Euphrates basin were regularly exchanging food and woven baskets for spices, precious stones and utensils made of copper with the seaport trading center of Dilmun and other parts of the ancient world. They also found thousands of 5000-year-old clay tablets where scribes recorded cuneiform versions of invoices, bills of lading, receipts for duty/tariff payments and even government-backed letters of credit. The players in these ancient transactions are very familiar:

- An importer (buyer) in Ur who wants 100 copper kettles.

- An exporter (seller) in Dilmun who is willing to trade 100 kettles for 500 woven baskets.

- An international shipping company willing to transport 500 baskets to Dilmun and 100 kettles back to Ur for a fee (20 kettles or 100 baskets).

- The export customs officer (export tax authority) charging a duty (5 kettles or 25 baskets) for goods shipped out of Dilmun.

- The import customs officer (import tax authority) charging a duty (5 kettles or 25 baskets) for any goods shipped into Ur for resale.

The clay records reveal that it only took a few hundred years for additional parties to be added to the transaction. Also, Sumerian coins, originally made from sea shells, began to be made from copper and silver and this promoted their use in international trade.

- With coins came bankers and soon, special clay "envelopes" were made to protect the clay banking documents that accompanied a shipment.

- To offer protection against loss, insurance companies began to divide a shipment among several different vessels. Clay "insurance policies" record these transactions.

- Since Sumeria was a region based upon law, attorneys became involved devising international sales contracts and those too were recorded on clay tablets.

Today, the number of individuals and entities involved in international trade has grown, and while some would say that trade has become more complex, othes maintain that it is easier, but we'll leave that question for the historians.

In this book we introduce all of the present-day players and explain the documents they generate, secure or require as part of modern international business transactions.

Edward G. Hinkelman
San Rafael, California

TABLE OF CONTENTS

CHAPTER 1

Introduction to Trade Documentation

DOCUMENTATION LIES AT THE HEART of all international trade transactions. It provides buyers and sellers with an accounting record; shipping and/or logistics firms with instructions of what to do with freight; countries of export and import with regulatory compliance, census and taxation information; and banks with instructions and accounting tools for collecting and disbursing payments. This book provides the reader with an explanation of the types of international trade documentation, examples of the most common documents, documentation requirements for the top 50 trading nations, checklists, a glossary, and a resource list. This text, however, is not exhaustive. By various estimates there are between 10,000 and 100,000 documents used in all facets of international trade for all nations on earth. The explanations and examples contained in this book are intended to give the reader sufficient familiarity and understanding of the vast majority of international trade documentation so as to ease the cross-border trading process in all countries of the world.

What is a Document?

The word "document" comes from the Latin *documentum* meaning official paper. The word also carries meanings of "proof" and "evidence." Therefore, a document is an official paper that serves as proof or evidence of something.

In the context of international trade, a document can serve many purposes including: proof of ownership of a shipment (the negotiable bill of lading), evidence of the particulars of a sale (the commercial invoice), proof or evidence of the country of origin of goods (the certificate of origin), proof of insurance coverage (the insurance certificate or document), and reassurance of the quality or quantity of goods in a shipment (the inspection certificate).

Recently, the definition of document as "official paper" has been expanded to include non-paper proof or evidence, such as faxes and pure electronic transmissions that are never actually printed.

Different forms of the term have distinct meanings in international trade:

- "Document" means an individual document or form.

- "The documents" or "the document package" means a grouping of individual documents that are required for the export or import of a particular shipment of goods or for a particular banking transaction.

- "Documentary" means that documents form the basis for concluding some agreed upon action or requirement between the parties to a transaction. In banking, for example, a "documentary credit" is the formal term for "letter of credit" because the buyer, seller and banks rely upon documentary evidence to show that an agreement has been fully performed before effecting payment.

The Purpose of Documents in International Trade

Documents serve a key role to each party involved in international trade.

- TO THE EXPORTER Documents provide an accounting record of a transaction, a receipt for goods shipped, the means for export clearance of the goods, as well as information and instructions to the many individuals, companies and governmental agencies who transport, handle, or inspect the shipment.

- TO THE IMPORTER Documents provide an accounting record of a transaction, assurances that the goods ordered are the goods shipped, and the means for clearing goods through customs at the country of destination.

- TO THE SHIPPING COMPANY AND FREIGHT FORWARDER Documents provide an accounting record of a transaction, instructions on where and how to ship the goods, and a statement giving instructions for handling the shipment.

- TO THE BANKS Documents provide instructions and accounting tools for collecting and disbursing payments.

- TO THE INSURER Documents provide a means of evaluating risks, valuing a shipment and tracing the point of loss in a coverage claim.

- TO THE COUNTRY OF EXPORT AND ITS REGULATORY AGENCIES Documents provide necessary proof of the right to export, statistical and census information regarding the goods exported, and an accounting tool for assessing duties and fees.

- TO THE COUNTRY OF IMPORT AND ITS REGULATORY AGENCIES Documents provide proof of the right to import, statistical and census information regarding the goods imported, evidence that the goods imported will not harm the health and safety of its citizens, and an accounting tool for assessing duties and fees.

- TO ALL OF THE ABOVE Documents provide proof of ownership of goods at any time and place throughout the transaction.

Categories of Documents Used in International Trade

There are several broad categories of documents used in international trade. A category indicates either that the documents are issued by a particular group (e.g. a shipping or logistics company) or are required by a particular entity (e.g. a bank or customs authority). In many cases, documents issued by one entity (e.g. the bill of lading issued by a shipping or logistics company) may be required by more than one entity (e.g. the importer, the country of import customs authority, etc.). In other cases, a single entity may both issue documentation as well as require documentation from other entities (e.g. banks issue documents related to letters of credit, but may require a number of specific documents from both the importer and exporter).

The following is a brief summary of the broad categories of international trade documentation. Each will be treated in detail in the chapters that follow.

TRANSACTION DOCUMENTS

These are the documents the buyer and seller generate to form the basis of their agreement to sell and purchase specific goods under specific terms and conditions. The quantity and formality of this type of documentation is greatly influenced by the nature of the relationship of the buyer and seller as well as the goods sold.

■ Transaction documents include the letter of inquiry, request for proposal (RFP), proposal, letter of intent, purchase order, contract of sale, pro-forma invoice, and commercial invoice.

Not all transactions require each of these documents. In the most simple transactions, the buyer and seller might speak by telephone and agree on terms, after which the seller simply prepares a commercial invoice.

EXPORT DOCUMENTS

These are the documents required by the export authority of a country. The quantity and formality of this type of documentation is greatly influenced by the requirements of the country of export and the nature of the goods being exported.

■ Export documents may include export licenses and permits, a commercial invoice, bill of lading, certificate of origin, export declaration, and inspection certificate(s). In certain countries an insurance certificate, foreign exchange documentation and a bank draft may be required.

Not all transactions require each of these documents. In even the most simple transactions, however, a commercial invoice, bill of lading, and simple export declaration are usually required.

TRANSPORT (SHIPPING) DOCUMENTS

These are the documents issued by the shipping line, airline, railroad, barge operator, international trucking company, freight-forwarder or logistics company as a receipt and contract for carriage of the goods to the stated destination. These organizations also issue insurance and inspection certificate(s).

■ The key document in international shipping is the bill of lading in one of its many forms.

NOTE: All international transactions involving the transport of goods require some form of bill of lading.

IMPORT DOCUMENTS

These are the documents required by the import (customs) authority of a country. The quantity and formality of this type of documentation is greatly influenced by the requirements of the country of import and the nature of the goods being imported.

■ Import documents generally include import licenses and permits, a commercial invoice, bill of lading, certificate of origin, import declaration, and inspection certificate(s). In certain countries a consular invoice, insurance certificate, foreign exchange documentation and a bank draft may be required.

Not all transactions require each of these documents. In even the most simple transactions, however, a commercial invoice, bill of lading, certificate of origin, and import declaration are usually required.

BANKING DOCUMENTS

These are the documents required by the banks participating in an international transaction, especially through a documentary letter of credit or documentary collection procedure. The quantity and formality of this type of documentation is greatly influenced by the requirements of the exporter and importer.

■ Banking documents include the application for letter of credit or documentary collection, collection order, draft or acceptance, order to open credit, documentary credit (numerous types), credit advice, order amendment, amendment notification, and order of assignment. Related documents include those made part of a document package for the importer for the import clearance of the goods in the country of destination.

Not all transactions require each of these documents. In many international transactions, the banks are only involved in the cashing of a check for the exporter/seller or the forwarding of a bank wire from the importer/buyer.

SPECIALIZED DOCUMENTS

These are documents required for export or import based on special requirements related to the country of export or import or the specialized nature of the goods being traded.

■ Specialized documents include export certifications for natural resource commodities; import permits for strategic goods such as arms, ammunition and radioactive materials; health certificate(s) for animals; phytosanitary certificate(s) for foodstuffs; and forms related to quotas.

Documentation related to specialized goods and trade sensitive countries provides the greatest challenge to traders. On the other hand, if you are dealing in non-sensitive commodities, this area will likely never become an issue.

Notes on Document Categories

1. There is a great deal of overlap from one category to another. This is because many of the same documents are required for business accounting, exporting, importing, transport, and banking.
2. Because several steps of the trade process require the same documentation (such as the bill of lading or commercial invoice), documents are commonly issued in a number of copies, often with a number of "original" copies.

Who Issues and Requires Documentation?

All parties to an international transaction either issue or require documentation. The type of documentation issued or required depends upon the nature of the transaction, the goods/services involved, the countries of export and import, and the involvement of specialized parties such as banks.

See "Introducing the Parties to International Trade Documentation" starting on page 15.

The Key Documents of International Trade

In the opening paragraph of this chapter is the statement that there are between 10,000 and 100,000 documents used in international trade throughout the world. Now for the good news: the vast majority of all international transactions are based on only five documents. These are:

1. The COMMERCIAL INVOICE (issued by the exporter/seller)
   This is the key transaction or accounting document. It identifies the seller and buyer, gives identifying numbers such as invoice number, date and shipping date, identifies the mode of transport, delivery and payment terms, and gives a complete list and description of the goods or services being sold including quantities, prices and discounts.

2. The BILL OF LADING (issued by the shipping line or carrier of the goods)
   This is the key transportation document. It is issued by a carrier (such as a shipping line or airline) to a shipper (the exporter or seller), signed by the captain, agent, or owner of a vessel and furnishes written evidence of the receipt of the goods (cargo), the conditions on which transportation is made (contract of carriage), and the engagement to deliver goods at the prescribed port of destination to the lawful holder of the bill of lading. A bill of lading is, therefore, both a receipt for merchandise and a contract to deliver it as freight. It can also serve as the title document, in which case whoever holds the document can claim possession of the goods.

3. The CERTIFICATE OF ORIGIN (issued by the exporter/seller, local exporting country chamber of commerce or other authorizing agency)
   This document establishes the country of origin of the goods shipped. The importer must typically submit it to the import authority of the country of import.

4. The EXPORT DECLARATION (issued by the exporter/seller)
   This is the formal statement by the exporter to the export authority identifying the seller, buyer, goods shipped, date of issuance, country of origin and country of final destination of the goods, quantity and description of the goods, and shipping details. This is used by the country of export to control exports, compile trade statistics and assess fees.

5. The IMPORT DECLARATION (prepared by the importer/buyer or a customs broker acting as agent for the importer)
   This is the formal statement by the importer to the import authority identifying the seller, buyer, goods shipped, date of issuance, country of origin and country of final destination of the goods, quantity and description of the goods, and shipping details. This is used by the country of import to control imports, compile trade statistics and assess duties.

Your Professional Partners

We highly recommend that you develop relationships with your "professional partners." These include your attorney (for sales/purchase contracts), your shipping line, freight forwarder or logistics company (for bills of lading, insurance documents, etc.), your banker (for letters of credit and other payment issues), and finally, your counterpart in the sale/purchase of the goods.

CHAPTER 2

Issues Concerning Trade Documentation

WITH SO MANY DOCUMENTS, issuers of documents, documentary requirements, different countries, different languages, unique laws, and the involvement of money, there are bound to be a number of issues that relate to the content, form, and presentation of documentation in international trade. Most of these can be described in broad categories, others are very specific and relate only to specialized transactions.

Fortunately, few traders will be faced with all the issues described in this chapter. However, being an informed trader will have a significant impact upon your ability to deal with issues as they come up.

RECOMMENDATION: Read this chapter now and then again after reading the whole book. Some concepts cannot be fully integrated without reading the chapters that follow.

Country of Export Document Requirements

Most countries require at least basic documentation for all export transactions. For simple transactions with non-regulated commodities and goods, this may only include a commercial invoice, bill of lading and export declaration.

At the other extreme, extensive documentary requirements may be required for certain goods including export licenses, export permits, authorization from other governmental agencies, and pre-shipment inspections. In extreme cases, export approval may require a vote of the country's national legislature or executive power. In certain countries, proof of pre-shipment payment or foreign exchange documentation may also be required.

EXCEPTION: Export from and import to member nations of a regional trade pact (such as the European Union) may require little or no documentation whatsoever.

See "Introducing the Export Authority" on page 21.

Country of Import Document Requirements

Most countries require at least basic documentation for all import transactions. For simple transactions with non-regulated commodities and goods from non-regulated countries of export, this may only include a commercial invoice, bill of lading and import declaration.

At the other extreme, extensive documentary requirements for the import of certain goods may require import licenses, import permits, authorization from other governmental agencies, and pre-shipment inspections. In certain countries, extensive regulations concerning payment in hard currencies add an additional set of restrictions and require extra documentation.

Some countries restrict imports by imposing difficult import documentation requirements with the view of protecting domestic producers. Such restrictions are non-tariff barriers to trade and are the subject of great controversy.

EXCEPTION: Export from and import to member nations of a regional trade pact (such as the European Union) may require little or no documentation whatsoever.

See "Introducing the Import Authority/Customs" on page 22.

Trade Relationship of the Countries of Import and Export

The nature of the trading relationship between the country of export and country of import can have a significant impact upon export/import requirements, tariffs and duties, as well as the number and type of documents required.

Most countries have a four-tier system of trade relationships with other nations. Each tier represents a different level of requirements regarding the ease of trade, amount of duties charged and documentation required.

TIER 1: SPECIAL TRADE STATUS

At tier one, two or more nations have entered into a special trade relationship. Examples include the European Union (EU), NAFTA (North American Free Trade Agreement), and Mercosur (Southern Common Market).

Nations that are a party to such an agreement pledge to remove most or all tariff and non-tariff barriers to trade. In the case of the EU, virtually all barriers have been removed. NAFTA is an example where tariff and documentation requirements are being gradually reduced, but not entirely eliminated.

TIER 2: NORMAL TRADE RELATIONS (FORMERLY MOST FAVORED NATION)

Normal trade relations are those between countries that are friendly but not part of a Regional Trade Agreement. This includes the vast majority of trading relationships in the world. Non-excessive trade requirements, tariffs and documentation requirements are the norm. Examples include the trading relationships between the USA and France or between Indonesia and Italy.

TIER 3: RESTRICTED TRADE RELATIONS

In restricted or limited trade relations, trade with a subject nation is permitted, but significant restrictions apply. Export or import of certain listed goods is restricted, quantities may be limited, high import duties or tariffs apply, and stringent documentation requirements exist.

An example of this was the trading relationship between the USA and China before the USA granted China Most Favored Nation (now called Normal Trade Relations) status. One could import goods to the USA from China, but the duty rates were extremely high and served to restrict trade.

TIER 4: EMBARGO

In this situation, all trade with the subject country is banned. An embargo can be unilateral (such as the USA's 30 year embargo of Cuba), or multi-lateral (such as the UN's sanctions of Iraq as a result of events related to the Gulf War of 1991).

Terms of Sale

The terms of sale establish the obligations of the buyer and the seller with respect to the place of delivery, who bears the cost of delivery, and who bears the risk of loss or damage to the goods while in transit. The terms of sale also have an impact upon who is responsible for providing documentation.

At one extreme, the seller may be required only to place the goods at the disposal of the buyer at the manufacturing facility. The buyer is responsible for picking up the goods, export formalities, transportation, import formalities and final delivery to his place of business in the country of destination. In this case, the seller may have no obligation to provide documentation other than a commercial invoice. The buyer, however, generally asks the seller to provide specific documentation to help in export and import formalities. This is generally handled by a documentation requirements clause in the sales contract or letter of credit.

At the other extreme, the seller may be required to deliver the goods to the buyer at the buyer's place of business in the destination country. In this case, the seller is responsible for providing and presenting all documentation required for export, transportation, insurance, and import formalities.

INCOTERMS 2000

The ICC (International Chamber of Commerce) in Paris developed INCOTERMS (INternational COmmercial TERMS), a set of uniform rules for the interpretation of international commercial terms defining the costs, risks, and obligations of buyers and sellers. First published in 1936, these rules have been periodically revised to account for changing modes of transport and document delivery. The current version is INCOTERMS 2000.

For an illustrated guide (29 pages) to the 13 Incoterms 2000 we recommend the *Dictionary of International Trade* (4th edition or later) also by World Trade Press.

Method of Payment

When the buyer and seller agree to prepayment or credit terms, banks are not involved other than with the cashing of a payment check, the sending of a bank wire or handling a credit card payment. However, with a documentary credit or documentary collection, bank involvement and documentation can be significant:

- **DOCUMENTARY LETTER OF CREDIT** In this case the buyer applies to the bank for the issuance of a letter of credit naming the seller as beneficiary. The buyer also lists specific documentation the seller must present as a requirement of getting paid. The documents listed are those required for import formalities as well as additional documents that might include inspection and insurance certificates.

- **DOCUMENTARY COLLECTIONS** In this case the seller instructs the bank to issue a collection order for an individual shipment to the buyer. The seller presents to the bank the documentation the buyer requires for the importation of the goods. The seller's bank transfers these documents to the buyer's bank which then requires payment or a promise of payment (according to the terms of the collection) from the buyer in exchange for the documents.

NOTE: As with all matters involving money and payments, the form and content of these documents is of great importance to all parties to the transaction. Subtle differences between forms and subtle changes in wording can tip the balance between a successful and an unsuccessful transaction.

See "Banking Documents" starting on page 76..

The Nature of the Goods Traded

Document requirements for export and import are very closely tied to the level of regulation of the goods by either the country of export or the country of import. The simple rule: each additional regulation adds an additional document that must be obtained from or presented to a governmental agency. In some cases, one document may be required for export from the country of origin while a different document is required for import to the country of destination.

Regulated goods fall into a number of categories:

RESTRICTED GOODS

Broadly, restricted goods are those that pose or have the potential of posing economic, health, environmental, safety, cultural or moral risk to the citizens of the country of export or import.

Examples include natural resource commodities, drugs, food, alcohol, animals, motor vehicles, medical devices, toys, chemicals, cultural relics, and morally or politically questionable literature. Another category includes products of threatened species of plants and animals (especially those covered by international treaty).

Documentation requirements include licenses, permits, sanitary certificates, and inspection certificates. These documents generally originate from or are submitted to governmental agencies with specific regulatory powers.

PROHIBITED GOODS

These include goods that are completely illegal to export either from the country of origin or to import to the country of destination. Note that some goods may be legal to export but illegal to import. Usually, these are goods that pose significant and demonstrated economic, health, environmental, safety, cultural or moral risk to the citizens of the country of import.

Examples include: certain natural resource commodities; drugs, animals, insects, food products and agricultural products; medical devices that have not met the standards of the country of import; toys, cultural relics (especially those covered by international treaty) and morally questionable literature; and agricultural products originating from an area infested with pests or plant or animal diseases.

STRATEGIC GOODS

These products and commodities relate to a country's security interests and may be heavily regulated, restricted, or prohibited.

Examples include arms and armaments, radioactive materials, high technology (including hardware and software), biological vectors, and aerospace products.

Documentation requirements include licenses, permits and inspection certificates and these originate from governmental agencies with specific regulatory powers.

Quotas are quantitative limits placed upon the importation of goods from all countries or specific countries. They are generally placed on manufactured goods that threaten a country's domestic industry and are a highly politicized issue. Examples of goods often subject to quotas include steel, automobiles, textiles, and textile products.

Documentation requirements include licenses, permits, and visas. A visa is an endorsement in the form of a country of export stamp on an invoice or export control license. Visas are a self-imposed restriction on exports to a particular country. Visa stamps are bought and sold as they guarantee the ability to export and then import certain products to the destination country.

Relationship Between the Exporter and the Importer

The relationship of the parties to a transaction make documentation either more or less complex. Parties who know each other well are more likely to trade on an open account basis. This eliminates the need for letters of credit or documentary collections procedures that involve banks. Also, with trust, the buyer is less likely to require inspection certificates. Examples include businesses that have long and successful trading histories, or companies that are owned by the same parent company. On the other hand, if the parties have not had previous dealings with each other, or are fearful of doing business with each other, one can expect intense banking and inspection requirements and documentation.

NOTE: Regardless of their relationship, both the exporter and importer will be required to fulfill country of export and country of import documentation requirements.

Distance and Geography

The greater the distance and the more varied the geography between the buyer and the seller, the greater the likelihood that multiple modes of transport will be required to get a shipment to its final destination.

This can result in either a shipment made in distinct and discreet stages with separate documentation required for each stage of the journey, or a combined multi-modal shipment made under a single set of documentation. However, even in the latter case, documentation and instructions tend to be more involved.

Originals vs. Copies

There are two broad issues that relate to "originals" in international trade documentation: 1) When are originals required?, and 2) What is an original?

WHEN ARE ORIGINALS REQUIRED?

Certain steps in the export and import process require the presentation of "original" documents. Export and import authorities, banks, government agencies and buyers often specify that they receive original documents.

The most important example of this is the "negotiable bill of lading." Along with the commercial invoice, this is one of the key documents of international trade. It may be even more important than an invoice when it is the "title document," possession of which is evidence of ownership of the particular shipment. Clearly, a "copy" of this document is not the same as the original.

In general, originals, of all specified documents should be included in the "document package" presented to the buyer, banks, or transport company, unless copies are requested or allowed.

NOTE: The original negotiable bill of lading should only be handed over when the seller is prepared to pass title to the shipment to the company receiving the document.

WHAT IS AN ORIGINAL?

Since several "originals" may be required, this can be an issue of some confusion. The general rule is that copies made on a copier or computer printer or even carbon copies can be an "original" provided they have been marked "ORIGINAL" and signed, in ink (blue ink is preferred) by the authorized individual and any required stamps or seals also appear.

The expanded use of electronic signatures makes this issue even more pressing as a computer printed document with an electronic signature can now be an original. The general rule is that copies marked "ORIGINAL" are accepted so long as the parties to the transaction agree.

BANKING CONSIDERATIONS

Unless otherwise noted in a letter of credit, banks are authorized to accept documents as originals, even if they were produced or appear to have been produced on a copy machine, by a computerized system, or by carbon copy, provided they have the notation "ORIGINAL" and are, when necessary, signed.

FAXED DOCUMENTS

In the 1980s the proliferation of fax machines created an interesting issue: Were documents received by fax considered "original" documents? "Fax" is an abbreviation of facsimile, which means exact copy. However, an exact copy is not an original. Worldwide trade practices needed to keep up with the times, and modern practice accepts that facsimiles can be used, at least for some documentation, so long as both parties to the transaction agree that it can be so used.

ELECTRONIC DOCUMENTS

In the 1980s and 1990s the proliferation of computers and EDI (Electronic Data Interchange) created a new question: Can an electronic document be "official" or "original"? In theory, if the document is in the computer system, there may never actually be a "hard copy." In most cases this has been answered, yes, so long as the parties to the transaction agree.

Ambiguity as to Issuers and Authentication of Documents

Most documents in international sales transactions are generated or obtained by the exporter in the country of export. Although this is a burden, it is considered a necessary part of providing good service to the buyer. The buyer assists in the process by specifying exactly what documents as well as what certifications or authorizations are required. The buyer specifies these needs in the context of the sales contract, letter of credit or even a letter sent by fax or e-mail.

Two types of problems arise, however, when the importer does not specify the requirements in sufficient detail. They are:

ISSUERS OF DOCUMENTS

If the importer/buyer does not name a specific issuer of a document, or if the issuer is referred to by such terms as "first class," "well-known," "qualified," "independent," "official," "competent," or "local" (especially a certificate of origin or an inspection certificate), the exporter/seller is essentially being asked to make its own decision as to who should issue the document.

In the case of documentary letters of credit, banks are authorized to accept whatever documents are presented, provided that the documents appear on their face to be in compliance with the terms of the credit and were not issued by the seller.

The import authority in the buyer's country of destination, however, may not accept a certificate of origin or an inspection certificate (such as a sanitary certificate) unless it was issued by a specific authority in the country of origin.

AUTHENTICATION OF DOCUMENTS

The importer/buyer may state that a document be "certified," "notarized," or "endorsed." What is meant by these terms varies considerably from country to country and an exporter, in good faith, may try to comply with the requirements for a specific document yet end up with a seal or signature that is unacceptable to the importer or import authority.

Once again, in documentary letter of credit transactions, banks are authorized to accept documents as presented so long as the authentication appears to be consistent with the requirements of the credit and other stipulated documents.

To avoid problems, the buyer should know what documents are required, what authentication is required, and whether a specific issuer is required. These requirements should be communicated to the seller in list form in the sales contract or in the documentary letter of credit.

Document Dates

There are a number of issues that revolve around document dates. Examples:

- What if a contract states that delivery to the shipping line must be made by February 15th and the bill of lading is dated February 16th?

- What if the seller is responsible for providing insurance coverage for a shipment, the date of the bill of lading is February 16th, but the insurance certificate establishes the start date of insurance as February 20th?

- What if a document has been dated 06/07/01? In the USA this means June 7, 2001. In Europe it means 6 July 2001.

In many cases exporters don't pay attention to the written and firm requirements of sales contracts and letters of credit and do a sloppy job of export documentation. Keep in mind that customs authorities and regulatory agencies are known to stick to the rules when traders present documents with even the slightest irregularities. The best approach is to be extremely conscious of all issues related to dates in sales contracts and letters of credit.

NOTE: Unless otherwise noted in a letter of credit, banks are authorized to accept documents dated prior to the issuance date of the credit, so long as all other terms of the credit have been satisfied.

Signatures and Seals

Most every form in existence has a signature line at the bottom and many documents in international trade need a signature to be valid. A signature is considered to be the formal certification by the person signing that the information in the form is true, or that they agree to be bound by the terms and conditions listed in the document.

A signature, often in blue ink to differentiate it from the black type of most documents and copies of documents, is also used in conjunction with the word "ORIGINAL" to indicate that a copy is to be considered an original copy.

In some instances, a company "seal" is used in addition to a signature to indicate that the company is an existing entity with authority to transact business.

With the advent of fax machines, electronic documents, and the Internet, the question of what constitutes a valid signature has become an issue; one that has not been completely resolved. Generally speaking, the parties to a transaction can agree upon what constitutes a valid signature. For example, many firms accept a faxed contract or inspection certificate as valid, while others maintain that only the actual hand-signed original is valid. Also, certain documents, such as the negotiable bill of lading must still be in its original hand signed form to be valid.

NOTE: Unless otherwise instructed, banks in letter of credit and documentary collection payment situations are authorized to accept documents that have been signed by facsimile, perforated signature, stamp, symbol, or other mechanical or electronic method.

Consistency Among Documents

The largest single issue in the preparation, presentation, and verification of documentation by sellers, buyers, and banks is consistency among documents.

EXAMPLE: In examining the documentation for a letter of credit transaction involving the sale of five pieces of machinery, the buyer noticed that the commercial invoice listed the net weight as 12,140 kilograms and the gross weight as 12,860 kilograms. The bill of lading, however, listed the gross weight as 9,612 kilograms.

What happened to the other 3,248 kilograms? Did the seller make a mistake in preparing the invoice? Did the shipping company make a mistake in preparing the bill of lading? Did the seller forget to ship one or more pieces of machinery? Did the shipping company misplace some machinery? Did someone steal the machinery?

The seller should have noticed the inconsistency before forwarding the documents to the advising bank, which should have noticed the inconsistency before forwarding the documents to the issuing bank, which should have noticed the inconsistency before forwarding the documents to the buyer. The buyer will certainly reject this documentation and withhold payment until account is made for the missing 3,248 kilograms.

Other consistency problems:

■ Incorrect names and addresses can divert a shipment to the wrong party or hold up a shipment until information is verified.

■ Different quantities of goods listed on invoices, packing lists and other documents add an element of uncertainty in the eyes of the importer, banks and authorities.

■ Errors in documents or failure to follow instructions in a documentary letter of credit can result in a refusal of payment by the bank or by the buyer.

■ Inconsistencies in paperwork are an automatic red flag to customs officers who become much more likely to order time consuming and costly inspections.

As each document is prepared, presented and verified, it should agree in all particulars with the information included in the contract of sale, the commercial invoice, the bill of lading and the documentary letter of credit (if used).

See "General Consistency Checklist" on page 174.

Document language

Some countries of import may require that all import documentation be in the language of that country. This can include the commercial invoice and other documents that must be translated before they will be accepted.

Securing Documentation

An international trader may come to a complete understanding of the documentation required for a transaction, but a complete standstill in trying to secure it in a timely manner or at all. This can be the result of a government's mindless bureaucracy, purposeful bureaucracy (as a non-tariff barrier to trade) or corruption at either low or high levels. Dealing with this issue in detail is not within the scope of this publication.

Generally...

Regretfully, the words "generally," "usually," and "often" appear many times in this book. International trade documentation is a business with many complicating factors and the particulars of each transaction determine document requirements.

The editorial format throughout this book is to describe the basic transaction first and then list the exceptions or complicating factors.

A complete understanding of international trade documentation, and its rules and exceptions, will come only from a combination of study and practice.

CHAPTER 3

Introducing the Parties to International Trade Documentation

AT THE CORE OF EVERY BUSINESS TRANSACTION is the buyer and the seller. However, in international transactions, a number of other individuals, organization and entities enter the picture as key players. Each party may have a minor or major role depending upon the goods or services being bought or sold, the countries of import or export, and the method of payment. Also, each party to the transaction may either issue, secure or require documentation.

In this chapter we introduce the parties to international transactions and describe their roles in either issuing or requiring documentation. Thankfully, few international transactions involve all the parties listed. A more exhaustive description of each party follows the list.

The reader will note some similarities in content between this chapter and successive chapters on Export, Import, and Banking Documentation. The purpose of each chapter is to describe documentation from a different perspective and replication is necessary. For example, the exporter may issue or secure one set of documents for export (see the Export Documentation chapter), but may have additional responsibilities to issue and secure other documents for the importer/buyer (see Introducing the Exporter in this chapter).

Who Issues/Secures/Requires Documentation?

- THE EXPORTER/SELLER
- THE IMPORTER/BUYER
- THE COUNTRY OF EXPORT (EXPORT AUTHORITY)
- THE COUNTRY OF IMPORT (IMPORT AUTHORITY)
- THE FREIGHT FORWARDER/LOGISTICS COMPANY
- THE CUSTOMS BROKER
- THE FREIGHT CARRIER
  (SHIPPING LINE, AIRLINE, RAILROAD, BARGE LINE, COURIER)
- THE GOVERNMENT REGULATORY AGENCY
- THE INTERNATIONAL BANKS
- THE INSURANCE COMPANY
- THE ATTORNEY
- THE INSPECTION SERVICE
- THE NOTARY PUBLIC
- THE CHAMBER OF COMMERCE
- THE CONSULAR OFFICE

Introducing the Exporter/Seller

BUSINESS/JOB DESCRIPTION

The exporter/seller is an individual or company engaged in the business of manufacturing, selling, or brokering raw materials, component parts, finished goods or services to the importer/buyer for manufacture, assembly, resale or direct consumption.

DOCUMENTARY RESPONSIBILITIES

The agreed upon terms of sale between the buyer and seller will have a direct effect upon the exporter's documentary responsibilities. In most transactions the exporter/seller is responsible for the documentation required for export clearance and the export clearance itself. In addition, the exporter generally assumes the responsibility of issuing and/or securing various documents at the request of the importer/buyer. These are the documents needed by the importer for import clearance in the country of destination.

NOTE: The primary responsibility for preparing and securing documentation falls to the exporter/seller.

DOCUMENTS ISSUED/SECURED/PRESENTED BY THE EXPORTER/SELLER

Below is a list of document categories and documents the exporter may issue, secure from third parties, present to the export authorities, present to the importer/buyer, or present to the bank in a documentary collection or letter of credit transaction.

In certain terms of sale (e.g., DDU (Delivered Duty Unpaid) and DDP (Delivered Duty Paid) terms) the exporter may be responsible for both export and import clearance of the goods. In this summary, however, it is assumed that the exporter is responsible for export documentation and export clearance only. Not all the documents listed below are required in all transactions. Further explanation and samples of documents are provided in the document category chapters that follow.

■ TRANSACTION DOCUMENTS — THE EXPORTER/SELLER. . .

▪ Issues a PROPOSAL, BID or QUOTATION in response to an RFP (REQUEST FOR PROPOSAL) or RFQ (REQUEST FOR QUOTATION) from the importer/buyer.

▪ Negotiates and issues (usually with the assistance of an attorney) a CONTRACT FOR THE SALE OF GOODS.

▪ Issues a PRO-FORMA INVOICE at the request of the importer.

▪ Issues a COMMERCIAL INVOICE.

■ EXPORT DOCUMENTS — THE EXPORTER/SELLER. . .

▪ Secures an EXPORT LICENSE and/or EXPORT PERMIT from the export authority (as required).

- Issues an EXPORT DECLARATION for the export authority.
  This includes DESTINATION CONTROL and ULTIMATE CONSIGNEE statements.

- Issues or secures an INSPECTION CERTIFICATE as required by the export authority.

■ TRANSPORT AND INSURANCE DOCUMENTS — THE EXPORTER/SELLER. . .

- Prepares a PACKING LIST for use by the shipping company, export and import authorities, and importer/buyer.

- Assists in the preparation and issuance of a BILL OF LADING/AIR WAYBILL (or other form of bill of lading) for use by the shipping company, export and import authorities, importer and bank(s) (if a documentary payment procedure is used).

■ BANKING DOCUMENTS — THE EXPORTER/SELLER. . .

  If a documentary collection is used:

- Prepares a DOCUMENTARY COLLECTION ORDER for the bank.

- Submits a BANK DRAFT/BILL OF EXCHANGE to the bank for payment.

- Issues and/or secures a "document package," which includes all the documents the importer needs for importation of the goods to the country of destination, plus any requested inspection documents (e.g., for verification of quantities and quality of the merchandise shipped).

  If a documentary letter of credit is used:

- Issues and/or secures a "document package," which includes all the documents required by the importer as stated in the LETTER OF CREDIT ADVICE. These are the documents the importer needs for importation of the goods to the country of destination, plus any requested inspection documents (e.g., for verification of quantities and quality of the merchandise shipped).

- Submits a BANK DRAFT/BILL OF EXCHANGE to the bank for payment.

■ IMPORT DOCUMENTS — USUALLY AT THE REQUEST OF THE IMPORTER/ BUYER.
  THE EXPORTER/SELLER. . .

- Issues or secures a CERTIFICATE OF ORIGIN from a chamber of commerce or government authority.

- Secures a CONSULAR INVOICE from a consulate of the importer/buyer's country of final destination of the goods.

- Secures an INSURANCE POLICY or INSURANCE CERTIFICATE.

- Secures an INSPECTION CERTIFICATE (for verification of quantities, quality and other specifications of the merchandise shipped).

- Secures a PHYTOSANITARY CERTIFICATE (for import of plants and foods).

- Secures SPECIALIZED INSPECTION CERTIFICATES as required.

- Secures or issues other documents as required.

Introducing the Importer/Buyer

BUSINESS/JOB DESCRIPTION

The importer/buyer is an individual or company engaged in the business of purchasing raw materials, component parts, finished goods or services from the exporter/seller for import to a domestic market for manufacture, assembly, resale, or direct consumption.

DOCUMENTARY RESPONSIBILITIES

The agreed upon terms of sale between the buyer and seller will have a direct effect upon the exporter's documentary responsibilities. In most transactions the exporter/seller is responsible for the documentation required for export clearance and the export clearance itself while the importer/buyer is responsible for import clearance.

In order to facilitate import clearance, the importer must secure a number of documents required by the customs authorities of the country of import. Since many (but not all) of these documents are generated by the exporter or are more easily secured by the exporter in the country of export, the importer is responsible for notifying the exporter of the documents required.

NOTE: While the exporter has primary responsibility for preparing and securing customs documentation, the importer is responsible for specifying the import documentation required.

REQUESTING DOCUMENTS OF THE EXPORTER

Requesting documents of the exporter is accomplished in several ways, depending upon the type of transaction:

■ PREPAYMENT OR CREDIT TERMS In these transactions the importer/buyer simply lists the required documentation in the sales contract or in a simple letter to the exporter/seller sent by post, courier, fax or e-mail.

■ DOCUMENTARY COLLECTIONS In these transactions the importer/buyer also lists the required documentation in the sales contract or in a letter to the exporter/seller.

■ DOCUMENTARY LETTERS OF CREDIT In these transactions the importer/buyer lists the required documentation in the body of the letter of credit itself.

RECEIVING DOCUMENTS FROM THE EXPORTER

Documents come into the possession of the importer from the exporter in several ways, depending upon the type of transaction:

■ PREPAYMENT OR CREDIT TERMS In these transactions the documents may simply be sent by mail, by courier or as a document package accompanying the shipment itself.

■ DOCUMENTARY COLLECTIONS In these transactions the documents are forwarded to the importer by a bank (typically the importer's bank by way of the exporter's bank) and handed over in exchange for payment (or in some cases the promise of future payment).

■ DOCUMENTARY LETTERS OF CREDIT In these transactions the documents are forwarded to the importer by a bank (typically the importer's bank by way of the exporter's bank) and handed over as part of a document package.

DOCUMENTS ISSUED OR REQUESTED BY THE IMPORTER

Below is a list of the document categories and documents the importer issues or requests or requires of the exporter.

In this summary it is assumed that the importer is responsible for import documentation and import clearance only. Not all the documents listed below are required in all transactions. Further explanation and samples of documents are provided in the document category chapters that follow.

■ TRANSACTION DOCUMENTS — THE IMPORTER/BUYER. . .

▫ Issues an RFP (REQUEST FOR PROPOSAL) or RFQ (REQUEST FOR QUOTATION) to the exporter/seller.

▫ Receives a PROPOSAL, BID or QUOTATION in response.

▫ Negotiates (usually with the assistance of an attorney) a CONTRACT FOR THE SALE OF GOODS with the exporter/seller.

▫ May request a PRO-FORMA INVOICE.

▫ Requires a COMMERCIAL INVOICE.

■ TRANSPORT DOCUMENTS — THE IMPORTER/BUYER. . .

▫ Requests or requires a PACKING LIST for use by the shipping company and import authorities.

▫ Requires a BILL OF LADING/AIR WAYBILL (or other form of bill of lading) for use by the shipping company, import authorities, and bank(s) (if a documentary payment procedure is used).

■ BANKING DOCUMENTS — THE IMPORTER/BUYER. . .

If a documentary collection is used:

▫ Prepares a list of documents to be included in the document package the exporter presents to the bank for transmittal to the importer's bank. This includes all the documents the importer needs to import the goods to the country of destination, plus any requested inspection documents (for verification of quantities, quality, and other properties of the merchandise shipped).

If a documentary letter of credit is used:

▫ Completes a LETTER OF CREDIT APPLICATION at the bank.

▫ Prepares a list of documents to be included in the document package the exporter presents to the bank for transmittal to the importer's bank. This includes all the documents the importer needs to import the goods to the country of destination, plus any requested inspection documents (for verification of quantities, quality, and other properties of the merchandise shipped).

■ SPECIALIZED DOCUMENTS (AS NEEDED) — THE IMPORTER/BUYER. . .

▦ Requires from the exporter/seller a CERTIFICATE OF ORIGIN from a chamber of commerce or government authority located in the country of origin of the shipment.

▦ Requires the exporter/seller to provide a CONSULAR INVOICE from a consulate of the importer/buyer's country of final destination of the goods located in the country of origin of the goods.

▦ Requires the exporter/seller to submit an INSURANCE POLICY or INSURANCE CERTIFICATE.

▦ Requires from the exporter/seller an INSPECTION CERTIFICATE (for verification of quantities, quality and other specifications of the merchandise shipped).

▦ Requires the exporter/seller to obtain a PHYTOSANITARY CERTIFICATE (for import of plants and foods).

▦ Requires the exporter/seller to provide SPECIALIZED INSPECTION CERTIFICATES if needed.

▦ Requires other product-specific documents as needed.

IMPORT DOCUMENTS NOT OBTAINED FROM THE EXPORTER

In addition to the documents the importer secures from the exporter, there are additional documents the importer must issue or secure for presentation to the import authorities. Some of these documents may be issued by the importer, some by government agencies of the country of import, while others may be produced by a customs broker or freight forwarder acting on behalf of the importer. Not all of the documents listed below are required in all import transactions. These documents include:

▦ IMPORT PERMIT

▦ IMPORT LICENSE

▦ SPECIAL CUSTOMS INVOICE

▦ CUSTOMS DECLARATION

▦ OTHER SPECIALIZED DOCUMENTATION

Introducing the Export Authority

JOB DESCRIPTION

The export authority has three major responsibilities:

1. LAW ENFORCEMENT To enforce the export and other laws and regulations of the country, and in the process regulate the flow of exported goods;

2. REVENUE COLLECTION To collect export duties, tariffs and fees; and

3. CENSUS To collect statistical data on the country's exports including the type, value and destination of exported products.

FULFILLMENT OF RESPONSIBILITIES

In the course of fulfilling its responsibilities, the export authority may:

- Examine and verify export documentation.

- Examine, classify and appraise merchandise for compliance with export requirements.

- Act as the "eyes and ears" of other regulatory agencies, looking for illegal exports (i.e., drugs, cultural relics, strategic goods), smuggling, or other evidence of "intent to defraud," as well as violations of trademark, copyright and marking laws.

- Require laboratory testing and analysis of merchandise.

- Require that additional information, documentation or permits be provided.

- Issue or deny permits to release merchandise for export, depending on whether the exporter has met legal and documentary requirements.

- Require verification of the accuracy and consistency of information provided by the exporter (or freight forwarder acting for the exporter) on all export documents.

REQUIRED EXPORT DOCUMENTATION

Documents provide the export authority with evidence that the exporter has complied with the laws and regulations of the country of export. The following is a list of the basic export documentation required by most countries:

- The EXPORT LICENSE (as required)

- The EXPORT PERMIT (as required, especially for restricted goods)

- The EXPORT DECLARATION as issued by the exporter, and sometimes including a DESTINATION CONTROL or ULTIMATE CONSIGNEE STATEMENT.

- The BILL OF LADING as issued by the carrier

- The COMMERCIAL INVOICE as issued by the exporter

- The CERTIFICATE OF ORIGIN (as required)

- The INSPECTION CERTIFICATE (as required)

NOTE: Exporters often use a freight forwarder to assist in export formalities.

See "Export Documents" starting on page 56.

Introducing the Import Authority/Customs

JOB DESCRIPTION

The import authority has three major responsibilities:

1. LAW ENFORCEMENT To enforce the import and other laws and regulations of the country, and in the process regulate the flow of imported goods;

2. REVENUE COLLECTION To collect import duties, tariffs and fees; and

3. CENSUS To collect statistical data on the country's imports including the type, value and final destination of imported products.

RANGE OF RESPONSIBILITIES

In the course of fulfilling its responsibilities, the import authority may:

- Examine and verify import documentation.
- Examine, classify and appraise merchandise for compliance with import requirements.
- Act as the "eyes and ears" of other regulatory agencies, looking for illegal imports (i.e., drugs, strategic goods), smuggling, or other evidence of "intent to defraud," as well as violations of trademark, copyright and marking laws.
- Require laboratory testing and analysis of merchandise.
- Require that additional information, documentation or permits be provided.
- Issue or deny permits to release merchandise for import, depending on whether the importer has met legal and documentary requirements.
- Require verification of the accuracy and consistency of information provided by the importer (or customs broker acting for the importer) on all import documents.

REQUIRED IMPORT DOCUMENTATION

Documents provide the import authority with evidence that the exporter and importer have complied with the laws and regulations of the country of import. The following is a list of the basic import documentation required by most countries:

- The IMPORT PERMIT (as required, especially for restricted goods)
- The IMPORT LICENSE (as required)
- The IMPORT DECLARATION as issued by the importer.
- The BILL OF LADING as issued by the carrier.
- The COMMERCIAL INVOICE as issued by the exporter.
- The CERTIFICATE OF ORIGIN (as required)
- The INSPECTION CERTIFICATE (as required, especially for restricted goods)

NOTE: Importers often use a customs broker to assist in import formalities.

See "Import Documents" starting on page 68.

Introducing the Freight Forwarder/Logistics Company

BUSINESS/JOB DESCRIPTION

International freight forwarders are in the business of moving goods from one country to another. Logistics firms are in the business of planning and controlling the flow of raw materials, work in progress, or finished products from point of origin to point of destination. The destination can include a factory for further processing, a warehouse for storage, or the marketplace for sale. With significant industry consolidation in recent years almost all companies in this field are now offering logistics services that include the services of import customs brokerage as well.

RANGE OF RESPONSIBILITIES

In the course of fulfilling their responsibilities logistics firms may handle:

- All aspects related to pre-shipment warehousing of goods,
- All documentation and formalities required for the export of goods,
- All aspects of shipping via all modes of transport including multi-modal,
- All documentation and formalities required for the import of goods,
- All aspects of foreign-country warehousing of goods,
- All aspects of packing, containerization and insurance, and
- All aspects of wholesale and retail fulfillment.

These firms are familiar with the rules and regulations of both the country of export and the country of import. They can also recommend appropriate packing methods and materials or arrange to have goods packed and/or containerized.

They can provide pre-shipment and pre-bidding advice on the costs of insuring, packing, and shipping goods, as well as documentation compliance, inspection services, fees, tariffs and taxes, thus allowing the exporter to make more accurate costings.

By working with overseas customs brokers, these firms ensure that goods comply with import requirements and that all customs duties, licenses and taxes are paid. In most countries, freight forwarders are required to be licensed by an agency of the national government.

DOCUMENTS ISSUED BY THE LOGISTICS COMPANY

Below is a list of documents that logistics firms generally issue or secure:

- The BILL OF LADING
- The INSURANCE CERTIFICATE
- Certain INSPECTION CERTIFICATES

DOCUMENTS REQUIRED BY THE LOGISTICS FIRM FOR EXPORT

In the course of exporting goods, the logistics company will require various documentation from the exporter. See "Export Documents" starting on page 56.

Introducing the Customs Broker

BUSINESS/JOB DESCRIPTION

A customs broker is an individual or company licensed by a government authority to act on behalf of others in customs (generally import) transactions. The customs broker assists in all aspects of clearing imported goods through customs. For example, in the USA customs brokers handle issues involving "entry and admissibility of goods, classification and valuation, the payment of duties, taxes, or other charges assessed or collected, or the refunds, rebate or drawback thereof." In essence, they handle the sequence of customs formalities and other details critical to the legal and speedy import and export of goods.

THE POWER OF ATTORNEY

The customs broker is acting on behalf of the importer in legal matters and therefore must first secure a LIMITED POWER OF ATTORNEY from the importer. This enables the customs broker to sign specified papers in the name of the importer.

RANGE OF RESPONSIBILITIES

In the course of fulfilling its responsibilities, a customs broker:

- Advises the importer about customs formalities, responsibilities, and tariffs,

- Advises the importer on legal strategies for securing the lowest import duty rate possible,

- Completes required customs documentation,

- Presents documentation to the customs authorities,

- Secures documentation to release imported merchandise from customs, and

- Provides additional services including insurance warehousing and other freight services.

DOCUMENTS ISSUED BY THE CUSTOMS BROKER

Below is a list of the documents generally issued by the customs broker:

- The APPLICATION FOR IMPORT LICENSE and IMPORT PERMITS

- The IMPORT DECLARATION

- The SPECIAL CUSTOMS INVOICE

- Documentation and applications related to refunds, rebates and drawback

DOCUMENTS REQUIRED BY THE CUSTOMS BROKER FOR IMPORT

In the course of securing the entry of goods through customs, the customs broker will require various documentation from the importer. See "Import Documents" starting on page 68.

Introducing the Freight Carrier
(Shipping Line/Airline/Railroad/Barge Line/Courier)

BUSINESS/JOB DESCRIPTION

International freight "carriers" are in the business of moving cargo from one country to another. Carriers range from huge ocean shipping lines that move ship load quantities of crude oil or grain, to courier companies that handle small package shipments of less than one-half kilogram (1.1 pound).

CARRIERS VS. FREIGHT FORWARDERS

In the past, only large-scale shippers went to the shipping lines and airlines directly, because small shippers needed the additional services that freight forwarders and logistics firms provided. Today, however, the distinctions have been blurred between freight forwarder, customs broker and carrier.

All carriers wish to provide the most comprehensive service possible to their clients in an attempt at full integration of logistics services. Many carriers now routinely provide export documentation and clearance as well as import documentation and clearance for both exporter and importer.

It is important to realize that some carriers are specialists in only one mode of transport. Since international shipments often require more than one mode of transport (sea, air, land) it may be necessary to use a shipper (or logistics firm) that can act as a "multi-modal transport operator" and take responsibility for the entire shipping process from point of origin to point of final destination.

NOTE: Many of the traditional "small package and document" courier companies offer door-to-door service and handle large freight shipments as well.

DOCUMENTS ISSUED BY FREIGHT CARRIERS

The key documents issued by freight carriers are:

- The BILL OF LADING (in one of its many forms)
- The AIRBILL (for shipments by air)
- The INSURANCE CERTIFICATE or DOCUMENT

See "Transport Documents" starting on page 38.

Introducing the Governmental Regulatory Agency

BUSINESS/JOB DESCRIPTION

Governmental regulatory agencies exist to enforce specific laws and regulations designed to protect the economic well-being in addition to the health and safety of their citizens.

RANGE OF RESPONSIBILITIES

Examples of the range of regulatory responsibilities (taking the USA as an illustration) include:

- **FOOD AND DRUG ADMINISTRATION (FDA)** Enforce laws regulating the import of food products and drugs.

- **ANIMAL AND PLANT HEALTH INSPECTION SERVICE** Enforce laws related to the inspection and importation of animals, plants, and products thereof.

- **CONSUMER PRODUCT SAFETY COMMISSION** Enforce laws regulating the importation of consumer products ranging from toys to guns.

RANGE OF RESPONSIBILITIES

In the course of fulfilling the above responsibilities, these agencies may:

- Examine exported or imported merchandise,

- Require specific and detailed documentation regarding the country of origin, region of origin, and even the manufacturing plant of origin of merchandise,

- Require documentation on the precise composition of imported merchandise,

- Require laboratory testing and analysis of merchandise,

- Require that special licenses and permits be obtained, and

- Issue or deny permits to release merchandise for export or import, depending on whether the exporter has met legal and documentary requirements.

SAMPLE DOCUMENTATION ISSUED OR REQUIRED

Documents provide evidence of compliance with specific laws and regulations. The following is a list of the sample documentation issued or required by regulatory agencies:

- The general CERTIFICATE OF INSPECTION
- The PHYTOSANITARY CERTIFICATE for plants and plant products
- The VETERINARY HEALTH CERTIFICATE for live animals, meat and meat by-products
- The SAFETY TESTING CERTIFICATE for consumer products (e.g., toys, electric heaters, automobiles)
- The FUMIGATION/STERILIZATION CERTIFICATE for wood or fiber packaging materials.
- The DANGEROUS GOODS CERTIFICATE for dangerous and hazardous materials.

Introducing the International Bank

BUSINESS/JOB DESCRIPTION

International banks handle all aspects of international payments for exporters and importers, including documentary collections and letters of credit.

RANGE OF RESPONSIBILITIES

In the course of fulfilling their responsibilities, international banks:

- Process checks, drafts, credit cards and bank wires in payment for transactions,
- Structure documentary collection transactions for exporters and importers, and
- Structure documentary letter of credit transactions for exporters and importers.

DIFFERENT ROLES BANKS PLAY

Banks play a number of different roles in international transactions:

- **ISSUING BANK** In letter of credit transactions, this bank opens a letter of credit at the request of the importer/buyer. Also called the buyer's bank or opening bank.

- **ADVISING BANK** In letter of credit transactions, this bank receives a letter of credit from the issuing bank and forwards it to the exporter/seller (beneficiary in banking terms). Also called the seller's bank or exporter's bank.

DOCUMENTS ISSUED BY INTERNATIONAL BANKS

Banks issue many documents, but the key documents are:

- The DOCUMENTARY COLLECTION ORDER
- The DOCUMENTARY LETTER OF CREDIT (in various forms)
- The DOCUMENTARY LETTER OF CREDIT AMENDMENT
- The DOCUMENTARY LETTER OF CREDIT ADVICE
- The BANK DRAFT/BILL OF EXCHANGE

DOCUMENTS REQUIRED BY THE BANKS

In the course of handling documentary collection or letter of credit transactions the banks will require various documentation from the exporter and importer. See "Banking Documents" starting on page 76.

Introducing the Insurance Company/Agent

BUSINESS/JOB DESCRIPTION

Insurance companies provide coverage by contract to indemnify or guarantee another party against risk of loss for a stated peril, such as the risk of loss or damage to shipments of cargo in international trade.

Importers and exporters can work directly with an insurance company or an agent. In many cases, freight forwarders, customs brokers, shipping lines, railroads and other carriers act as agents for insurance companies. Some of the larger logistics firms have an insurance company as a subsidiary.

RANGE OF SERVICES

Insurance companies can provide a full range of insurance coverage in international trade. These include:

- Export credit insurance
- Insurance for risk of loss or damage to cargo
- Kidnapping insurance
- Insurance of foreign office, manufacturing and distribution facilities.

Insurance coverage against risk of loss or damage to cargo is a requirement in nearly all international transactions. Coverage is generally determined by what is often called "insurable interest." Insurable interest relates to the risk an individual firm has with regard to a particular shipment.

EXAMPLE: If the exporter sells on a pre-payment EXW (Ex Works) basis, meaning that the goods merely need to be made available to the importer/buyer at the exporter's loading dock, the exporter ceases to have insurable interest once paid and the goods are picked up by the importer or an agent.

Some countries of export and import require that insurance coverage be made with a company headquartered in that country.

DOCUMENTS ISSUED BY THE INSURANCE COMPANY

The key documents issued by the insurance company are:

- The INSURANCE POLICY, or
- The INSURANCE CERTIFICATE

See "Insurance Documents" starting on page 101.

Introducing the International Attorney

BUSINESS/JOB DESCRIPTION

Attorneys and law firms are in the business of providing legal advice to clients. Individual attorneys and firms have developed different areas of specialization. Note that the role of attorneys varies greatly from country to country.

RANGE OF RESPONSIBILITIES

In the course of fulfilling their responsibilities international attorneys may:
- Advise regarding contracts for the sale of goods,
- Advise concerning joint venture and intellectual property right (IPR) issues,
- Advise concerning issues related to export from or import to a country,
- Advise concerning issues related to the export or import of difficult commodities,
- Advise and handle litigation against suppliers or buyers,
- Represent exporters or importers in the customs courts of various countries
- Write contracts.

WORKING WITH AN ATTORNEY

The particulars of an international contract can differ significantly from domestic ones. The prudent trader will have an attorney who is familiar with international trade law consult while negotiating a contract of sale.

DOCUMENTS ISSUED BY THE ATTORNEY

With regard to the context of this book, attorneys draft:

- The CONTRACT FOR SALE OF GOODS (or SERVICES).

Introducing the Inspection Company

BUSINESS/JOB DESCRIPTION

Inspection companies are in the business of providing testing services for exporters, importers, export authorities and import authorities. Inspection companies are often licensed by government agencies or have professional affiliations with recognized industry groups.

In order to protect the health, safety and economic well-being of its citizens, many countries require inspections for products before they may be imported. Some countries require that samples of products be sent in advance of the full shipment for testing by laboratories within the country of import, while others are satisfied with certificates generated in the country of export prior to shipment.

RANGE OF SERVICES

In the course of fulfilling its responsibilities, an inspection company may:

- Inspect shipments for verification of quantities,
- Inspect shipments for product quality, and
- Inspect shipments for compliance with country of export or country of import regulations.

DOCUMENTS ISSUED BY INSPECTION FIRMS

Documents issued by inspection firms include:

- The general CERTIFICATE OF INSPECTION

- The PHYTOSANITARY CERTIFICATES for plants and plant products.

- The VETERINARY HEALTH CERTIFICATE for live animals, meat and meat by-products.

- The SAFETY TESTING CERTIFICATE for consumer products (i.e. toys, electric heaters, automobiles, etc.).

- The FUMIGATION/STERILIZATION CERTIFICATE for wood or fiber packaging materials.

- The DANGEROUS GOODS CERTIFICATE for dangerous and hazardous materials.

- The QUALITY CERTIFICATE for everything from milk, butter and cosmetics to woven baskets, rolled steel sheeting, and human hair wigs.

Introducing the Document Authenticator (Notary Public)

JOB DESCRIPTION

Import authorities may require some documents to be certified or notarized. Most countries have appointed or commissioned individuals who are given authority to identify and certify the identity of persons who sign documents with proof of their signature. In some countries, such as England, France and Germany, these individuals often have special legal training, while in other countries they can be qualified after a short course, test and background check. Some countries have no provision for such commissioned persons, in which event consular, judicial or legal professionals will often be used to fulfill authentication requirements. In the United States, these individuals are called notaries public.

DOCUMENTS NEEDING AUTHENTICATION

The key documents "certified" or "notarized" by notaries are:

- The LIMITED POWER OF ATTORNEY for customs brokers
- Certain CONTRACTS that need to be recorded or otherwise require proof of the signature
- Certain INSPECTION CERTIFICATES
- The certified CONSULAR INVOICE

Introducing the Chamber of Commerce

BUSINESS/JOB DESCRIPTION

Chambers of commerce provide a wide range of services to the international trader. These include export education, country market information, assistance with export documentation and trade leads.

With regard to international trade documentation, many local chambers of commerce can assist the exporter by "certifying" certain documents.

DOCUMENTS ISSUED OR CERTIFIED BY CHAMBERS OF COMMERCE

Many countries require a local chamber of commerce to certify documents as the following:

- The CERTIFICATE OF ORIGIN
- The CERTIFICATE OF FREE SALE

Introducing the Consular Official

BUSINESS/JOB DESCRIPTION

The consular official or office of the country of importation, located in the country of export, is often empowered to "certify" certain documents or forms required for the eventual import of goods.

Some countries require that before goods bound for their country can be admitted for import, the documents which accompany the shipment must be "certified" by an official of their own consulate or embassy residing in the country of export. The process is very similar to that done by a notary public and a fee is charged for each page or document processed by the official.

DOCUMENTARY RESPONSIBILITIES

Examples of documents that may require consular certification include:

- The COMMERCIAL INVOICE
- The CUSTOMS INVOICE
- The CONSULAR INVOICE

CHAPTER 4

Transaction Documents

TRANSACTION DOCUMENTS are generated by the buyer and seller to define their business relationship and provide an accounting record of individual transactions. These documents range from a simple letter of inquiry to a contract for the sale of goods and a commercial invoice. This category does not include specific export, transport, import, or bank documentation.

In the most straightforward sale the buyer might call or fax the seller and order a quantity of goods, and the seller simply issues an invoice. At the other end of the spectrum, the process can be much more formal with an importer/buyer submitting an RFP (Request for Proposal) for bids on a product with 100 pages of detailed specifications, engineering charts and the like.

Fortunately, most businesspeople are already familiar with basic transaction documents because these are virtually the same as the ones used in domestic business.

The Flow of Transaction Documents

A typical exchange of documents between buyer and seller proceeds in the following pattern:

1. The prospective importer/buyer (buyer) sends a LETTER OF INQUIRY to the proposed exporter/seller (seller) asking if the company either has certain products available or would like to bid on a project.

2. The seller sends a REPLY LETTER stating an interest in bidding and perhaps includes a CAPABILITIES STATEMENT.

3. The buyer sends a REQUEST FOR QUOTATION (RFQ) (generally if the goods already exist in the exporter's product line) or a REQUEST FOR PROPOSAL (RFP) (generally if the goods have to be designed or manufactured to the buyer's specification as outlined in the RFP.

4. The seller prepares and sends the buyer a formal PROPOSAL including product specifications, quantities, prices and terms and conditions.

5. The buyer and seller negotiate specifications quantities, prices, terms and conditions.

6. The buyer issues a LETTER OF ACCEPTANCE or signs an ORDER FORM.

7. The buyer and seller prepare and sign a CONTRACT FOR THE SALE OF GOODS.

8. The seller prepares a COMMERCIAL INVOICE

NOTE: The above documents can be exchanged by letter, fax, courier or e-mail. Some of the early steps may occur by telephone.

International Transaction Documents

The following table and notes will help you identify the various documents needed in an international sale. Not all will be required for any single transaction, but you should be able to identify those you need for a particular sale.

Document	Notes	Sample Page
Letter of Inquiry	A	-
Request for Quotation (RFQ)	B	-
Request for Proposal (RFP)	C	page 33
Proposal/Bid/Quotation/Offer	D	page 34
Pro-forma Invoice	E	-
Contract for the Sale of Goods or Services	F	page 35
Commercial Invoice (C/I)	G	page 36

■ A—LETTER OF INQUIRY This is a simple letter written by the buyer asking the seller if a product is available or if the seller will bid on the supply of a product. This letter is generally short and does not include detailed specifications.

■ B—REQUEST FOR QUOTATION (RFQ) A letter written by the buyer asking the seller to submit a formal price quotation for a specified product and quantity.

NOTE: An RFQ is generally used for a one time sale of an existing product from the seller's inventory or product line, or a fungible product (one that is identical with other goods of the same nature; for example crude oil #3).

■ C—REQUEST FOR PROPOSAL (RFP) A letter written by the buyer asking the seller to submit a formal proposal for a specified product and quantity.

NOTE: An RFP is generally used when envisioning an ongoing relationship with multiple deliveries over time or where a product has detailed specifications (for example, an engineered product that requires custom manufacturing).

■ D—PROPOSAL/BID/QUOTATION/OFFER This is the seller's written offer to sell specified products under specified terms and conditions. This can be as simple as a one page letter listing a stock number, quantities, price per unit and sales terms, or it can be a 1,000 page proposal complete with engineering drawings, and complicated terms and conditions.

■ E—PRO-FORMA INVOICE This is a preliminary invoice made up by the exporter at the importer's request prior to a shipment of merchandise. It identifies the parties to the transaction and includes the kinds and quantities of goods to be sent, their value and specifications and shipping costs. The pro-forma invoice is used by the importer to see what the purchase will cost, obtain any necessary import licenses and foreign exchange approval, and apply for a letter of credit.

■ F—CONTRACT FOR THE SALE OF GOODS (OR SERVICES) This is the formal, legal agreement between the exporter and the importer stating products and prices, responsibilities and rights, and terms and conditions.

■ G—COMMERCIAL INVOICE This is the prime transaction document. It lists the date, buyer and seller, products, quantities, prices, delivery terms and other important information.

Notes on Transaction Documents

1. The quantity and formality of transaction documentation is influenced by the relationship of the buyer and seller, the countries of export and import, as well as the goods sold. For example, if the buyer and seller know each other, the preliminaries may be handled by telephone and the only transaction document issued will be the commercial invoice.

2. The key document in this category is the commercial invoice. Copies of this document will be retained by the exporter and presented to the export authorities, the freight carrier, the import authorities, the importer and the bank (if a documentary collection or letter of credit is used).

3. Transaction documents may need to have additional information and/or be in the language of the country of export or import.

Request for a Proposal (RFP)

DEFINITION

An RFP is a request for a formal proposal for the sale, supply or manufacture of products.

✔ KEY ELEMENTS

An RFP includes the following elements:

1. Name and address of importer/buyer (as on a letterhead)
2. Name and address of proposed exporter/seller
3. Date
4. Statement of request for a formal proposal
5. Product specifications
6. Quantities
7. Required delivery time
8. Deadline for submission (optional)

! CAUTIONS & NOTES

The key element is the product specification list. This can be a simple statement of a known item (such as a commodity known by international standards) or as complex as a book-length listing of engineering drawings, raw material specifications, delivery schedules, packaging and shipping instructions, compliance documents, inspection requirements and more.

 Proposal

DEFINITION

A proposal is a seller's formal written offer to sell specified products under specified terms and conditions.

ISSUED BY

The proposal is issued by the proposed seller.

✔ **KEY ELEMENTS**

A formal proposal includes the following key elements:

1. Name and address of exporter/seller (as on a letterhead)
2. Name and address of proposed importer/buyer
3. Date
4. Statement that the document is a proposal or offer to sell
5. Product specifications list
6. Proposed quantities
7. Proposed delivery time
8. Proposed delivery method
9. Proposed packaging
10. Terms and conditions
11. Deadline for acceptance or validity term of proposal

! CAUTIONS & NOTES

The key element in a proposal is generally the product specification list, but can also be the terms and conditions of sale or other factors. As stated earlier, the product specifications list can be a very simple statement of a known item (such as a commodity known by international standards) or as complex as a book-length listing of engineering drawings, raw material specifications, delivery schedules, packaging and shipping instructions, compliance documents, inspection requirements and more.

A limited term of validity of the proposal is given so that if business conditions change, the seller has the option of modifying the terms and conditions of the proposal.

Contract for the Sale of Goods

DEFINITION

This is the formal, written agreement between buyer and seller naming the parties to the transaction, products and prices, responsibilities and rights, and terms and conditions. Issued by either the seller or buyer, with the drafter having the advantage of claiming greater influence on contract terms, but the disadvantage of being subject to strict interpretation of the terms should there be a dispute.

✔ KEY ELEMENTS AND CHECKLIST

The following provisions are for a complete international contract for a one time sale of goods. Not every provision is applicable to every transaction.

1. Contract date ❑
2. Identification of parties ❑
3. Goods—description ❑
4. Goods—quantity ❑
5. Goods—price ❑
6. Payment—method of payment ❑
7. Payment—medium of exchange ❑
8. Payment—exchange rate ❑
9. Costs and charges—duties and taxes ❑
10. Costs and charges—insurance ❑
11. Costs and charges—handling and transport ❑
12. Packaging arrangements ❑
13. Delivery—date ❑
14. Delivery—place ❑
15. Delivery—transfer of title ❑
16. Transportation—carrier ❑
17. Transportation—storage ❑
18. Transportation—notice provisions ❑
19. Transportation—shipping time ❑
20. Transportation—insurance ❑
21. Import/export documentation ❑
22. Invoice preparation and delivery ❑

23. Re-exportation prohibition ❑
24. Inspection rights ❑
25. Indemnities ❑
26. Intellectual property rights ❑
27. Warranties ❑
28. Enforcement and remedies ❑
29. Arbitration provisions ❑
30. Time is of the essence ❑
31. Modification of contract ❑
32. Cancellation ❑
33. Liquidated damages ❑
34. Attorneys' fees ❑
35. Force majeure ❑
36. Inurement and assignment ❑
37. Conditions precedent ❑
38. Governing law ❑
39. Choice of forum ❑
40. Severability of provisions ❑
41. Integration of provisions ❑
42. Notices ❑
43. Authority to bind ❑
44. Independent counsel ❑
45. Acceptance and execution ❑

! CAUTIONS & NOTES

Regardless of whether you draft the terms of the contract by yourself, or hire an attorney, you need to be aware of key contract provisions. It is up to you to insist on the protection of your own interests. The best course of action is to define all of the provisions of your agreement in writing at the time you enter into it. See also *International Contracts* by Karla Shippey, J.D. from World Trade Press.

Commercial Invoice

DEFINITION

The commercial invoice is the key accounting document describing a commercial transaction between a buyer and seller.

ISSUER

The commercial invoice is issued by the exporter/seller.

✔ KEY ELEMENTS

The commercial invoice includes the following elements:

1. Name and address of seller
2. Name and address of buyer
3. Date of issuance
4. Invoice number
5. Order or contract number
6. Quantity and description of the goods
7. Unit price, total price, other agreed upon charges, and total invoice amount
8. Shipping details including: weight of the goods, number of packages, and shipping marks and numbers
9. Terms of delivery and payment
10. Any other information as required by the seller (e.g., country of origin)

! CAUTIONS & NOTES RE DESCRIPTION OF GOODS

It is vitally important that the description of the goods and the terms listed in the commercial invoice correspond precisely with the description of goods in the contract of sale and with a documentary letter of credit (if that form of payment is used).

! CAUTIONS & NOTES IN LETTER OF CREDIT PAYMENT TERMS

▪ INVOICE AMOUNT The invoice amount should match exactly or at least should not exceed the amount specified in the letter of credit. Banks and buyers have the right to refuse invoices issued for amounts in excess of the amount stated in the credit. The exception: when a documentary credit specifies "about" in relation to the currency amount and quantity of merchandise, in which case the invoice may specify an amount equal to plus or minus 10 percent of the stipulated amount of the credit.

▪ CURRENCY The invoice should be made out in the same currency as the letter of credit.

▪ APPLICANT Unless otherwise stipulated in the letter of credit, the commercial invoice must be made out in the name of the applicant (importer/buyer). The exception: In a transferable documentary credit the invoice may be made out to a third party.

▪ INCONSISTENCIES The buyer, seller, and bank(s) should all carefully check for discrepancies in the invoice. The details specified therein should not be inconsistent with those of any other documents and should exactly conform to the specifications of the credit.

SAMPLE COMMERCIAL INVOICE

Indonesia Coffee Export Co.
Jalan Sudirman
Jakarta 10420, Indonesia

INVOICE

June 27, 1998
Invoice No. 98-123456

American Caffeine Import Company
125 Main Street
Seattle, Washington

Description of goods:
15 metric tons of 60-kilo bags of New Crop D.P. Sumatra Mandheling Arabica Grade 1 - Green Coffee - As per buyer's purchase order No. 1234

TOTAL CIF Seattle, Washington, USA US$65,000.00

Payment:	By irrevocable documentary letter of credit No. 1234567 dated May 27, 1998 of The American Import Bank, Seattle, Washington USA
Payment Terms:	At 120 days' sight, draft drawn on San Francisco International Bank, San Francisco, California, USA
Country of Origin:	Indonesia
Number of bags:	250 bags
Weights:	Gross 15,000 kilo, Net 15,000 kilo
Marks/No.:	USA Made in Indonesia No. 12345.67
Dispatch:	Through ABC Freight Services, by sea from Jakarta via Sea Maritime Steamship Line to Seattle

Indonesia Coffee Export Co.

Indonesia Coffee Export Company

CHAPTER 5

Transport Documents

INTERNATIONAL SHIPMENTS OF GOODS can be made by ocean going vessel, airplane, rail, truck, barge on inland waterways, courier or any combination of modes (multi-modal). An individual shipment may also be placed or packed in an ocean container, airfreight container (unit load device or ULD), in less than container load (LCL) shipments, in dry or wet bulk (such as grain, iron ore or crude oil) or in drums, sacks, or crates.

The one document that all these modes of transport and means of packing share is the bill of lading, or B/L, in one of its many forms. It is not the only transport document, but it is the most important.

MINI GLOSSARY

CONSIGNOR: The individual, company or entity that ships goods (the shipper, not the shipping company), or gives goods to another for care. This is the exporter/seller.

CONSIGNEE: The person or firm named in a freight contract to whom goods have been shipped or turned over for care. This is generally the importer/buyer.

International Transport Documents

The following table and notes will introduce you to the various transport documents used in international shipments. Rarely are all of these documents used in a single shipment, but you should understand each conceptually as requirements for obscure documents do arise from time to time.

Document	Notes	Sample
Bill of Lading (in various forms)	A	page 40
Packing List	B	page 53
Shipping Instructions	C	-
Forwarder's Instructions	D	-
Stowage Instructions	E	-
Hazardous Materials Instructions/Declaration	F	-
Dock Receipt	G	-
Mate's Receipt	H	-
Captain's (or Master's) Protest	I	-

■ A—BILL OF LADING This is the key transport document that identifies the consignor, the consignee, the carrier, the mode of transport and other facts about the shipment. See the following pages for detailed information about bills of lading.

- B—PACKING LIST (or BILL OF PARCELS) This form identifies the consignor and consignee, the number of packages in the shipment, package and container contents, weights, dimensions, marks and numbers. It does not contain prices. Even when not required, a packing list is a good idea. It enables the consignee to check that the correct number of units have been received.

- C—SHIPPING INSTRUCTIONS This form or letter is issued by the consignor and gives specific instructions to the shipping company regarding a shipment. The bill of lading is drawn up from this information. Many shipping lines have pre-printed forms or computerized entry systems for this information. Consignors who provide their own bill of lading must attach a copy of any shipping instructions.

- D—FORWARDER'S INSTRUCTIONS This form, issued by the consignor, gives specific and formal instructions to the freight forwarder regarding the booking of a shipment and information for completing transport documents. Most freight forwarders and logistics firms have their own printed form but the necessary information may also be presented on the consignor's letterhead.

- E—STOWAGE INSTRUCTIONS These are specific instructions given by the consignor in a letter or on a shipping line or freight forwarder's pre-printed form regarding how or where a shipment should be stowed during transport. For example, a shipper may require that the shipment be placed below deck and amidships for greater protection from the elements and movement of the ship.

- F—HAZARDOUS MATERIALS/DANGEROUS GOODS INSTRUCTIONS A hazardous material is a substance or product that is capable of posing a risk to health, safety or property when transported in commerce. The same material is classified as a dangerous good when transported by air. Hazards are classified as "Other Regulated Materials" (ORM-A through ORM-E) and include irritating, corrosive, caustic, flammable, radioactive and other life or health threatening materials. Special handling instructions must be provided and containers must be properly emblazoned with international warning labels/stickers.

- G—DOCK RECEIPT This is a receipt issued by a port officer or warehouse supervisor certifying that a shipment of goods has been received from the domestic carrier or consignor and that accountability for the goods has transferred to the named transport company.

- H—MATE'S RECEIPT This is a document issued by the captain or mate of a vessel as a receipt for goods shipped. If the captain or mate sees a discrepancy in the number of units received or damage to a package, it will be noted on the receipt (which is then said to be a "claused" or "unclean" receipt). This information is then included in or attached to the bill of lading, which then also becomes claused or unclean. A signed copy of the mate's receipt is given to the consignor in exchange for the original bill of lading.

- I—CAPTAIN'S (OR MASTER'S) PROTEST This is prepared by a ship's captain (or master) and details unusual conditions encountered during a voyage (i.e., "Acts of God," catastrophic natural events, piracy, mutiny, collisions, etc.) that might affect the vessel's cargo. This is a means of relieving the ship owner of liability for loss or damage, thus directing the cargo owner to look to its insurance company for reimbursement.

The Bill of Lading

DEFINED

A bill of lading is a document issued by a carrier to a shipper (exporter/seller/consignor), signed by the captain, agent, or owner of a vessel, furnishing written evidence regarding receipt of the goods (cargo), the conditions on which transportation is made (contract of carriage), and the engagement to deliver goods at the prescribed port of destination to the lawful holder of the bill of lading.

A bill of lading is, therefore, both a receipt for merchandise and a contract to deliver it as freight. There are a number of different types of bills of lading and a number of issues that relate to them as a group of documents.

MINI GLOSSARY

NEGOTIABLE INSTRUMENT A written document (instrument) that can be transferred merely by endorsement (signing) or delivery. Checks, bills of exchange, bills of lading, and warehouse receipts (if marked negotiable), and promissory notes are examples of negotiable instruments and can be bought, sold or traded. Endorsement of such a document transfers the rights to money or goods as described in the negotiable instrument to the holder of the document.

TYPES OF BILLS OF LADING DEFINED

- **STRAIGHT BILL OF LADING** (non-negotiable) A straight bill of lading indicates that the shipper will deliver the goods to the consignee. This is a non-negotiable document. The consignee need only present identification to claim the goods. A straight bill of lading is often used when payment for the goods has already been made in advance or when the goods are shipped on open account. A straight bill of lading, therefore, cannot be transferred by endorsement.

- **SHIPPER'S ORDER (NEGOTIABLE) BILL OF LADING** A shipper's order bill of lading is a title document to the goods (negotiable instrument), issued "to the order of" a party, usually the shipper, whose endorsement is required to effect its negotiation. Because it is negotiable, a shipper's order bill of lading can be bought, sold, or traded while goods are in transit. These are highly favored for documentary letter of credit transactions. The buyer usually needs the original or a signed copy as proof of ownership to take possession of the goods.

- **BLANK ENDORSED NEGOTIABLE BILL OF LADING** A blank endorsed negotiable bill of lading is one that has been endorsed without naming an endorsee. In simple terms, any person in possession of a blank endorsed negotiable bill of lading may claim possession of the goods. Possession of this document equals rights to possession of the shipment.

- **AIR WAYBILL** An air waybill is a form of bill of lading used for the air transport of goods and is not negotiable.

- **COURIER RECEIPT** A courier receipt is a document issued by a courier or delivery service evidencing receipt of goods for delivery to a named consignee and is not negotiable.

- **POST RECEIPT** A post receipt is a document issued by the postal service of a country evidencing receipt of goods for delivery to a named consignee.

- **MULTI-MODAL BILL OF LADING** A multi-modal bill of lading is a single bill of lading covering a single shipment by more than one mode of transport (for example by truck, then by rail and then by ship to its final destination).

- **CLEAN BILL OF LADING** A clean bill of lading is one where the carrier has noted that the merchandise has been received in apparent good condition (no apparent damage, loss, etc.) and that does not bear such notations as "Shipper's Load and Count," etc. Most forms of documentary payments require a "clean" bill of lading in order for the seller to obtain payment.

- **CLAUSED BILL OF LADING** Opposite of clean bill of lading, a claused bill of lading is one that contains notations that specify a shortfall in quantity or deficient condition of the goods and/or packaging. There are some circumstances in which transport documents with clauses are acceptable. For example, in the steel trade, such notations are the rule rather than the exception. If this is the case, the letter of credit should explicitly state which clause(s) will be deemed acceptable.

ISSUES AND NOTES REGARDING BILLS OF LADING

Many issues concerning bills of lading come up with regard to satisfying the written instructions of the buyer for documentation in letter of credit transactions.

- **MULTIPLE MODES OF TRANSPORT** In documentary letter of credit transactions, if multiple modes of transport are permitted, or partial shipments allowed, and part of the goods will be shipped by one mode of transport and part by another, it is necessary to put "or" or "and/or" between the names of the required transport documents. For example, if the goods are to be shipped by both sea and air, the letter of credit might specify "marine bill of lading and/or air waybill."

- **ORIGINALS** In documentary credit transactions, the full set of original transport documents (one or more) must be presented. If the full set of transport documents consists of several originals, all of the originals should be submitted. The buyer can stipulate in the letter of credit the number of originals to be issued in a set, but many countries prefer or require that a set contain only one original of each document.

- **NAMED CARRIER** A transport document must appear on its face to have been issued by a named carrier or its agent. This does not mean that the buyer must name the carrier in the documentary credit application. It merely means that the transport document must indicate the name of the carrier. The applicant is free to stipulate a particular carrier, although this could cause delay in shipment.

- **ON DECK** An "on deck" notation on a transport document indicates that the goods have been placed above the deck level on the ship (subject to wind and weather). Such a notation will not be acceptable in letter of credit transactions unless specifically authorized. If the transport document shows that the goods are loaded on deck, any accompanying insurance document must show cover against "on deck" risks. Bear in mind, however, that dangerous or specialized cargo (including certain chemicals and live animals) often are or must be carried on deck.

- **ON BOARD** An "on board" notation on a bill of lading indicates that the goods have in fact been loaded on board or shipped on a named vessel. This notation is made by the carrier, the master of the ship, or the carrier's or master's agent. Unless expressly authorized, the transport document issued by the carrier must reflect that it is "on board" in order for the seller to obtain payment under a documentary credit.

Marine/Ocean/Port-to-Port Negotiable Bill of Lading

DEFINITION

A marine bill of lading is a transport document covering port-to-port shipments of goods (for carriage of goods solely by sea).

✔ KEY ELEMENTS

The marine bill of lading contains the following elements:

1. Name of carrier with a signature identified as that of the carrier, or ship's master, or an agent of the carrier or ship's master
2. An indication or notation that the goods have been loaded "on board" or shipped on a named vessel. Also, the date of issuance or date of loading
3. An indication of the port of loading and the port of discharge
4. A sole original, or if issued in multiple originals, the full set of originals
5. The terms and conditions of carriage or a reference to the terms and conditions of carriage in another source or document
6. No indication that the document is subject to a charter party and no indication that the named vessel is propelled by sail only
7. Meets any other stipulations of the letter of credit (when applicable)

! CAUTIONS & NOTES

Most notes relate to rules concerning bills of lading in transactions involving a letter of credit payment.

- VESSEL NAME If the bill of lading includes the notation "intended vessel," it must also contain an "on board" notation of a named vessel along with the date of loading, even if the named vessel is the same as the intended vessel.
- PORT OF LOADING If the document indicates a place where the goods were received by the carrier different from the port of loading, the document must also contain an "on-board" notation indicating the port of loading as named in the letter of credit and the named vessel, along with the date.
- TRANSPORT DOCUMENTS If a documentary letter of credit calls for a port-to-port shipment but does not call specifically for a marine bill of lading, the banks will accept a transport document, however named, that contains the above information. Banks will normally accept the following documents under this title: ocean bill of lading, combined transport bill of lading, short form bill of lading, or received for shipment bill of lading, provided it carries the notation "on board."
- ENDORSEMENT If the documents are drawn up "to the order of" the exporter or "to order," they must be endorsed.
- TRANSSHIPMENT If the letter of credit prohibits transshipment, this document will be rejected if it specifically states that the goods will be transshipped.
- TRANSFER IN TRANSIT Since this is a negotiable instrument, it may be endorsed and transferred to a third party while the goods are in transit.

SAMPLE MARINE/OCEAN/PORT-TO-PORT BILL OF LADING

Carrier:
Hapag-Lloyd Container Linie GmbH, Hamburg

Bill of Lading
Multimodal Transport or Port to Port Shipment

PAGE 2

Hapag-Lloyd

Shipper: WATSON/SHAKLEY RICE INTERNATIONAL 8176 WILLOW STREET WINDSOR, CALIFORNIA CA 95492-9305	**Hapag-Lloyd Reference:** 14013696 **B/L-No.:** HLCUOAK980300049 **Export References:** SHPR REF: JFC(UK) LTD FWDR REF: SF01078226 C.H.B.NO: 5118
Consignee or Order: TO THE ORDER BANK OF LLOYDS LONDON L/C# 3892XVGR012965	**Forwarding Agent:** F.M.C.NO: 0087 NALDUZAK ASSOCIATES, INC. 5088A DIAMOND HEIGHTS BLVD. SAN FRANCISCO, CA 94131-1605 **Consignee's Reference:**
Notify Address (Carrier not responsible for failure to notify; see clause 20 (1) hereof): CONNOLLY (UK) LIMITED #1 1000 NORTH CIRCLE ROAD EAST STAPLES CORNER LONDON NW2 7JP ENGLAND	**Place of Receipt:**
Pre-Carriage by:	**Place of Receipt by Pre-Carrier:**	**Place of Delivery:**

Ocean Vessel: 50E04	Port of Loading:
HEIDELBERG EXPRES	OAKLAND, CA
Port of Discharge: THAMESPORT	**Place of Delivery by On-Carrier:**

Container Nos., Seal Nos.; Marks and Nos.	Number and Kind of Packages: Description of Goods	Gross Weight (kg)	Measurement (cbm)
HLCU 2254295 SEAL: 136427	1 FCL/FCL 20' CONTAINER STC: 1420 PACKAGES MILLED RICE COMMODITY: 1006000000	43020# 19513K	

```
SHIPPED ON BOARD DATE: MAR/05/1998
PORT OF LOADING: OAKLAND, CA
VESSEL NAME:     KOELN EXPRESS

SHIPMENT PURSUANT TO SC NO. 98-302
SHIPPER'S LOAD, STOWAGE AND COUNT
FREIGHT PREPAID - ORIGIN TERMINAL CHARGE PREPAID
NO S.E.D. REQUIRED, SECTION 30.39 FTSR, C.A.S. - JL.
THESE COMMODITIES, TECHNOLOGY OR SOFTWARE WERE EXPORTED FROM
THE UNITED STATES IN ACCORDANCE WITH THE EXPORT ADMINISTRATION
REGULATIONS.     DIVERSION CONTRARY TO U.S. LAW PROHIBITED, NLR
```

ORIGINAL

Above Particulars as declared by Shipper. Without responsibility or warranty as to correctness by carrier (see clause 11(1) and 11(2))

Total No. of Containers/Packages received by the Carrier:	Shipper's declared value (see clause 7(1) and 7(2) hereof): 1	**Received** by the Carrier from the Shipper in apparent good order and condition (unless otherwise noted herein) the total number or quantity of Containers or other packages or units indicated in the box opposite entitled "Total No. of Containers/Packages received by the Carrier" for Carriage subject to all the terms and conditions hereof **(including the Terms and Conditions on the Reverse hereof and the Terms and Conditions of the Carrier's Applicable Tariff)** from the Place of Receipt or the Port of Loading, whichever is applicable, to the Port of Discharge or the Place of Delivery, whichever is applicable. One original Bill of Lading, duly endorsed, must be surrendered by the Merchant to the Carrier in exchange for the Goods or a delivery order. In accepting this Bill of Lading the Merchant expressly accepts and agrees to all its terms and conditions whether printed, stamped or written, or otherwise incorporated, notwithstanding the non-signing of this Bill of Lading by the Merchant. **In Witness whereof** the number of original Bills of Lading stated below all of this tenor and date has been signed, one of which being accomplished the others to stand void.

Movement	FCL/FCL	Currency	USD

Charge	Rate	Basis	WT/MEA/VAL	Payment	Amount
THO	420.00	CTR	1	P	420.00
SEA	1530.00	CTR	1	P	1530.00
BAF	40.00	CTR	1	P	40.00
CAF	6.00	PCT	1530	P	91.80
THD	185.00	CTR	1	C	185.00

Place and Date of Issue:
CORTE MADERA, CA   MAR/05/1998

Freight Payable at:	Number of original Bs/l:
CORTE MADERA, CA	3/3

For above named carrier
Hapag-Lloyd (America) Inc.
(as agent)   *Alen Miller*

Total Freight Prepaid	Total Freight Collect	Total Freight
2081.80	185.00	2266.80

Non-Negotiable Sea Waybill

DEFINITION

A non-negotiable sea waybill is a transport document covering port-to-port shipments. It is not a title document, is not negotiable, and cannot be endorsed.

✔ KEY ELEMENTS

The non-negotiable sea waybill contains the following elements:

1. Name of carrier with a signature identified as that of the carrier, ship's master, or agent for the carrier or ship's master

2. An indication or notation that the goods have been loaded "on board" or shipped on a named vessel. Also, the date of issuance or date of loading

3. An indication of the port of loading and the port of discharge

4. A sole original, or if issued in multiple originals, the full set of originals

5. The terms and conditions of carriage or a reference to the terms and conditions of carriage in another source or document

6. No indication that the document is subject to a charter party and no indication that the named vessel is propelled by sail only

7. Meets any other stipulations of the letter of credit (when applicable)

! CAUTIONS & NOTES

Most notes relate to rules concerning bills of lading in transactions involving a letter of credit payment.

■ VESSEL NAME If the document includes the notation "intended vessel," it must also contain an "on board" notation of a named vessel along with the date of loading, even if the named vessel is the same as the intended vessel.

■ PORT OF LOADING If the document indicates a place where the goods were received by the carrier different from the port of loading, the document must also contain an "on-board" notation indicating the port of loading as named in the letter of credit and the named vessel, along with the date.

■ TRANSPORT DOCUMENTS If the letter of credit calls for a port-to-port shipment but does not call specifically for a marine bill of lading, the banks will accept a transport document, however named, that contains the above information. Banks will normally accept the following documents under this title: ocean bill of lading, combined transport bill of lading, short form bill of lading, or received for shipment bill of lading, provided it carries the notation "on board."

■ WAYBILLS Because they are not title documents, sea waybills eliminate many of the inconveniences of a bill of lading and offer advantages in situations where the rigid security of a bill of lading is not required. Waybills reduce the opportunity for fraud and they remove the problems of goods arriving ahead of documents.

Sea waybills are appropriate for shipments between associated companies, for shipments to an agent for sale at destination on an open account basis, and for shipments between companies that have established mutual trust.

SAMPLE NON-NEGOTIABLE SEA WAYBILL

Express Cargo Bill

Carrier:
Hapag-Lloyd Container Linie GmbH, Hamburg

Multimodal Transport or Port to Port Shipment

PAGE 2

Hapag-Lloyd

Shipper:	Hapag-Lloyd Reference:	ECB-No.:
ABC WINE COMPANY 1234 SPAIN STREET SONOMA, CA 96476	10347784	HLCUOAK980300071

Export References:
USS-NL-000-008

C.H.B.NO: 5118

Consignee:	Forwarding Agent: F.M.C.NO: 0087
DELAHAY WINE ENTERPRISES, LTD. HAZELDONK 1408 - 1412 NL 4386 LH BREDA THE NETHERLANDS	NALDUZAK ASSOCIATES, INC. 5088A DIAMOND HEIGHTS BLVD. SAN FRANCISCO, CA 94131-1605

Consignee's Reference:

Notify Address (Carrier not responsible for failure to notify):	Place of Receipt:
DELAHAY WINE ENTERPRISES, LTD. HAZELDONK 1408 - 1412 NL 4386 LH BREDA THE NETHERLANDS	

Pre-Carriage by:	Place of Receipt by Pre-Carrier:	Place of Delivery:

Ocean Vessel: 06E07	Port of Loading:
KOELN EXPRESS	OAKLAND, CA

Port of Discharge:	Place of Delivery by On-Carrier:
ROTTERDAM	

Container Nos.; Seal Nos.; Marks and Nos	Number and Kind of Packages; Description of Goods	Gross Weight (kg)	Measurement (cbm)
HLCU 4073300 SEAL: 2902455 PO-DS: 3327-04G PO-C1: EL100093	1 X 40' CONTAINER SAID TO CONTAIN: 1246 CS CALIFORNIA WINES LESS THAN 14% ALCOHOL. COMMODITY: 2204000000	19872 KGM	

SHIPPED ON BOARD DATE: MAR/06/1998
PORT OF LOADING: OAKLAND, CA
VESSEL NAME: KOELN EXPRESS

SHIPMENT PURSUANT TO SC NO. 98-500
SHIPPER'S LOAD, STOWAGE AND COUNT
FREIGHT COLLECT
PROTECT AGAINST EXTREME TEMPERATURES
THESE COMMODITIES LICENSED BY THE U.S. FOR ULTIMATE DESTINATION
THE NETHERLANDS.   DIVERSION CONTRARY TO U.S. LAW PROHIBITED.

Above Particulars as declared by Shipper. Without responsibility or warranty as to correctness by carrier

RECEIPT

Total No. of Containers/Packages received by the Carrier	Shipper's declared value (see clause 7(1) and 7(2) hereof):
1	

Movement	ECL/ECL	Currency	USD

Charge	Rate	Bass	WT/MEA/VAL	Payment	Amount
THO	500.00	CTR	1	C	500.00
SEA	1701.00	CTR	1	C	1701.00
BAF	80.00	CTR	1	C	80.00
CAF	21.00	PCT	1701	C	357.21
THO	343.00	CTR	1	C	167.33

RECEIVED by the Carrier from the Shipper in apparent good order and condition (unless otherwise noted herein) the total number or quantity of Containers or other packages or units indicated in the box opposite entitled "Total No. of Containers/Packages received by the Carrier" for Carriage subject to all the terms and conditions hereof (INCLUDING THE TERMS AND CONDITIONS ON THE REVERSE HEREOF AND THE TERMS AND CONDITIONS OF THE CARRIER'S APPLICABLE TARIFF) from the Place of Receipt or the Port of Loading, whichever is applicable, to the Port of Discharge or the Place of Delivery, whichever is applicable. In accepting this Express Cargo Bill the Merchant expressly accepts and agrees to all its terms and conditions whether printed, stamped or written, or otherwise incorporated, notwithstanding the non-signing of this Express Cargo Bill by the Merchant

Place and Date of Issue:
CORTE MADERA, CA   MAR/05/1998

Freight Payable at:
BARKING, U.K.

For above named carrier
Hapag-Lloyd (America) Inc.
(as agent)

Total Freight Prepaid	Total Freight Collect	Total Freight
	2805.54	2805.54

90115743

Express Cargo Bill · Not Negotiable

Charter Party Bill of Lading

DEFINITION

A charter party bill of lading is a transport document covering port-to-port shipments of goods issued by a party chartering a vessel (as opposed to a named carrier or shipping line).

ISSUED BY

The charter party bill of lading is issued by the party chartering a vessel; specifically not a carrier.

✔ KEY ELEMENTS

The charter party bill of lading contains the following elements:

1. An indication that the bill of lading is subject to a charter party
2. A signature or authentication by the ship's master or owner, or an agent for the ship's master or owner
3. Does not name a carrier
4. An indication or notation that the goods have been loaded "on board" or shipped on a named vessel. Also, the date of issuance or date of loading
5. An indication of the port of loading and the port of discharge
6. A sole original, or if issued in multiple originals, the full set of originals
7. No indication that the named vessel is propelled by sail only
8. Meets any other stipulations of the letter of credit (when applicable)

! CAUTIONS & NOTES

The charter party bill of lading may have preprinted wording indicating that the shipment has been loaded "on board" the "named vessel," but the document must still be signed as per number two above.

If preprinted wording is used, the date of issuance is deemed to be the date of loading on board. In all other cases the document must contain an "on board" "named vessel" notation along with the date the shipment was loaded on board.

SAMPLE CHARTER PARTY BILL OF LADING

CODE NAME: "CONGENBILL" . EDITION 1978

Shipper Swiss Export Ltd. Industriestrasse 200 CH-8050 Zürich-Oerlikon	**BILL OF LADING** B/L No. TO BE USED WITH CHARTER-PARTIES GGG/mzf 101

Consignee

TO ORDER OF SHIPPER

Reference No.
1150.01.23.

SHIPCRAFT TRANSPORT INC.

General Agents:

SHIPCRAFT A/S
(Hovedgaden 16)
P O Box 142
DK-2970 Hoersholm, Denmark
Phone: 4 2-571033
Telex: 37584 Shpcr Dk
Fax: 4 2-571044

Notify address

1st: ViaMAT (Far East)
     1-10-7 Higashi Gotanda
     Sinagawa-Ku, TOKYO 141

2nd: Suzuki K.K.
     Saitama

Agent for Switzerland:

MAT TRANSPORT AG
Erlenstrasse 95
P.O. Box
CH-4002 Basel, Switzerland

Vessel M/V TIGER	Port of loading Cherbourg
Port of discharge Yokohama	

Phone: 061 68 68 000
Fax: 061 68 68 001

Shipper's description of goods			Gross weight	
92HBFC0803T 1 - 240	240 packages ============	MACHINERY as per contract PQ 733 054 dated 12.10.19.. Letter of credit No. MC986CH34 dated 4.12.19..	452'500 kg ==========	1202 m3

ORIGINAL

(of which -0-(none) on deck at Shipper's risk; the Carrier not
being responsible for loss or damage howsoever arising)

Freight payable as per CHARTER-PARTY dated .... 7. March 19.. FREIGHT ADVANCE. Received on account of freight: PREPAID AS AGREED Time used for loading .... 0 .. days .. 23 .... hours.	S H I P P E D at the Port of Loading in apparent good order and condition on board the Vessel for carriage to the Port of Discharge or so near thereto as she may safely get the goods specified above. Weight, measure, quality, quantity, condition, contents and value unknown. IN WITNESS whereof the Master or Agent of the said Vessel has signed the number of Bills of Lading indicated below all of this tenor and date, any one of which being accomplished the others shall be void. FOR CONDITIONS OF CARRIAGE SEE OVERLEAF
Freight payable at Basel/Switzerland	Place and date of issue Basel, - 6. Mai 19..
Number of original Bs/L 3/3 (Three)	Signature **MAT TRANSPORT AG** as agent of the owner i.e. Shipcraft Transport Inc.

Printed and sold
by Carl Svanberg Tryckeri AB. Box 91, 35103 Vaxjö.
by authority of The Baltic and International Maritime Conference,
Copenhagen

Multimodal (Combined) Transport Document

DEFINITION

A multimodal transport document is a bill of lading covering a shipment by two or more modes of transport, such as shipping by rail and by sea.

ISSUED BY

The multimodal transport document is issued by a freight-forwarder, logistics firm, or carrier. In some instances the document may be filled out by the exporter/consignor, but then signed by an agent of the carrier.

✔ KEY ELEMENTS

The multimodal transport document contains the following elements:

1. Name of carrier or multimodal transport operator with a signature identified as that of the carrier, transport operator, ship's master, or agent of one of these

2. An indication that the shipment has been "dispatched," "taken in charge," or "loaded on board," along with a date

3. Indication of the place of receipt of the shipment, which may be different from the place of actual loading "on board" and the place of delivery of the shipment, which may be different from the place of discharge

4. A sole original, or if issued in multiple originals, the full set of originals

5. The terms and conditions of carriage or a reference to the terms and conditions of carriage in another source or document other than the multimodal transport document

6. No indication that the document is subject to a charter party and no indication that the named vessel is propelled by sail only

7. Meets any other stipulations of the letter of credit (when applicable)

! CAUTIONS & NOTES

■ RECEIPT OF GOODS In multimodal situations the contract of carriage and liability is for a combined transport from the place of shipment to the place of delivery. Thus, the document evidences receipt of goods and not shipment on board.

■ DATE OF ISSUANCE The date of issuance of the document is deemed to be the date of dispatch unless there is a specific date of dispatch, taking in charge, or loading on board, in which case the latter date is deemed to be the date of dispatch.

■ TRANSPORT DOCUMENTS Even if a letter of credit prohibits transshipment, banks will accept a multimodal transport document that indicates that transshipment will or may take place, provided that the entire carriage is covered by one transport document.

A combined transport document issued by a freight forwarder is acceptable to banks in a letter of credit unless the credit stipulates otherwise or unless the credit specifically calls for a "marine bill of lading." The issuing freight forwarder accepts carrier responsibility for performance of the entire contract of carriage and liability for loss or damage wherever and however it occurs.

■ NEGOTIABILITY As a rule, multimodal transport documents are not negotiable.

SAMPLE MULTIMODAL (COMBINED) TRANSPORT DOCUMENT

Bill of Lading   PAGE 2   **Hapag-Lloyd**

Carrier:
Hapag-Lloyd Container Linie GmbH, Hamburg   Multimodal Transport or Port to Port Shipment

Shipper:	Hapag-Lloyd Reference:	B/L-No.:
WILSON COMMODITIES INTERNATIONAL 100 MEADOWCREEK DRIVE CORTE MADERA, CA 94125	10347484	HLCUOAK980204041

Export References:

REF#156008
REF#156008
C.H.B.NO: 12330

Consignee or Order:	Forwarding Agent: F.M.C.NO: 0953
ZAIDNERS INTERNATIONAL B.V. POSTBUS 27 4870 AA ETTEN-LEUR THE NETHERLANDS	NALOUZAK ASSOCIATES, INC. 5088A DIAMOND HEIGHTS BLVD. SAN FRANCISCO, CA 94131-1605 Consignee's Reference:

Notify Address (Carrier not responsible for failure to notify; see clause 20 (1) hereof)	Place of Receipt:
GARCIA ROTTERDAM B.V. POSTBUS 425 3200 AK SPIJKENISSE THE NTHERLANDS	FRESNO, CA

Pre-Carriage by:	Place of Receipt by Pre-Carrier:	Place of Delivery:

Ocean Vessel: 23E06	Port of Loading:	
ROTTERDAM EXPRESS	OAKLAND, CA	
Port of Discharge:	Place of Delivery by On-Carrier:	
ROTTERDAM		

Container Nos.. Seal Nos.. Marks and Nos.	Number and Kind of Packages: Description of Goods	Gross Weight (kg)	Measurement (cbm)
HLXU 4787302 SEAL: 3814	1 40' HC REEFER CONTAINER STC: 791 CARTONS OF RASPBERRIES SEEDLESS COMMODITY: 0811000003 MAINTAIN TEMPERATURE AT -18.0 CELSIUS OR LOWER	42857LBS	

SHIPPED ON BOARD DATE: FEB/17/1998
PORT OF LOADING: OAKLAND, CA
VESSEL NAME: CAPE HENRY

CARGO STOWED UNDER REFRIGERATION
SHIPPER'S LOAD, STOWAGE AND COUNT
FREIGHT COLLECT
THESE COMMODITIES, TECHNOLOGY OR SOFTWARE WERE EXPORTED FROM
THE UNITED STATES IN ACCORDANCE WITH THE EXPORT ADMINISTRATION
REGULATIONS.   DIVERSION CONTRARY TO U.S. LAW PROHIBITED. NLR

ORIGINAL

Above Particulars as declared by Shipper. Without responsibility or warranty as to correctness by carrier (see clause 11(1) and 11(2))

Total No. of Containers/Packages received by the Carrier	Shipper's declared value (see clause 7(1) and 7(2) hereof):	
1		

Movement   FCL/FCL

Charge	Rate	Basis	WT/MEA/VAL	Payment	Amount
OLF	490.00	CTR	1	C	490.00
THO	500.00	CTR	1	C	500.00
SEA	3805.00	CTR	1	C	3805.00
BAF	80.00	CTR	1	C	80.00
CAF	21.00	PCT	3805	C	799.05
THD	343.00	CTR	1	C	170.12

Currency   USD

Received by the Carrier from the Shipper in apparent good order and condition (unless otherwise noted herein) the total number or quantity of Containers or other packages or units indicated in the box opposite entitled "Total No. of Containers/Packages received by the Carrier" for Carriage subject to all the terms and conditions hereof **(including the Terms and Conditions on the Reverse hereof and the Terms and Conditions of the Carrier's Applicable Tariff)** from the Place of Receipt or the Port of Loading, whichever is applicable, to the Port of Discharge or the Place of Delivery, whichever is applicable. One original Bill of Lading, duly endorsed, must be surrendered by the Merchant to the Carrier in exchange for the Goods or a delivery order. In accepting this Bill of Lading the Merchant expressly accepts and agrees to all its terms and conditions whether printed, stamped or written, or otherwise incorporated, notwithstanding the non-signing of this Bill of Lading by the Merchant.

In Witness whereof the number of original Bills of Lading stated below all of this tenor and date has been signed, one of which being accomplished the others to stand void.

Place and Date of Issue:
CORTE MADERA, CA   FEB/23/1998

Freight Payable at:	Number of original Bs/l:
DESTINATION	3/3

For above named carrier
Hapag-Lloyd (America) Inc.
(as agent)   *Allen Miller*

Total Freight Prepaid	Total Freight Collect	Total Freight
	5844.17	5844.17

90116741

Air Transport Document (Air Waybill)

DEFINITION
An air waybill is a non-negotiable transport document covering transport of cargo by air from airport to airport.

ISSUED BY
The air waybill is issued by the air carrier (or by a freight forwarder or logistics company). In some instances the document may be filled out by the exporter/seller/consignor, but then signed by an agent of the airline.

✔ KEY ELEMENTS
The air waybill contains the following elements:

1. Name of carrier with a signature identified as that of the carrier or its named agent
2. An indication that the goods have been accepted for carriage. Also, the date of issuance or date of loading
3. An indication of the actual date of dispatch (if required by a documentary credit), or, if the actual date of dispatch is not required by the letter of credit, the issuance date of the document is deemed to be the date of shipment
4. An indication of the airport of departure and airport of destination
5. Appears on its face to be the original
6. The terms and conditions of carriage or a reference to the terms and conditions of carriage in another source or document
7. Meets any other stipulations of the letter of credit (when applicable)

! CAUTIONS & NOTES
■ FLIGHT DATA Information contained in the "for carrier use only" box concerning flight number and date are not considered to be the actual flight number and date. The air waybill should not be required to indicate an "actual flight date" since IATA regulations specify that reservations requested by the shipper shall not be inserted under "Flight/Date."

■ ORIGINALS Since air waybills are issued in three originals—one for the issuing carrier, one for the consignee (buyer), and one for the shipper/consignor (seller)—a documentary letter of credit should not require presentation of more than one original. Nor should it call for a "full set of original air waybills."

■ NEGOTIABILITY The air waybill is not a negotiable document. It indicates only acceptance of goods for carriage.

The air waybill must name a consignee (who can be the buyer). In a letter of credit payment situation the waybill should not be required to be issued "to order" and/or "to be endorsed" (since it is not a negotiable instrument). Also, since it is not negotiable, and it does not evidence title to the goods, in order to maintain some control of goods not paid for by cash in advance, sellers often consign air shipments to their sales agents or freight forwarders' agents in the buyer's country.

SAMPLE AIR WAYBILL

| 085 | BSL | 7260 2751 | | | | | | | | | | | | 085-7260-2751 |

Shipper's Name and Address	Shipper's account Number	NOT NEGOTIABLE
SWISS EXPORT LTD AIRFREIGHT DIVISION ZUERICH		**AIR WAYBILL** **swissair** ✈ AIR CONSIGNMENT NOTE Issued by: Swiss Air Transport Co., Ltd., Zurich, Switzerland Member of IATA (International Air Transport Association)

Copies 1, 2 and 3 of this Air Waybill are originals and have the same validity

Consignee's Name and Address	Consignee's account Number	
IMPORT KONTOR VIENNA Phone: 633 7876		It is agreed that the goods described herein are accepted in apparent good order and condition (except as noted) for carriage SUBJECT O THE CONDITIONS OF CONTRACT ON THE REVERSE HEREOF. THE SHIPPER'S ATTENTION IS DRAWN TO THE NOTICE CONCERNING CARRIERS' LIMITATION OF LIABILITY. Shipper may increase such limitation of liability by declaring a higher value for carriage and paying a supplemental charge if required.

Issuing Carrier's Agent Name and City	Accounting information
FORWARDING LTD BASLE	

Agent's IATA Code	Account No.
81-4 0000	

Airport of Departure (Addr. of the Carrier) and requested Routing
BSL-VIE

to	By first Carrier	Routing and Destination	to	by	to	by	Currency	CHGS Code	WT/VAL PPD COLL	Other PPD COLL	Declared Value for Carriage	Declared Value for Customs
VIE	SWISSAIR						SFR		CO PP		NVD	

Airport of Destination	Flight/Date	For Carrier Use only Flight/Date	Amount of Insurance	INSURANCE - If carrier offers insurance and such insurance is requested in accordance with conditions on reverse hereof, indicate amount to be insured in figures in box marked amount of insurance.
VIENNA	SR436/8.7.			

Handling Information

No of Pieces RCP	Gross Weight	kg lb	Rate Class	Commodity Item No.	Chargeable Weight	Rate Charge	Total	Nature and Quantity of Goods (incl. Dimensions or Volume)
8	200,6	K	C	6750	201	1.90	381.90	CHEMICALS NOT RESTRICTED CONTRACT No 100-15-2
8	200,6							

Prepaid	Weight Charge	Collect	Other Charges
		381.90	AWA 15.00
	Valuation Charge		
	Tax		

Total other Charges Due Agent	Shipper certifies that the particulars on the face hereof are correct and that insofar as any part of the consignment contains dangerous goods, such part is properly described by name and is in proper condition for carriage by air according to the applicable Dangerous Goods Regulations.
15.00	
Total other Charges Due Carrier	SWISS EXPORT LTD / p.o Forwarding LTD
	--
	Signature of Shipper or his Agent

Total Prepaid	Total Collect	
15.00	381.90	

Currency Conversion Rates	cc charges in Dest. Currency	07.07.	BASLE	Forwarding LTD
		Executed on (Date)	at (Place)	Signature of Issuing Carrier or its Agent
Charges at Destination	Total collect Charges			
For Carrier's Use only at Destination				085-7260 2751

No. 3 - ORIGINAL for SHIPPER

Form 30.301
Printed in the Fed. Rep. Germany - Bartsch Verlag, Munich-Ottobrunn 600j (III)

Road, Rail or Inland Waterway Transport Documents

DEFINITION

Road, rail, or inland waterway bills of lading are transport documents covering transport of cargo from named points via truck, rail or barge transport.

ISSUED BY

The road, rail or inland waterway transport document is issued by the carrier. In some cases, this document may be filled out by the consignor but then signed by an agent of the carrier.

✔ KEY ELEMENTS

Road, rail, or inland waterway bills of lading contain the following elements:

1. Name of carrier with a signature or authentication identified as that of the carrier or its named agent and/or a reception stamp or other mark noting receipt by the carrier or its named agent
2. An indication that the goods have been accepted for shipment, dispatch or carriage. Also, the date of issuance or date of shipment
3. An indication of the place of shipment and place of destination
4. The terms and conditions of carriage or a reference to the terms and conditions of carriage in another source or document
5. Meets any other stipulations of the letter of credit (when applicable)

! CAUTIONS & NOTES

- DATE OF SHIPMENT In road, rail, or inland waterway transport documents the date of issuance is considered the date of shipment unless there is a reception stamp, in which case that date is deemed to be the date of shipment.

- TRANSPORT DOCUMENTS Unless otherwise stipulated in a documentary credit, banks will accept transport document(s) as presented as a "full set."

- ORIGINALS Unless otherwise stipulated in a documentary credit, banks will accept road, rail, or inland waterway transport documents as originals whether marked as such or not.

Packing List/Bill of Parcels

DEFINITION

A packing list is a document prepared by the shipper listing the kinds and quantities of merchandise in a particular shipment.

A copy of the packing list is often attached to the shipment itself and another copy sent directly to the consignee to assist in checking the shipment when received. It is also called a bill of parcels.

ISSUED BY

The packing list is issued by the exporter/shipper/consignor.

✔ KEY ELEMENTS

The packing list contains the following elements:

1. Name and address of seller (consignor)
2. Name and address of buyer (consignee)
3. Date of issuance
4. Invoice number (reference to invoice that covers the particular shipment)
5. Order or contract number
6. Quantity and description of the goods
7. Weight of the goods
8. Number of packages
9. Shipping marks and numbers
10. Quantity and description of contents of each package, carton, crate or container
11. Any other information as required in the shipper's instructions (e.g., country of origin)

! CAUTIONS & NOTES

The packing list is a more detailed version of the commercial invoice but without price information. The type of each container is identified, as well as its individual weight and measurements. The packing list is attached to the outside of its respective container in a waterproof envelope marked "Packing List Enclosed," and is immediately available to authorities in both the countries of export and import.

A packing list is not required in all transactions, but is a standard requirement by the export or import laws of certain countries and by some buyers. A packing list helps the consignee at the point of delivery and warehouse personnel to identify which contents may be found in which packages. Also, if custom authorities require an inspection, it allows them to easily identify the specific package they wish to open.

Courier Receipt

DEFINITION
A courier receipt is a document issued by a courier or expedited delivery service evidencing receipt of goods for delivery to a named consignee.

ISSUED BY
The courier receipt is typically filled out by the exporter/seller/consignor, but then signed by an agent of the courier company.

✔ KEY ELEMENTS
Courier receipts should include the following elements:

1. Appears on its face to name the issuer
2. Appears on its face to be stamped, signed, or authenticated by the service
3. Name and address of the shipper/consignor (seller)
4. Name and address of the consignee (buyer)
5. The date of pick-up or receipt of the goods by the service
6. Meets any other stipulations of the letter of credit (when applicable)

! CAUTIONS & NOTES
Unless a documentary credit names a specific courier or expedited delivery service, banks will accept a document issued by any courier or service.

Post Receipt

DEFINITION
A post receipt is a document issued by the postal service of a country evidencing receipt of goods for delivery to a named consignee.

ISSUED BY
The post receipt for an expedited shipment is typically filled out by the exporter/seller/consignor, but then signed by an agent of the postal authority.

✔ KEY ELEMENTS
Postal receipts should include the following elements:

1. A stamp or authentication by the postal service
2. The date of pick-up or receipt of the goods by the postal service
3. Name and address of the shipper/consignor (seller)
4. Name and address of the consignee (buyer)
5. Meets any other stipulations of the letter of credit (when applicable)

SAMPLE COURIER RECEIPT

PLEASE TYPE. SEE INSTRUCTIONS ON BACK.

UPS SHIPPER NO. / BILLING NO.

SHIPPER'S IDENTIFICATION NO.
FOR CUSTOMS PURPOSES (E.I.N.)

SHIPPER

NAME OF SENDER

TELEPHONE NO. (VERY IMPORTANT)

COMPANY NAME AND ADDRESS (include Postal ZIP Code)

COUNTRY

CONSIGNEE'S UPS ACCOUNT NO.

CONSIGNEE'S IDENTIFICATION NO. FOR CUSTOMS
PURPOSES (V.A.T., IMPORTERS NO. ETC.)

CONSIGNEE

NAME OF CONTACT PERSON

TELEPHONE NO. (VERY IMPORTANT)

COMPANY NAME AND ADDRESS (include Postal ZIP Code)

COUNTRY

PAYMENT OF CHARGES

BILLING OPTION (SELECT ONE OPTION ONLY)
REFER TO APPROPRIATE SERVICE GUIDE FOR OPTIONS AVAILABLE BY COUNTRY

PREPAID · FREIGHT COLLECT · FOB · C&F · DELIVERED DUTY PAID, V.A.T. UNPAID · BILL DUTY, TAX AND SHIPPING CHARGES TO SHIPPER

BILL "SHIPPER'S" PORTION OF SHIPPING CHARGES TO PARTY LISTED BELOW (COMPLETE THIS SECTION IF SHIPPER'S PORTION OF SHIPPING CHARGES IS TO BE BILLED TO ANY PARTY OTHER THAN THE SHIPPER LISTED ABOVE)

COMPANY NAME

COUNTRY

UPS ACCOUNT NO.

02876501 3/94 W

FOR INTERNATIONAL INFORMATION OR ASSISTANCE CALL 1-800-782-7892

UPS Waybill / Tracking No. 4857 0744 248

United Parcel Service

UPS WORLDWIDE SERVICES WAYBILL (non-negotiable)

SPECIAL INSTRUCTIONS

SERVICE LEVEL (PLEASE MARK A LARGE X . SELECT ONE LEVEL ONLY)
REFER TO THE APPROPRIATE SERVICE GUIDE FOR LEVELS AVAILABLE)

EXPRESS
EXPEDITED
STANDARD

SHIPMENT INFORMATION

NO. OF PACKAGES IN SHIPMENT · TOTAL ACTUAL WEIGHT OF SHIPMENT · TOTAL BILLABLE WEIGHT OF SHIPMENT (DIMENSIONAL CHARGES, IF APPLICABLE) · ZONE

DESCRIPTION OF GOODS

INDICATE IF DOCUMENTS ONLY

DECLARED VALUE OF SHIPMENT FOR INSURANCE ONLY (US $) · DECLARED VALUE OF SHIPMENT FOR CUSTOMS ONLY (US $)

REFERENCE NO. 1

REFERENCE NO. 2

Unless a greater value for insurance is declared in writing in the space provided on this waybill, the carrier's liability is limited by the Warsaw Convention and any amendments thereto.

RECEIVED FOR UPS BY: · DATE: · TIME:

U.S. SHIPPER'S EXPORT DECLARATION (S.E.D.)

An S.E.D. is required when the value of any commodity is greater than $2,500 U.S. or when a validated export license is required.
☐ Check here if S.E.D. is included with Export Documents
☐ Check here if S.E.D. is electronically filed and enter your C.A.S. (S.A.S.) no.
☐ Check here and complete section below if you want UPS to prepare an S.E.D. on your behalf

HARMONIZED TARIFF CODE

VALIDATED LICENSE NUMBER & EXPIRATION DATE OR GENERAL LICENSE NUMBER

PARTIES TO TRANSACTION · COUNTRY OF ORIGIN (WHERE MANUFACTURED)

☐ RELATED
☐ NON-RELATED

COUNTRY OF ULTIMATE DESTINATION

The shipper agrees to the terms and conditions on the reverse of this waybill. The shipper authorizes UPS to act as forwarding agent for export controls and customs purposes.

SHIPPER'S SIGNATURE · DATE OF SHIPMENT

The shipper certifies that these commodities/technical data are licensed by the United States for shipment to the ultimate destination country recorded in the Consignee section or the U.S. Shipper's Export Declaration section of this waybill. Diversion contrary to U.S. law is prohibited.

SHIPPER'S COPY

SAMPLE POST RECEIPT

POST OFFICE TO ADDRESSEE **EXPRESS MAIL** **EMS**

EG762575732US

ORIGIN (POSTAL USE ONLY)

INTERNATIONAL SHIPMENTS ONLY
☐ Business Papers
☐ Merchandise

Customs forms and commercial invoice may be required.
See Pub 273 and International Mail Manual

P.O. ZIP

Date in
Mo. Day Yr.

Time in
☐ AM ☐ PM

Weight
lbs oz.

No Delivery
☐ Weekend ☐ Holiday

Day of Delivery
☐ Next ☐ Second
☐ 12 Noon ☐ 3 PM

Military
☐ 2nd Day ☐ 3rd Day

Int'l Alpha Country Code

Acceptance
Clerk Initials

☐ Flat Rate Envelope

Postage
$

Return Receipt

C.O.D.

Total Postage & Fees
$

DELIVERY (POSTAL USE ONLY)

Delivery Attempt · Time ☐ AM ☐ PM · Employee Signature

Delivery Attempt · Time ☐ AM ☐ PM · Employee Signature

Delivery Attempt · Time ☐ AM ☐ PM · Employee Signature

Signature of Addressee or Agent
X

Name - Please Print
X

MAILING COPY

CUSTOMER USE ONLY

METHOD OF PAYMENT:
Express Mail Corporate Acct. No.
Federal Agency Acct. No. or
Postal Service Acct. No.

☐ WAIVER OF SIGNATURE (Domestic Only) I wish delivery to be made without obtaining the signature of the addressee or the addressee's agent (if in the judgement of the delivery employee, the article can be left in a secure location) and I authorize the delivery employee to sign that the shipment was delivered and understand that the signature of the delivery employee will constitute valid proof of delivery.

NO DELIVERY
☐ WEEKEND ☐ HOLIDAY

Customer Signature

FROM: (PLEASE PRINT) PHONE

TO: (PLEASE PRINT) PHONE

PLEASE PRESS HARD

YOU ARE MAKING 3 COPIES

LABEL 11-B 5/94

For Pickup or Tracking Call 1-800-222-1811

CHAPTER 6

Export Documents

THIS CHAPTER PROVIDES A BROAD OVERVIEW of export documentation. The good news is that for many transactions, export documentation is extremely simple. Exports of non-regulated goods from many countries may require only a commercial invoice, a bill of lading, and an export declaration. It's that easy.

One way to think about export (and import) documentation is that the basic process is very simple, but that each complicating factor adds another document to the process. One complicating factor adds one document, three complicating factors add three documents.

Therefore, the key to understanding export documentation is to understand documentation for a basic transaction and then to understand the documentation for the complicating factors. Let's start with the most straightforward export transaction and then we'll provide "cheat sheets" for the complicating factors.

NOTES

1. Throughout this chapter we will assume that the exporter and importer have already made a contract to sell and purchase a set amount of goods.
2. Many documents required for export are also required for shipping, import formalities and banking/payment. Details will be given step-by-step.
3. Many documents mentioned in this chapter are more fully described in other chapters in which case a cross reference to a specific chapter or page is given.

A fundamental issue is the difference between "required for export" and "required of the exporter." The difference is that certain documents are required of the exporter by the export authority whereas other documents are required of the exporter for other purposes including transportation and to satisfy the needs of the importer. The primary concern of this chapter is documentation required for export.

Basic Export Documentation

DEFINITION
Basic export transactions are those with no complicating factors whatsoever and therefore require the most minimal documentation. In this example, documentation requirements are for export only and do not include any documentation for import to the country of destination.

CONDITIONS AND ASSUMPTIONS
For a basic export transaction, all of the following must apply:

- A written or verbal agreement has been made between the parties specifying the product, quantity, price, delivery date, delivery method and all other conditions of sale including who will pay for shipping, insurance, duties and other costs.

▨ The countries of export and import have normal trade relations.

▨ The country of export is economically and politically stable and does not have excessive export or foreign exchange regulations. No export licensing is required.

▨ The country of import is economically and politically stable and does not have excessive import or foreign exchange regulations.

▨ The country of import does not require consular certifications or invoices.

▨ The goods traded are unregulated and do not require export licenses or permits.

▨ The buyer is familiar with the goods traded and has no reason to believe that the goods shipped will be anything other than the goods ordered.

▨ The parties to the transaction either know each other, have traded successfully in the past, or have no reason to expect duplicity or dishonesty from the other party.

▨ The terms are payment in advance, by cash, check, wire-transfer, or credit card, or on open account with future payment by check, wire-transfer, or credit card.

REVIEW OF CONDITIONS AND ASSUMPTIONS

Sound like a lot of conditions? Not really. Most apply to normal domestic transactions: The parties come to agreement, they know each other, they know the merchandise, there is a stable trading environment, and payment is either in advance or on credit terms. The seller issues a commercial invoice and a bill of lading (or waybill) for shipping the goods. The only "complicating factor" in this transaction is that the goods are exported and one complicating factor adds one additional document. In this case the EXPORT DECLARATION.

BASIC EXPORT DOCUMENTS

Document	Notes	Sample
Commercial Invoice	A	page 36
Bill of Lading/Air Waybill (B/L)	B	page 40
(Shipper's) Export Declaration	C	page 66

SUPPLEMENTAL BASIC EXPORT DOCUMENTS (AS REQUIRED)

Document	Notes	Sample
Packing List	D	page 53
Certificate of Origin	E	page 107
Insurance Documents	F	page 104

NOTES

■ A—COMMERCIAL INVOICE (issued by the exporter/seller)
This is the key transaction or accounting document. It identifies the seller and buyer, gives identifying numbers such as invoice number, the date, shipping date, mode of transport, delivery and payment terms, and a complete list and description of the goods being sold including quantities, prices, and discounts. It is virtually identical to a domestic commercial invoice. Export invoices are often signed by the exporter

and state the country of origin of the goods.
See "Transaction Documents" starting on page 31.

- B—BILL OF LADING (issued by the shipping line or carrier of the goods)
  This is the key transportation document. It is issued by a carrier (such as a shipping line or airline) to a shipper (exporter or seller), signed by the captain, agent, or owner of a vessel, furnishing written evidence regarding receipt of the goods (cargo), the conditions on which transportation is made (contract of carriage), and the engagement to deliver goods at the prescribed port of destination to the lawful holder of the bill of lading. A bill of lading is, therefore, both a receipt for merchandise and a contract to deliver it as freight. It can also serve as the title document, in which case whoever holds it can claim possession of the goods.
  See "Transport Documents" starting on page 38.

- C—EXPORT DECLARATION (issued by the exporter)
  This is the formal statement by the exporter to the export authority identifying the seller, buyer, goods shipped, date of issuance, country of origin and country of final destination, quantity and description of the goods, and other shipping details. This is required by the country of export to control exports, assess duties (if any) and compile trade statistics.
  See "(Shipper's) Export Declaration (SED)" on page 66.

- D— PACKING LIST (or BILL OF PARCELS) (issued by the exporter)
  This identifies the consignor (exporter/seller/shipper) and consignee (importer/buyer), total packages in the shipment, package and container contents, weights, dimensions, marks and numbers. This is typically a copy of the invoice, with prices deleted and shipping details added. Even when not required, a packing list is a good idea. It enables the consignee to check that the full shipment has been received.
  See "Transport Documents" starting on page 38.

- E—CERTIFICATE OF ORIGIN (issued by the exporter/seller, local exporting country chamber of commerce or other authorizing agency)
  This document declares the country of origin of the goods shipped. It is typically required by the importer for the import authority of the country of import, but may also be required by the export authority. In the most straightforward transactions the exporter/seller makes a notation on the export declaration or at the bottom of the invoice: "Made in ___(country name)___".
  See "Special Documents" starting on page 100.

- F—INSURANCE DOCUMENT (issued by the insurance company or its agent)
  This document provides proof of insurance for a shipment. In the most straightforward transactions, insurance is provided by the carrier and may be noted on the bill of lading itself.
  See "Special Documents" starting on page 100.

Exporter's Instruction Documents

Instruction documents issued by the exporter are generally not required for export, but are highly recommended to facilitate the export process and make certain everyone is performing according to the exporter's specific instructions.

EXPORTER'S INSTRUCTION DOCUMENTS

Document	Notes	Sample
Forwarder's Instructions	A	-
Shipping Instructions	B	-
Stowage Instructions	C	-
Hazardous Materials/Dangerous Goods Instructions	D	-
Bank Instructions	E	-

- A—FORWARDER'S INSTRUCTIONS (issued by the consignor) This form or letter contains instructions for booking the shipment of cargo and completing the transport documents. Most freight forwarders and logistics firms have their own printed form but the necessary information may also be typed on the exporter's letterhead.

- B—SHIPPING INSTRUCTIONS (issued by the consignor)
  This form or letter gives specific instructions to the shipping company or freight forwarder regarding the shipment. It is virtually identical to the FORWARDER'S INSTRUCTIONS. The bill of lading is typically drawn up from this information. Many shipping lines have pre-printed forms or computerized entry systems to aid the exporter/shipper. Consignors who provide their own bill of lading generally attach a copy of their shipping instructions to the bill of lading.

- C—STOWAGE INSTRUCTIONS (issued by the consignor)
  This form or letter issued by the consignor contains specific instructions regarding how or where a cargo should be stowed during transport. For example, a shipper may require that the shipment is placed below deck and amidships for greater protection from the elements.

- D—HAZARDOUS MATERIALS/DANGEROUS GOODS INSTRUCTIONS (issued by the consignor) This form or letter is issued by the consignor and contains information regarding a shipment of hazardous material or dangerous goods. A hazardous material is a substance or product that has been determined to be capable of posing an unreasonable risk to health, safety and property when transported in commerce. The same material is classified as dangerous goods when transported by air. Hazards are classified as "Other Regulated Materials" (ORM-A through ORM-E) and include irritating, corrosive, caustic, flammable, radioactive and other life or health threatening materials. Special handling instructions must be provided and containers must be properly emblazoned with warning labels and stickers.

- E—BANK INSTRUCTIONS (issued by the consignor)
  This form or letter to the bank contains information about how the exporter/ seller wishes to have payment secured for a shipment when a documentary collection or documentary letter of credit is used.
  See "Banking Documents" starting on page 76.

Additional Export Documentation ("Complicating" Factors)

While many export transactions require minimal documentation, many more require that the exporter issue or secure additional documentation. These documents follow in lock-step with various export or import requirements and fall into a small number of broad categories.

Listed below are the categories of additional export documentation required. Following the list are more complete explanations of the regulatory context, the documents themselves, and, where appropriate, cross references to other parts of this book where additional information can be found.

- Export Licenses, Permits and Inspections
- Special Transport Documents
- Banking and Foreign Exchange Documents
- Import Documents (issued or secured for the importer)

Export Licenses, Permits, Declarations and Inspections

All countries seek to control their exports for political, economic or security purposes. Governments also seek to control who exports, what is exported and the country of final destination of their exports.

In some cases, an outright export ban on a commodity or product might exist, or a product may be banned only to certain countries, while in other cases it may be permissible to export a product but only under certain specified conditions. In all cases, governments use various forms of export licenses, permits and declarations to control and track their exports.

EXPORT LICENSES, PERMITS AND DECLARATIONS

Document	Notes	Sample
Export License	A	page 65
Export Permit	A	-
Destination Control Statement	B	-
Hazardous Materials/Dangerous Goods Declaration	C	-
Exchange Control Documents	D	-
Inspection Certificates	E	page 100

- A—EXPORT LICENSE/PERMIT (issued by the export authority) Export licenses and permits are either general (license or permit to export any goods) or specific (license or permit to export specific goods). In some instances, a general license to export and a specific permit to export a restricted product must both be obtained.

- B—DESTINATION CONTROL STATEMENT (made by the exporter/consignor) Most exporting countries restrict the export of certain commodities and products to certain destination countries. These restrictions can be motivated by political, economic or strategic reasons. The most common example is the restricted export of high-technology products with military application to "unfriendly" nations. Countries with these export restrictions require that the exporter make statements that they are not selling restricted products or diverting such products to restricted countries. This can be accomplished on a specific declaration form or on a standard export declaration form that all exporters must complete. For example, when exporting from the USA, the correct wording to be printed, written, typed or stamped on the export declaration must read: "These commodities, technology, or software were exported from the United States in accordance with the export administration regulations. Diversion contrary to U.S. law is prohibited."

- C—DANGEROUS GOODS DECLARATION (issued by the consignor) Countries put special procedures in place for handling and documenting shipments of hazardous materials/dangerous goods including biohazards and toxic and radioactive wastes. This declaration is a formal statement about the contents of a specific shipment and is used by both export authorities and the carrier.

- D—EXCHANGE CONTROL DOCUMENTS Certain countries seek to control the flow of their national currency by controlling imports and exports (e.g., Russia, Nigeria, India). Such countries require that the exporter (and importer) make a statement or declaration that the flow of goods and payments follow prescribed regulations. Exporters may be required to submit documentation that payment has been received prior to the export of the goods, or importers may be required to apply for approval to obtain hard currency to pay for an import shipment.

- E—INSPECTION CERTIFICATES Certain products and commodities may require export inspections and certification. See "Special Documents" starting on page 100.

Special Transport Documents

Special transport documents may be issued in place of a standard ocean bill of lading, used to notify the carrier and export authorities of special or dangerous cargo, or to document certain transactions between the carrier and the consignor.

These documents may be issued by the consignor or the carrier and may be presented to the consignor, the carrier, banks, the buyer, or the export authorities.

SPECIAL TRANSPORT DOCUMENTS

Document	Notes	Sample
Special (form of) Bill of Lading	A	page 40
Shipping Instructions	B	-
Stowage Instructions	C	-
Hazardous Materials/Dangerous Goods Declaration	D	-
Dock Receipt	E	-
Mate's Receipt	F	-

- A—SPECIAL (FORM OF) BILL OF LADING (issued by the carrier) Different forms of the bill of lading are issued by carriers depending upon the mode of transport and the needs of the exporter and importer as defined by the terms of their transaction. For example, the importer, in a letter of credit, may require presentation of an "air waybill." See "The Bill of Lading" on page 40.

- B—SHIPPING INSTRUCTIONS (issued by the consignor) This form gives specific instructions to the shipping company or freight forwarder regarding the shipment. The bill of lading is typically drawn up from this information. Many shipping lines have pre-printed forms or computerized entry systems to aid the shipper/exporter. Consignors who provide their own bill of lading generally attach a copy of any additional shipping instructions to the bill of lading. See "Exporter's Instruction Documents" on page 59.

- C—STOWAGE INSTRUCTIONS (issued by the consignor) These are specific instructions given to the shipping line or freight forwarder regarding how and/or where a shipment should be stowed during transport. See "Exporter's Instruction Documents" on page 59.

- D—DANGEROUS GOODS DECLARATION (issued by the consignor) All carriers will require notification if a shipment contains hazardous materials or dangerous goods. This declaration is a formal statement about the contents of a specific shipment and is used by the carrier to safely handle the cargo.

- E—DOCK RECEIPT This receipt is issued by a port officer or warehouse supervisor certifying that the goods have been received from a domestic carrier and that accountability for the goods has transferred to the international carrier.

- F—MATE'S RECEIPT This is a document issued by the captain or mate of a vessel as a receipt for goods shipped.

For all the above see "Transport Documents" starting on page 38.

Bank and Finance Documents

The exporter's contact with banks is determined principally by the terms of payment agreed to with the importer/buyer. If the terms are payment in advance by cash, check, wire-transfer, or credit card, or on open account with future payment by cash, check, wire-transfer, or credit card, the exporter's only contact with the bank will be to deposit the buyer's check, to have the buyer's wire transfer funds be deposited into an account, or bank processing of a credit card payment.

However, if a documentary collection or documentary letter of credit are used as the payment mechanism, much greater involvement with the bank is required. See "Banking Documents" starting on page 76.

Documents Issued or Secured for the Importer

The following documents are not generally required by the export authorities or by the transport carrier. However, exporters are generally asked (or required) by the importer/buyer to provide documentation to assist in the process of importing goods to the country of destination. Many of the documents listed here have already been mentioned; this list is given for easy reference purposes only.

Note that the list of required import documents will have the addition of documents issued or supplied by the importer. See "Import Documents" starting on page 68.

IMPORT DOCUMENTS ISSUED OR SECURED BY THE EXPORTER

Document	Notes	Sample
Commercial Invoice	A	page 36
Bill of Lading/Air Waybill (B/L)	B	page 40
Packing List	C	page 53
Packing Declaration	D	-
Certificate of Origin	E	page 107
Certified Consular Invoice	F	-
Insurance Certificate	G	page 104
(Quality) Inspection Certificates	H	page 112
Special Inspection Certificates	I	-

■ A—COMMERCIAL INVOICE (issued by the exporter/seller)
This is the key transaction or accounting document.
See "Transaction Documents" starting on page 31.

■ B—BILL OF LADING (issued by the shipping line or carrier of the goods)
This is the key transportation document.
See "Transport Documents" starting on page 38.

■ C—PACKING LIST (or BILL OF PARCELS) (issued by the exporter)
This identifies the contents of the shipment.
See "Transport Documents" starting on page 38.

■ D—PACKING DECLARATION (issued by the shipper/exporter or forwarder)
This document certifies that packing materials are free from pests.
See "Special Documents" starting on page 100.

■ E—CERTIFICATE OF ORIGIN (issued by the exporter/seller, local exporting country chamber of commerce or other authorizing agency)
This document establishes the country of origin of the goods shipped. A special Regional Trade Association certificate of origin may be required to obtain special duty rates.
See "Special Documents" starting on page 100.

■ F—CERTIFIED CONSULAR INVOICE (issued by a consulate or chamber of commerce of the country of final destination located in the country of export)
This establishes country of origin, description and values of goods shipped.
See "Special Documents" starting on page 100.

■ G—INSURANCE CERTIFICATE (issued by an insurance company or its agent)
This document offers proof of insurance for a shipment.
See "Special Documents" starting on page 100.

■ H—(QUALITY) INSPECTION CERTIFICATE (generally issued by a third-party independent testing company)

This document offers independent certification of product quality, quantity or adherence to certain specifications.
See "Special Documents" starting on page 100.

■ I—SPECIALIZED INSPECTION CERTIFICATES (generally issued by a third-party independent testing company or government authority)
This is a large category of inspection certificates and can include:
The PHYTOSANITARY CERTIFICATE
The FUMIGATION CERTIFICATE
The VETERINARY CERTIFICATE
The PUBLIC HEALTH CERTIFICATES
See "Special Documents" starting on page 100.

Electronic Filing of Documents

Increasingly, certain export documents are required to be filed electronically. Many systems are now in place (or soon will be implemented) whereby the same electronic document format may be used for exporting/importing between dozens of different countries. This standardization is proving to be of great benefit to the international exporter/importer.
See "Electronic Documents" starting on page 114.

Export Document Assistance

As this chapter has demonstrated, export documentation can be extremely simple or exceedingly complex. Many exporters rely upon the services of freight forwarders and logistics professionals. Often, their services are quite reasonable in comparison to the total freight bill. Many exporters whose goal is to handle all export documentation internally often rely upon these professionals until they become well versed in the regulatory and documentation requirements for their commodities and countries of destination.

Export License/Permit

DEFINITION

An export license is a document granting an individual or business entity the general right to export or the right to export a specific shipment of a commodity or good to a named country.

An export license, therefore, can be required of all exporters or required only for a particular export. Export licenses are often required for the export of certain natural resources, cultural relics, drugs, technology, live animals, food products, strategic commodities, and arms and armaments.

ISSUED BY

Export licenses are issued by the export authority or government agency with regulatory authority of a country of export.

✔ KEY ELEMENTS

Each country's export license will have its own form and content. Certain elements are likely to be included in all export licenses:

1. Name and address of seller

2. Name and address of buyer

3. Date of issuance

4. Validity date

5. Description of goods covered by license

6. Name of country of origin

7. Name of country of ultimate destination

8. Statement that the goods will not be diverted to another country contrary to the laws of the exporting country.

! CAUTIONS & NOTES

Some countries require export licenses for virtually all commodities and products. The license is a means of control, taxation and statistical reporting. In some cases the lack of an export license can be cited as a reason why goods cannot be shipped, even though payment has been made. Buyers should be especially careful about buying sensitive goods from countries with a demonstrated lack of rule by law.

The export license is typically the seller's responsibility. However, a buyer who is dealing in sensitive goods should research the need for an export license beforehand. Failure to secure such a license can delay or prevent shipment and can jeopardize the validity of a payment such as a documentary letter of credit.

(Shipper's) Export Declaration (SED)

DEFINITION

An export declaration is a document specifying the particulars of an export transaction.

Note that different countries have different names for the export declaration. In the USA it is called the SED or Shipper's Export Declaration.

ISSUED BY

The export declaration is issued by the exporter/seller/consignor and presented to the export authority of the country of export. In some cases, it must be certified by the export authority.

✔ KEY ELEMENTS

Each country has its own export declaration form. The shipper's export declaration typically includes the following elements:

1. Name and address of seller
2. Name and address of buyer
3. Date of issuance
4. Quantity and description of the goods
5. Country of origin of the goods shipped
6. Country of final destination of the goods
7. Quantity and description of the goods
8. Shipping details including: weight of the goods, number of packages, and shipping marks and numbers
9. Statement that the goods will not be diverted to another country contrary to the laws of the exporting country

! CAUTIONS & NOTES

The shipper's export declaration is used by a nation's customs authorities to control exports and compile trade statistics. The SED is rarely a requirement of the importer, but rather is required of the exporter by the export authorities.

SAMPLE EXPORT DECLARATION FOR THE UNITED STATES

U.S. DEPARTMENT OF COMMERCE ○ U.S. CENSUS BUREAU ⋔ Economics and Statistics Administration ○ BUREAU OF EXPORT ADMINISTRATION

FORM **7525-V**   (7-25-2000)   **SHIPPER íS EXPORT DECLARATION**   OMB No. 0607-0152

1a. U.S. PRINCIPAL PARTY IN INTEREST (USPPI) *(Complete name and address)*

ZIP CODE

2. DATE OF EXPORTATION

3. TRANSPORTATION REFERENCE NO.

b. USPPI EIN (IRS) OR ID NO.

c. PARTIES TO TRANSACTION
☐ Related   ☐ Non-related

4a. ULTIMATE CONSIGNEE *(Complete name and address)*

b. INTERMEDIATE CONSIGNEE *(Complete name and address)*

5. FORWARDING AGENT *(Complete name and address)*

6. POINT (STATE) OF ORIGIN OR FTZ NO.

7. COUNTRY OF ULTIMATE DESTINATION

8. LOADING PIER *(Vessel only)*

9. METHOD OF TRANSPORTATION *(Specify)*

14. CARRIER IDENTIFICATION CODE

15. SHIPMENT REFERENCE NO.

10. EXPORTING CARRIER

11. PORT OF EXPORT

16. ENTRY NUMBER

17. HAZARDOUS MATERIALS
☐ Yes   ☐ No

12. PORT OF UNLOADING *(Vessel and air only)*

13. CONTAINERIZED *(Vessel only)*
☐ Yes   ☐ No

18. IN BOND CODE

19. ROUTED EXPORT TRANSACTION
☐ Yes   ☐ No

20. SCHEDULE B DESCRIPTION OF COMMODITIES *(Use columns 22ñ24)*

D/F or M (21)	SCHEDULE B NUMBER (22)	QUANTITY ñ SCHEDULE B UNIT(S) (23)	SHIPPING WEIGHT (Kilograms) (24)	VIN/PRODUCT NUMBER/ VEHICLE TITLE NUMBER (25)	VALUE (U.S. dollars, omit cents) (Selling price or cost if not sold) (26)

27. LICENSE NO./LICENSE EXCEPTION SYMBOL/AUTHORIZATION

28. ECCN *(When required)*

29. Duly authorized officer or employee

The USPPI authorizes the forwarder named above to act as forwarding agent for export control and customs purposes.

30. I certify that all statements made and all information contained herein are true and correct and that I have read and understand the instructions for preparation of this document, set forth in the **"Correct Way to Fill Out the Shipperís Export Declaration."** I understand that civil and criminal penalties, including forfeiture and sale, may be imposed for making false or fraudulent statements herein, failing to provide the requested information or for violation of U.S. laws on exportation (13 U.S.C. Sec. 305; 22 U.S.C. Sec. 401; 18 U.S.C. Sec. 1001; 50 U.S.C. App. 2410).

Signature

Confidential ñ For use solely for official purposes authorized by the Secretary of Commerce (13 U.S.C. 301 (g)).

Title

Export shipments are subject to inspection by U.S. Customs Service and/or Office of Export Enforcement.

Date

31. AUTHENTICATION *(When required)*

Telephone No. *(Include Area Code)*

E-mail address

This form may be printed by private parties provided it conforms to the official form. For sale by the Superintendent of Documents, Government Printing Office, Washington, DC 20402, and local Customs District Directors. The **"Correct Way to Fill Out the Shipperís Export Declaration"** is available from the U.S. Census Bureau, Washington, DC 20233.

CHAPTER 7

Import Documents

THIS CHAPTER PROVIDES A BROAD OVERVIEW of import documentation. For many basic transactions, import documentation is simple. Importers of non-regulated goods from many countries can present a commercial invoice, a bill of lading, and an import declaration, and they're done.

As with export documentation, each complicating factor adds another document to the process. One complicating factor adds one document, three complicating factors add three documents.

The chapter structure is to start with the most basic import transaction and then to proceed to more complicated transactions with both specialized requirements and specialized documentation.

NOTES

1. Throughout this chapter we will assume that the exporter and importer have already made a contract to sell and purchase a set amount of goods.

2. Many documents required for import are also required for export formalities, shipping, and banking/payment. Details will be given step-by-step.

3. Many documents mentioned in this chapter are more fully described in other chapters in which case we give a cross reference to a specific chapter or page.

Import documents are issued or secured by both the exporter, the importer (or a customs broker working for the importer) or by third parties. In each case, we will name a document, see where it comes from and offer a full description. In many cases, we'll also give a cross reference to another chapter where a more complete description is given.

Basic Import Documentation

DEFINITION

Basic import transactions are those with no complicating factors whatsoever and therefore require the most minimal documentation. In this example, documentation requirements are for import only and do not include any documentation for export from the country of origin.

CONDITIONS AND ASSUMPTIONS

For a basic import transaction, all of the following terms and conditions must apply:

- A written or verbal agreement has been made between the parties specifying the product, quantity, price, delivery date, delivery method and all other conditions of sale including who will pay for shipping, insurance, duties and other costs.

- The countries of export and import have normal trade relations.

- The country of export is economically and politically stable and does not have excessive foreign exchange regulations.

- The country of import does not have excessive import or foreign exchange regulations.

- The country of import does not require consular certifications or invoices.

- The goods traded are unregulated and do not require import licenses or permits.

- The buyer is familiar with the goods traded and has no reason to believe that the goods shipped will be anything other than the goods ordered.

- The parties to the transaction either know each other, have traded successfully in the past, or have no reason to expect duplicity or dishonesty from the other party.

- The terms are payment in advance, by cash, check, wire-transfer, or credit card, or on open account with future payment by check, wire-transfer, or credit card.

REVIEW OF CONDITIONS AND ASSUMPTIONS

Most of the above conditions already apply to normal domestic transactions: The parties come to agreement, they know each other, they know the merchandise, there is a stable trading environment, and payment is either in advance or on credit terms. The buyer gets a commercial invoice and a bill of lading (or waybill) from the seller. The only "complicating factor" in this transaction is that the goods are imported and one complicating factor adds one additional document. In this case the IMPORT DECLARATION.

BASIC IMPORT DOCUMENTS

Document	Notes	Sample
Commercial Invoice	A	page 36
Bill of Lading/Air Waybill (B/L)	B	page 40
Import Declaration/Entry Manifest	C	-

SUPPLEMENTAL BASIC IMPORT DOCUMENTS (AS REQUIRED)

Document	Notes	Sample
Packing List	D	page 53
Certificate of Origin	E	page 107
Insurance Documents	F	page 104

NOTES

- **A—COMMERCIAL INVOICE** (issued by the exporter/seller)
  This is the key transaction or accounting document.
  See "Transaction Documents" starting on page 31.

- **B—BILL OF LADING** (issued by the shipping line or carrier of the goods)
  This is the key transportation document.
  See "Transport Documents" starting on page 38.

■ C—IMPORT DECLARATION (issued by the importer or a customs broker working as agent for the importer)
This is the formal statement by the importer to the import authority identifying the seller, buyer, goods shipped, date of issuance, country of origin and country of final destination, quantity, description and cost of the goods, and shipping details. This is required by the country of import to control imports, assess duties, and compile trade statistics. Note that some countries assess duty on the landed cost, CIF (cost of goods, insurance and freight). This form has different names in different countries. In the USA it is called the entry manifest.
See "Import Documents" starting on page 68.

■ D—PACKING LIST (or BILL OF PARCELS) (issued by the exporter)
This identifies the contents of the shipment.
See "Transport Documents" starting on page 38.

■ E—CERTIFICATE OF ORIGIN (issued by the exporter/seller, local exporting country chamber of commerce or other authorizing agency)
This document declares the country of origin of the goods shipped. It is typically required by the importer for the import authority of the country of import. In the most straightforward transactions the exporter/seller makes a notation on the export declaration or at the bottom of the invoice: "Made in ___(country name)___". A special Certificate of Origin form (such as a NAFTA Certificate of Origin) may be required to take advantage of preferential import duties.
See "Special Documents" starting on page 100.

■ F—INSURANCE DOCUMENT (issued by the insurance company or its agent)
This document provides proof of insurance for a shipment.
See "Special Documents" starting on page 100.

Additional Import Documentation ("Complicating" Factors)

While many import transactions require minimal documentation, others require that the importer issue or secure additional documentation. These document requirements follow various import requirements and fall into a small number of broad categories.

Listed below are the categories of additional import documentation required. Following the list are more complete explanations of the regulatory context, the documents themselves, and, where appropriate, cross references to other parts of this book where more information can be found.

■ Import Licenses, Permits and Declarations

■ Additional Documents Required by the Import Authority

■ Special Transport Documents

■ Banking and Foreign Exchange Documents

Import Licenses, Permits and Declarations

All countries seek to control their imports for political, economic or security purposes. Governments also seek to control who imports, what is imported and the country of origin of their imports.

In some cases an outright import ban on a commodity or product might exist. In other cases, import of a product may be banned only from certain countries, while sometimes it may be permissible to import a product only under certain specified conditions. In all cases, governments use various forms of import licenses, permits and declarations to control and track their imports.

IMPORT LICENSES, PERMITS AND DECLARATIONS

Document	Notes	Sample
Import License	A	-
Import Permit	A	-
Hazardous Materials/Dangerous Goods Declaration	B	-
Exchange Control Documents	C	-

■ A—IMPORT LICENSE/PERMIT (issued by the import authority)
Import licenses and permits are either general (license or permit to import any goods) or specific (license or permit to import specific goods). In some instances, a general license to import and a specific permit to import a restricted product must both be obtained.

■ B—DANGEROUS GOODS DECLARATION (issued by the importer)
Countries put special procedures in place for handling and documenting shipments of hazardous materials/dangerous goods including biohazards and toxic and radioactive wastes. This declaration is a formal statement about the contents of a specific shipment and is used by both import authorities and the carrier.

■ C—EXCHANGE CONTROL DOCUMENTS Certain countries seek to control the flow of their national currency by controlling imports and exports (i.e., Russia, Nigeria, India). Such countries require that the importer make a statement or declaration that the flow of goods and payments follow prescribed regulations. Importers may be required to apply for prior approval to obtain hard currency to pay for an import shipment.

Additional Documents Required by the Import Authority

These are additional documents required by the import authorities and cover a wide range of import related issues. These documents may be issued by the exporter, the importer, foreign governments, country of import governmental agencies and third party organizations and organizations.

ADDITIONAL IMPORT DOCUMENTS

Document	Notes	Sample
Special Certificate of Origin	A	page 108
Customs Bond	B	-
Packing Declaration	C	-
Certified Consular Invoice	D	-
Insurance Certificate	E	page 104
Inspection Certificate	F	page 110
Quality Certificate	G	-
Phytosanitary Certificate	H	-
Fumigation Certificate	I	-
Veterinary Certificate	J	-
Public Health Certificate	K	-
ATA Carnet	L	-
Free Sale Certificate	M	-

- A—SPECIAL CERTIFICATE OF ORIGIN (issued by the shipper/exporter or special authorizing agency of the country of export)
  This document certifies the country of origin of a shipment within the context of a regional trade agreement (e.g., the NAFTA Certificate of Origin).

- B—CUSTOMS BOND (issued by the insurance company or its agent)
  This offers evidence that a financial guarantee by an insurance company has been made to the import authority regarding a particular import shipment.

- C—PACKING DECLARATION (issued by the shipper/exporter or forwarder)
  This document certifies that packing materials are free from pests.

- D—CERTIFIED CONSULAR INVOICE (issued or certified by a consulate of the country of final destination located in the country of export)
  This establishes country of origin and description and value of goods shipped.

- E—INSURANCE CERTIFICATE (issued by an insurance agent or company)
  This document offers proof of insurance for a shipment.

- F—INSPECTION CERTIFICATE (generally issued by a third-party independent testing company) This document certifies product quality, quantity or adherence to certain specifications. These certificates are required by certain nations as a means of controlling techniques commonly used to circumvent exchange control regulations (i.e., overstated quantities or under-declared valuations). The import license usually requires a "clean report of findings" by an authorized inspection organization before goods can clear customs or payment can be made.

- G—QUALITY CERTIFICATE (issued by independent testing companies)
  This document certifies that the products contained in the shipment meet the standards of the importing country. Most countries require that this certification be provided by the exporter and be approved and filed by the appropriate governmental control agency (i.e., the exporting country Department of Consumer Safety) prior to shipment.

- H—PHYTOSANITARY CERTIFICATE (generally issued by a third-party independent testing company or government authority)
  This document certifies that a shipment of imported plants or plant products (i.e., seeds, bulbs, flowers, fruits, vegetables, etc.) is free from pests or disease. This certificate requires on-site inspection(s) of the plants during the growing season and is usually provided by the agricultural ministry or department of the country of export.

- I—FUMIGATION CERTIFICATE (generally issued by a third-party independent testing company or government authority)
  This document certifies that wood-based packing materials, used clothing or packaging (i.e., coffee or cocoa bean bags) and certain other commodities have been fumigated or sterilized to kill any pests. These certificates are issued by private companies authorized to carry out these procedures and include details of the specific process, temperature range, chemicals and concentrations used.

- J—VETERINARY CERTIFICATE (generally issued by a third-party independent testing company or government authority)
  This document certifies that a shipment of live animals, fresh, chilled and frozen meats (and sometimes even canned meats) has been inspected for disease.

- K—PUBLIC HEALTH CERTIFICATE (generally issued by a third-party independent testing company or government authority)
  This document certifies that a shipment has been inspected for disease.

- L—ATA CARNET (issued by national chambers of commerce affiliated with the Paris-based International Chamber of Commerce (ICC))
  An international customs document used for the temporary duty-free admission of certain goods into a country in lieu of the usual customs documents.

- M—FREE SALE CERTIFICATE (issued by a local chamber of commerce in the exporter's country)
  This certifies that certain commodities (i.e., medicines, vitamins, other health products) are freely sold in the country of origin.

For all of the above see "Special Documents" on page 100.

Special Transport Documents

Special transport documents may be issued in place of a standard ocean bill of lading, used to notify the carrier and import authorities of special or dangerous cargo, or prepared to document certain transactions between the carrier and the consignor or consignee.

These documents may be issued by the carrier or the consignor and may be presented to the consignor, the carrier, the banks, the buyer/consignee, or the import authorities.

SPECIAL TRANSPORT DOCUMENTS

Document	Notes	Sample
Special (Form of) Bill of Lading	A	page 40
Shipping Instructions	B	-
Stowage Instructions	C	-

- **A—SPECIAL (FORM OF) BILL OF LADING** (issued by the carrier)
  Different forms of the bill of lading are issued by carriers depending upon the mode of transport and the needs of the exporter and importer as defined by the terms of their transaction. For example, the importer, in a letter of credit, may require presentation of an "air waybill" as proof of shipment by air.
  See "The Bill of Lading" starting on page 40.

- **B—SHIPPING INSTRUCTIONS** (generally issued by the consignor/shipper/exporter, but often at the request of the importer/buyer/consignee)
  This form gives specific instructions to the shipping company about how to handle a shipment. The bill of lading is typically drawn up from this information.

- **C—STOWAGE INSTRUCTIONS** (issued by the consignor/shipper/exporter)
  This form gives specific instructions to the shipping line about how and where to stow cargo during transport and is typically used when shipping hazardous, oversize, fragile, live or other unusual cargo.

For instructions see "Exporter's Instruction Documents" on page 59.

Banking and Foreign Exchange Documents

The importer's contact with banks is determined principally by the terms of payment agreed to with the exporter/seller. If the terms are payment in advance by cash, check, wire-transfer, or credit card, or on open account with future payment by cash, check, wire-transfer, or credit card, the importer's only contact with the bank will be to write a bank check, to have the bank send a wire transfer of funds to the exporter, or to process a credit card payment.

However, if a documentary collection or documentary letter of credit is used as the payment mechanism, much greater involvement with the bank is required.

See "Banking Documents" starting on page 76.

Electronic Filing of Documents

Increasingly, customs documents are required to be filed electronically. Many systems are now in place whereby the same electronic document format may be used for exporting/importing between dozens of different countries. This standardization is proving to be of great benefit to the international trader.

See "Electronic Documents" starting on page 114.

Import Document Assistance/Customs Brokers

Import documentation can be extremely simple or exceedingly complex. Many importers rely upon the services of a customs broker for assistance. Even importers whose goal is to handle all import documentation internally often rely upon these professionals until they become well versed in import requirements for their range of commodities.

If you do use a customs broker you will be required to sign a LIMITED POWER OF ATTORNEY. This gives your customs broker the right to act on your behalf with the customs authority and to sign customs documents in your name.

CHAPTER 8

Banking Documents

BECAUSE INTERNATIONAL TRADE always involves the transfer of money between different business entities in different national jurisdictions using different currencies, banks are almost always involved—and so are the all-important banking documents. In fact, documentation is so much a part of the process that banks refer to them as documentary transactions. Bankers rely upon these packets of paper because they spell out every nuance of who, what, where, when, and how much money will be paid.

Method of Payment

The key factor with regard to banking documentation relates to the method of payment used in the transaction. Depending upon the method of payment, bank documentation can be minimal or extremely complex.

PREPAID/CASH-IN-ADVANCE/CASH WITH ORDER

This is the most straightforward international transaction where the buyer negotiates the purchase of goods and prepays with cash, bank wire transfer, credit card, travelers' checks or perhaps even a personal or business check. The importer/buyer either picks up the goods on the spot, or they are shipped after payment has been received. In this case, the banks are hardly involved other than cashing a check, handling a bank wire transfer, arranging for traveler's checks or processing a credit card payment.

Prepaid terms are common, especially where the transaction value is not great or where the importer/buyer trusts the exporter/seller sufficiently to prepay for the shipment. Obviously, this is the best arrangement for the exporter/seller.

NOTE: The exporter/seller and importer/buyer are still responsible for all export and import regulatory and documentary requirements.

OPEN ACCOUNT

On open credit terms the exporter/seller ships goods to the importer/buyer on the expectation that payment will be made at a set future date. This can be 30, 60, 90 or even 180 or 360 days after shipment. Payment on the due date may still be made by cash, bank wire transfer, credit card, traveler's checks or even a personal or business check. Once again, the banks are hardly involved at all.

Open account terms are also common, especially where the exporter/seller sufficiently trusts that the importer/buyer will pay for the shipment at a later date. Obviously, this is the best arrangement for the importer/buyer.

NOTE: The exporter/seller and importer/buyer are still responsible for all export and import regulatory and documentary requirements.

DOCUMENTARY COLLECTIONS

In a documentary collection transaction, the seller uses banks as intermediaries to ensure that the documents conveying title to the shipment are not transferred to the buyer until payment (or a suitable promise of payment) has been made. It is a "documentary" collection because documents form the basis of the procedure. Documentary collection transactions require a great deal of documentation.

NOTE: Documentary collections are explained in the pages that follow.

DOCUMENTARY LETTERS OF CREDIT

In a letter of credit transaction, the buyer uses banks as intermediaries to ensure that payment to the seller is made only after certain terms and conditions have been met. All the terms and conditions involve presentation of documents. This is why the technical name for this procedure is "documentary letter of credit."

Letter of credit transactions require a great deal of documentation.

NOTE: Letters of credit are explained in the pages that follow.

International Banking Documents

The following table and notes will introduce you to the various documents used in international banking. Detailed information will be given for Drafts, Documentary Collections and Documentary Letters of Credit after this section.

DOCUMENTARY COLLECTION PAYMENT DOCUMENTS

Document	Notes	Sample
Documentary Collection Order	A	page 96
Negotiable Bill of Lading	B	page 48
Document Package for the Importer/Buyer	C	-
Draft/Bill of Exchange	D	page 79

DOCUMENTARY LETTER OF CREDIT PAYMENT DOCUMENTS

Document	Notes	Sample
Letter of Credit (L/C) Application	E	page 86
Letter of Credit (L/C)	F	page 92
Letter of Credit (L/C) Advice/Notification	G	-
Request for Amendment (to the Letter of Credit)	H	-
Amendment (to the Letter of Credit)	I	-
Amendment Notification (to the Letter of Credit)	J	-
Negotiable Bill of Lading	B	page 42
Document Package for the Importer/Buyer	C	-
Draft/Bill of Exchange	D	page 79

- A—DOCUMENTARY COLLECTION ORDER (prepared by the seller)
This is the key documentary collection document. It states the terms and conditions under which the bank is to hand over documents (including the title document) to the buyer and to receive payment.

- B—NEGOTIABLE BILL OF LADING (issued by the carrier)
This is the negotiable transport document possession of which confers ownership of the shipment to the holder. See "The Bill of Lading" starting on page 40.

NOTE: Technically, the bill of lading is part of the document package. See below.

- C—DOCUMENT PACKAGE FOR THE IMPORTER/BUYER (prepared by the exporter) This is the group of documents that the exporter prepares for the importer and that are needed to secure the shipment from the carrier and clear customs in the country of import. At the least, this includes a commercial invoice and a certificate of origin, but may also include inspection, insurance and other documents. Technically, the negotiable bill of lading is part of the document package.

- D—BANK DRAFT/BILL OF EXCHANGE (prepared by the exporter/seller)
This is the formal written demand for payment that accompanies the documents sent to the importer/buyer. This demand can be for immediate payment (a sight draft) or for payment at a future fixed date (a time or usance draft).

- E—DOCUMENTARY LETTER OF CREDIT (L/C) APPLICATION (prepared by the importer/buyer)
This is the application the importer/buyer makes to the bank to open a letter of credit naming the exporter/seller as beneficiary. It is both an application for credit (with the bank) and a listing of the terms and conditions under which the bank is to collect documents from the exporter and make payment.

- F—DOCUMENTARY LETTER OF CREDIT (L/C) (issued by the buyer's bank)
This is the actual letter of credit document that the importer's bank prepares (based upon the importer's L/C application) and that is forwarded to the exporter's bank. It details the terms and conditions under which the bank will transfer payment to the seller.

- G—DOCUMENTARY LETTER OF CREDIT (L/C) ADVICE/NOTIFICATION
(issued by the seller's/advising bank) This is the formal notification of the letter of credit presented to the exporter and issued by the seller's/advising bank on behalf of the importer/buyer. It details the terms and conditions under which the bank will transfer payment to the seller.

- H—REQUEST FOR AMENDMENT (TO THE LETTER OF CREDIT) (issued/initiated by the exporter/seller) A seller who wishes to change a term or condition of the letter of credit does so by making a request of the importer/buyer. This can be done verbally, but a formal letter is the preferred method.

- I—AMENDMENT (TO LETTER OF CREDIT) (issued by the importer/buyer's bank)
This is the formal document by the importer/buyer's bank stating the terms of the amendment to the existing letter of credit.

- J—AMENDMENT NOTIFICATION (TO THE LETTER OF CREDIT) (issued by the seller's advising bank) This is the formal notification of the amendment to the letter of credit issued by the seller's advising bank to the exporter/seller.

Drafts, Bills of Exchange and Acceptances

In documentary transactions, sellers make a written demand upon either a bank or the buyer to pay for the shipment of goods. This demand accompanies the documentation package the seller presents to the bank. Such a formal written demand for payment is called a "draft."

DRAFTS

A draft is an unconditional order in writing, signed by a person (drawer) such as a buyer, and addressed to another person (drawee), typically a bank, ordering the drawee to pay a stated sum of money to yet another person (payee), often the seller, on demand or at a fixed or determinable future time. The most common versions of drafts are: (1) SIGHT DRAFTS which are payable when presented, and (2) TIME DRAFTS (also called usance drafts) which are payable at a future fixed (specific) date or determinable (e.g., 30, 60, 90 days) date.

ACCEPTANCES

An acceptance is a time draft that has been accepted and signed by the drawee (the buyer or the bank) for payment at maturity. If a time draft is accepted by a buyer of merchandise, it is called a TRADE ACCEPTANCE. If a time draft is accepted by a bank, it is called a BANKERS' ACCEPTANCE.

In most cases, obviously, a draft accepted by a bank enjoys higher credit standing than a draft accepted by a company or individual, since a bank is presumed to meet its obligation at maturity, and a company or individual in a foreign country may not as readily comply with its obligation.

HOLDING OR DISCOUNTING ACCEPTANCES

In documentary transactions, the seller has two options, once its time draft is accepted. The seller may either hold it until maturity and collect full face value, or discount the draft, most likely with the accepting bank, and take the net value in cash immediately. In these ways, trade and bankers' acceptances often represent the easiest, least expensive way for a seller to provide credit to a buyer, while enjoying the security provided by the documentary transaction.

FINANCING TRANSACTIONS USING ACCEPTANCES

Thus, foreign buyers may indicate that they wish to provide a "time" documentary credit (rather than a "sight" documentary credit). In the case of a time documentary credit, the buyer may agree to allow the seller to increase the sales price slightly in order to offset the acceptance commission and discount costs.

In most cases, the buyer and the buyer's bank will absorb the charges involved, and the seller will receive the full contract sales amount. Since the charges are usually lower than conventional financing charges, the buyer is still better off than if financing had been obtained through a traditional bank loan.

SAMPLE DRAFT AND ACCEPTANCE

① Place/Date **Basle, 10th October 19..**	② **US$ 23'400.--**

③ At **120 days' sight** _please pay against this_ **sole** BILL of EXCHANGE (④ _____ being unpaid)

⑤ to the order of **Swiss Bank Corporation, Basle** _the amount of_

② **US Dollars twentythreethousandfourhundred** -----------------------

⑥ Drawn under L/C No. **26784** _dated_ **15th September 19..**

of **Universal Bank Inc., New York**

⑦ **Universal Bank Inc.**
Park Street
New York, N.Y. 10005

MUELLER AG BASEL
Muller Reg ⑧

---

① **Basle , 10th October 19..** ② **US$**

③ At **120 days' sight** _please pay against this_ ④ **sole**

⑤ to the order of **ourselves**

② **US Dollars twentythreethousandfourhundred** -------------

⑥ Value **in goods. Drawn under documentary credit No 26784 of Unive...**

⑦ M **New York Trading Co.**
1, Wall Street
New York, N.Y. 10048

⑨

New York

MUELLER AG BASEL
Muller Reg ⑧

No

Payable

---

① Place drawn and date
② Currency and amount in numbers and words
③ Validity period
④ Number of originals (sole or first/second)
⑤ If issued to own order: endorsement required

⑥ Reference to credit
⑦ Drawee
⑧ Drawer (handwritten signature)
⑨ Endorsement

"CLEAN" ACCEPTANCES

A "clean" acceptance is one that does not have any notations attached that would compromise its value. In a trade acceptance, the customer promises to pay the bank the full amount of the draft no later than the date of maturity, or upon demand of the bank. The accepted draft, when discounted, becomes a negotiable instrument that can be sold in the acceptance market, which is an over-the-counter market of brokers, dealers, and banks.

Bankers acceptances are generally short-term (up to 180 days). Bankers' acceptances become money market instruments once they are accepted by a major bank, which means that the bank has undertaken to honor the note at its maturity. Because of this characteristic, bankers' acceptances often result in lower financing costs. The difference can range from 1 to 3 percent depending on the transaction and the bank involved. Thus, they are important sources of financing.

Documentary Letters of Credit

A letter of credit is the written promise of a bank, undertaken on behalf of a buyer, to pay a seller the amount specified in the credit provided the seller complies with the terms and conditions set forth in the credit. The terms and conditions of a documentary credit revolve around two issues: (1) the presentation of documents that evidence title to goods shipped by the seller, and (2) payment.

In simple terms, banks act as intermediaries to collect payment from the buyer in exchange for the transfer of documents that enable the holder to take possession of the goods.

Letter of credit (L/C) is the historic and popular term (and abbreviation) used because such credits were and are transmitted in the form of a letter from the buyer's bank. However, the formal term is "documentary" letter of credit because of the importance of documents in the transaction.

REVOCABLE VS. IRREVOCABLE LETTERS OF CREDIT

Letters of credit may be issued by the buyer and issuing bank as revocable or irrevocable. Each has a distinct advantage for buyers and sellers.

- **REVOCABLE CREDIT** A revocable documentary credit gives the buyer and/or issuing bank the ability to amend or cancel the credit at any time right up to the moment of intended payment without approval by, or notice to, the seller. Revocable credits are, therefore, of great advantage to the buyer.

- **IRREVOCABLE CREDIT** An irrevocable documentary credit constitutes a firm contractual obligation on the part of the issuing bank to honor the terms of payment of the credit as issued. The buyer and issuing bank cannot amend or cancel the credit without the express approval of the seller.

NOTE: Irrevocable credits are of advantage to the seller. Virtually all documentary credits issued are irrevocable and so state on their face.

CONFIRMED VS. UNCONFIRMED LETTERS OF CREDIT

Payment under an irrevocable letter of credit is guaranteed by the issuing bank. However, from the seller's perspective, this guarantee may have limited value as the issuing bank may be (1) in a foreign country, (2) beholden to the buyer, (3) small and unknown to the seller, or (4) subject to unknown foreign exchange control restrictions. The seller, therefore, might wish that another, more local bank add its guarantee (confirmation) of payment to that of the issuing bank.

- **UNCONFIRMED (OR ADVISED) LETTER OF CREDIT** In this form of letter of credit, only the issuing bank assumes the undertaking to pay, thus payment is the sole responsibility of the issuing bank.

- **CONFIRMED LETTER OF CREDIT** In this form of letter of credit, both the issuing and advising banks carry the commitment to pay the seller.

The most popular letter of credit for sellers is the irrevocable confirmed letter of credit because it cannot be cancelled by the buyer, and a second bank (usually the seller's bank) adds its guarantee of payment to that of the buyer's bank.

SPECIAL DOCUMENTARY LETTERS OF CREDIT

There are a number of special letters of credit designed to meet the specific needs of buyers, suppliers, and intermediaries. These include:

- REVOLVING CREDIT This is a commitment on the part of the issuing bank to restore the credit to the original amount after it has been used or drawn down.

- RED CLAUSE CREDIT This credit has a special (red) clause that authorizes the confirming bank to make advances to the seller prior to the presentation of the shipping documents, in essence, extending pre-shipment financing to the seller.

- TRANSFERABLE CREDIT In this credit, the original beneficiary transfers all or part of the proceeds of an existing credit to another party (typically the ultimate supplier of the goods). It is normally used by brokers as a financing tool.

- BACK-TO-BACK CREDIT This is a new credit opened on the basis of an already existing, nontransferable credit. It is used by traders to make payment to the ultimate supplier. A trader receives a credit from the buyer and then opens another in favor of the supplier. The first credit is used as collateral for the second credit. The second credit makes price adjustments from which comes the trader's profit.

ROLE OF BANKS

It is important to note that banks are responsible for issues relating to documents and the specific wording of the letter of credit as opposed to issues relating to the goods themselves. See "Important Principles Regarding the Role of Banks" on page 99.

ELECTRONIC APPLICATIONS FOR DOCUMENTARY CREDITS

Electronic applications for documentary credits are becoming more and more common. Buyers install software on their office PCs that enable them to fill out an application and send it to their bank's processing center. Security is provided using encryption and password systems. Electronic applications enable the repeat letter of credit applicant faster turnaround and cuts paperwork for everybody.

CONTRACT PROVISION

It is recommended that buyers and sellers insert a payment provision in their contract that they wish to use a letter of credit as the payment method. The following is a sample contract provision.

PAYMENT: To secure payment, the BUYER NAME shall have ISSUING BANK NAME open an IRREVOCABLE documentary credit naming SELLER as beneficiary. The documentary credit is to be CONFIRMED by CONFIRMING BANK NAME. The documentary credit must remain valid for NUMBER OF MONTHS after issuance and be available AT SIGHT against presentation of the following documents: 1. . . ., 2. . . ., 3. etc. The cost of the credit is to be paid by BUYER NAME. The credit shall be subject to the Uniform Customs and Practice for Documentary Credits (1993 Revision), ICC, Publication Number 500.

The items in UNDERLINED CAPITAL LETTERS are the variables. As with all legal matters, it is best to consult with an experienced attorney for exact wording.

Document Movement for Issuance of an L/C

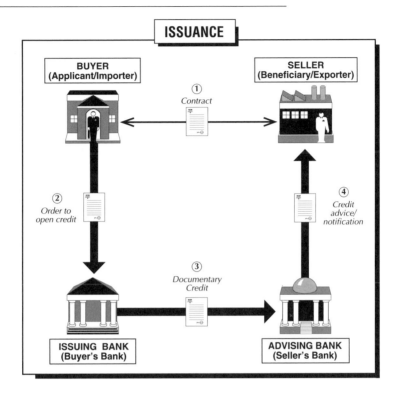

BUYER AND SELLER

1. The buyer and seller make a written or verbal contract agreeing on the terms of sale: (a) specifying a documentary credit as the means of payment, (b) naming an advising bank (usually the seller's bank), and (c) listing required documents.

BUYER (APPLICANT/IMPORTER)

2. The buyer applies to his bank (issuing bank) and opens a documentary credit naming the seller as beneficiary based on specific terms and conditions that are listed in the credit (the documents required).

ISSUING (BUYER'S) BANK

3. The issuing bank sends the documentary credit to the advising bank named in the credit.

ADVISING (SELLER'S) BANK

4. The advising bank informs (advises) the seller of the documentary credit.

Document Movement for Amendment to an L/C

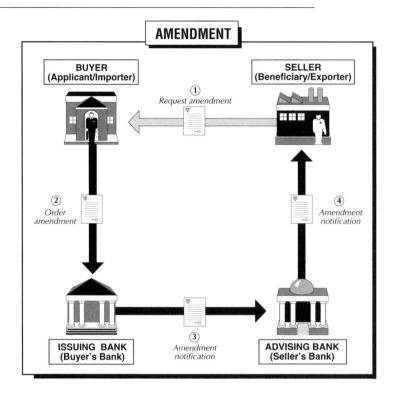

SELLER

1. The seller requests that the buyer make an amendment to the letter of credit. This can be made by a telephone call, a fax letter, e-mail, or by face-to-face negotiation.

BUYER

2. If the buyer agrees, the buyer orders the issuing bank to issue the amendment.

ISSUING (BUYER'S) BANK

3. The issuing bank amends the credit and notifies the advising bank of the amendment.

ADVISING (SELLER'S) BANK

4. The advising bank notifies (advises) the seller of the amendment.

Opening a Documentary Credit

INTRODUCTION

The success or failure of a documentary credit transaction can turn upon the wording of the documentary credit itself. As such, the buyer (whose responsibility it is to open the credit) should adhere to the greatest extent possible to the terms and conditions of the original contractual agreement, keeping the specifications clear and concise and as simple as possible.

REFER TO DOCUMENTS

The buyer's instructions to the issuing bank should be given in clear, professional wording, and should pertain only to documentation, not to the goods themselves. It is very important to demand documents in the credit that clearly reflect the agreements reached.

EXAMPLE 1: Require <u>confirmation</u> that goods are shipped by Conference vessel no more than twenty years old, rather than that the goods be shipped by Conference vessel no more than twenty years old.

EXAMPLE 2: Require <u>confirmation</u> that the goods were packaged in double-strength, waterproof containers, rather than requiring that the goods be packaged in double-strength, waterproof containers.

EXAMPLE 3: Require <u>proof</u> of notification to buyer (such as a copy of the cable or telex) that goods were shipped, rather than requiring that the buyer be notified that the goods were shipped.

Remember, when checking compliance with the documentary credit terms, the banks are concerned only with the documents presented, not with whether a party has complied with individual clauses of a contract.

BE CLEAR AND CONCISE

The wording in a documentary credit should be simple but specific. The more detailed the documentary credit is, the more likely the seller will reject it as too difficult to fulfill. It is also more likely that the banks will find a discrepancy in the details, thus voiding the credit, even though simpler terms might have been found to be in compliance with the credit.

The buyer should, however, completely and precisely set forth the details of the agreement as it relates to credit terms and conditions and the presentation of documents.

DO NOT SPECIFY IMPOSSIBLE DOCUMENTATION

The documentary credit should not require documents that the seller cannot obtain; nor should it call for details in a document that are beyond the knowledge of the issuer of the document. The documents specified should be limited to those required to smoothly and completely conclude an international sale of goods.

Documentary Letter of Credit Application

PROCEDURE

Refer to the application form on the next page for each numbered step.

BUYER

1. BENEFICIARY   Always write the seller's company name and address completely and correctly. A simple mistake here may result in the seller preparing inconsistent or improper documentation on the other end.

2. AMOUNT   State the actual amount of the credit. You may state a maximum amount in a situation where actual count or quantity is in question. You also may use the words APPROXIMATE, CIRCA, or ABOUT to indicate an acceptable 10 percent plus or minus amount from the stated amount. If you use such wording, you will need to be consistent and use it also in connection with the quantity as well.

3. VALIDITY PERIOD   The validity and period for presentation of the documents following shipment of the goods should be sufficiently long to allow the exporter time to prepare the necessary documents and send them to the bank.

4. BENEFICIARY'S BANK   Either leave blank to indicate that the issuing bank may freely select the correspondent bank or name the seller's bank.

5. TYPE OF PAYMENT AVAILABILITY   Sight drafts, time drafts, or deferred payment may be used, as previously agreed to by the seller and buyer.

6. DESIRED DOCUMENTS   The buyer specifies which documents are needed. Buyer can list, for example, a bill of lading, a commercial invoice, a certificate of origin, certificates of analysis, and so on.

7. NOTIFY ADDRESS   An address is given for notification of the imminent arrival of goods at the port or airport of destination. This address can also be used for notification of damage to the shipment while en route. The buyer's business or shipping agent is most often used.

8. MERCHANDISE DESCRIPTION   A short, precise description of the goods is given, along with quantity. Note the comments in number two above concerning approximate amounts.

9. CONFIRMATION ORDER   If the foreign beneficiary (exporter) insists on having the credit confirmed by a bank in his or her country it will be so noted in this space.

SAMPLE DOCUMENTARY LETTER OF CREDIT APPLICATION FORM

	Instructions **to open a Documentary Credit**
Sender Argentine Trading Company Lavalle 1716, Piso 2 1048 Buenos Aires Argentina Our reference AB/02	Buenos Aires, 30th September 2001 Place / Date

Please open the following [X] irrevocable [ ] revocable documentary credit	**Argentine Bank Corporation** Documentary Credits P.O. Box 1040 Buenos Aires, Argentina

Beneficiary ① American Import-Export Co., Inc. 123 Main Street San Francisco, California USA	Beneficiary's bank (if known) ④ US Domestic Bank 525 Main Street San Francisco, CA 94105 USA

Amount ② US$726,000.--	
Date and place of expiry ③ 25th November 2001 in San Francisco	Please advise this bank [ ] by letter [X] by letter, cabling main details in advance [ ] by telex / telegram with full text of credit

Partial shipments [X] allowed [ ] not allowed	Transhipment [ ] allowed [X] not allowed	Terms of shipment (FOB, C & F, CIF) CIF Buenos Aires

Despatch from / Taking in charge at Oakland	For transportation to Buenos Aires	Latest date of shipment 10th Nov. 2001 ③	Documents must be presented not later than 15 days after date of despatch

Beneficiary may dispose of the credit amount as follows [X] at sight upon presentation of documents ⑤ [ ] after ....days, calculated from date of	[ ] by a draft due .... drawn on [ ] you [ ] your correspondents which you / your correspondents will please accept

against surrender of the following documents ⑥
[X] invoice   (....3......copies)
 	
Shipping document
[X] sea: bill of lading, to order, endorsed in blank
[ ] rail: dublicate waybill
[ ] air: air consignment note
[ ]
	[X] insurance policy, certifcte (.................. copies)
	covering the following risks:
	 "all risks" including war up to
	[ ] Additional documents final destination in
	                     Argentina
	[X] Confirmation of the carrier that the
	  ship is not more than 15 years old
	
	[X] packing list (3 copies)

Notify address in bill of lading / goods addressed to ⑦ Argentine Trading Company Lavalle 1716, Piso 2 1048 Buenos Aires Argentina	Goods insured by [ ] us [X] seller

Goods ⑧
 	
1,000 "Computers model Pentium 4 as per pro forma invoice
     no. 74/1853 dd 10th September 2001"
 	
     at US$726.00 per unit

Your correspondents to advise beneficiary [ ] adding their confirmation [X] without adding their confirmation ⑨ Payments to be debited to our...U.S. Dollars................account no 10-32679150

NB. The applicable text is marked by [X]

Argentine Trading Company

Signature _____

For mailing please see overleaf

(left margin, rotated text): This credit is subject to the «Uniform customs and practice for documentary credits» fixed by the International Chamber of Commerce. It is understood that you do not assume any responsibility neither for the correctness, validity or genuineness of the documents which will be remitted to you nor for the description, quality, quantity and weight of the goods thereby represented.

Document and Goods Movement for Utilization of an L/C

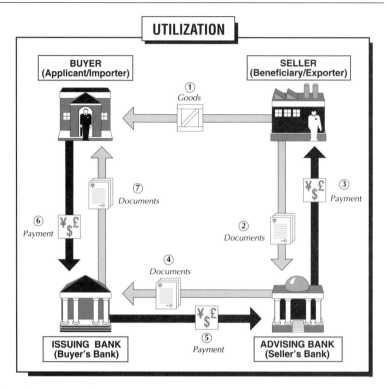

1. The seller ships the goods to the buyer and obtains a negotiable bill of lading from the shipping firm/agent.
2. The seller prepares and presents a document package to the bank (the advising bank) consisting of (a) the negotiable transport document, and (b) other documents as required by the buyer in the documentary credit.
3. The advising bank (a) reviews the document package making certain the documents are in conformity with the terms of the credit and (b) pays the seller (based upon the terms of the credit).
4. The advising bank sends the document package by mail or courier to the issuing bank.
5. The issuing bank (1) reviews the document package making certain the documents are in conformity with the terms of the credit, (b) pays the advising bank (based upon the terms of the credit), and (c) advises the buyer that the documents have arrived.
6. The buyer (a) reviews the document package making certain the documents are in conformity with the terms of the credit, and (b) makes a cash payment (signs a sight draft) to the issuing bank, or if the collection order allows, signs an acceptance (promise to pay at a future date).
7. The issuing bank sends the document package by mail or courier to the buyer who then takes possession of the shipment.

Irrevocable Straight Documentary Credit

DEFINITION

An irrevocable straight documentary credit conveys a commitment by the issuing bank to only honor drafts or documents as presented by the beneficiary of the credit.

EXPLANATION

This means that the beneficiary of the documentary credit (the seller) is supposed to deal directly with the issuing bank in presenting drafts and documents under the terms of the credit.

It is quite normal for banks and other financial institutions to purchase the drafts and documents of a beneficiary at a discount. For example, a seller may possess a draft obligating the issuing bank to pay a stated sum in 90 days. If the seller needs the money, he may wish to sell it to his bank at a discount for immediate cash. In an irrevocable straight documentary credit, the issuing bank has no formal obligation to such a purchaser/holder of the draft.

USES

The irrevocable straight documentary credit is typically used in domestic trade and for standby credits. In both situations confirmation or negotiation is considered unnecessary because of the reputation of the issuing bank.

ADVANTAGES/DISADVANTAGES

The irrevocable straight documentary credit is of greatest advantage to the buyer who does not incur a liability to pay the seller until his own bank reviews the documents.

KEY WORDING/ENGAGEMENT CLAUSE

The obligation of the issuing bank in an irrevocable straight documentary credit is typically stated in the credit itself with wording such as:

We hereby engage with you that each draft drawn and presented to us under and in compliance with the terms of this documentary credit will be duly honored by us.

and

This credit is subject to the Uniform Customs and Practice for Documentary Credits (1993 Revision), International Chamber of Commerce, Publication Number 500, and engages us in accordance with the terms thereof.

Irrevocable Negotiation Documentary Credit

DEFINITION

An irrevocable negotiation documentary credit conveys a commitment by the issuing bank to honor drafts or documents as presented by the beneficiary or any third parties who might negotiate or purchase the beneficiary's drafts or documents as presented under the documentary credit.

EXPLANATION

This means that the beneficiary of the documentary credit (the seller) may ask a third party bank or financial institution to negotiate or purchase and resell drafts and documents as presented under the documentary credit. The issuing bank commits to honoring drafts and documents held by third parties so long as the beneficiary and third parties comply with the terms and conditions of the documentary credit.

USES

The great majority of documentary credits are freely negotiable. They are common in international trade because a foreign seller typically wants to be able to obtain payment for a shipment immediately from the local bank.

ADVANTAGES/DISADVANTAGES

This form of credit is of advantage to the seller who does not have to wait until the buyer's bank reviews the documents to get paid the proceeds of the credit.

KEY WORDING/ENGAGEMENT CLAUSE

The obligation of the issuing bank in an irrevocable negotiation documentary credit is typically stated in the credit itself with wording such as:

Credit available with any bank, by negotiation for payment of beneficiary's draft at sight...

and

This credit is subject to the Uniform Customs and Practice for Documentary Credits (1993 Revision), International Chamber of Commerce, Publication Number 500, and engages us in accordance with the terms thereof.

Irrevocable Unconfirmed Documentary Credit

DEFINITION

An irrevocable unconfirmed documentary credit conveys a commitment by the issuing bank to honor drafts or documents as presented by the beneficiary of the credit. Such a credit is advised (notification to the beneficiary) through an advising bank.

EXPLANATION

The advising bank is often the seller's bank in the seller's country and acts as an agent of the issuing bank. The advising bank's responsibility is limited to a reasonable review of the documents forwarded by the issuing bank prior to their being passed on to the beneficiary of the credit.

The advising bank specifically does not confirm (add its guarantee of) payment of the credit. This means that the beneficiary of the documentary credit (the seller) will be paid by and has recourse to the issuing bank only.

USES

The irrevocable unconfirmed documentary credit is used when the reputation of the issuing bank is strong enough to give confidence to the seller that he will get paid.

ADVANTAGES/DISADVANTAGES

There is a slight advantage to the buyer as the buyer is typically responsible for paying the documentary credit fees. Since confirmation incurs a fee, the buyer would have a small savings.

KEY WORDING/ENGAGEMENT CLAUSE

The obligation of the issuing bank in an irrevocable unconfirmed documentary credit is typically stated in the credit itself with wording such as:

Confirmation instructions: Without.

and

This credit is subject to the Uniform Customs and Practice for Documentary Credits (1993 Revision), International Chamber of Commerce, Publication Number 500, and engages us in accordance with the terms thereof.

ADVICE WORDING

The advising bank passes on the issuing bank's documentary credit to the beneficiary and adds wording such as:

The enclosed advice is sent to you without confirmation.

Irrevocable Confirmed Documentary Credit

DEFINITION

An irrevocable confirmed documentary credit is one that contains a guarantee on the part of both the issuing and advising banks of payment to the beneficiary (seller) so long as the terms and conditions of the credit are met.

EXPLANATION

Confirmation is only added to an irrevocable credit at the request of the issuing bank. Confirmation of an irrevocable documentary credit adds the guarantee of a second bank (usually the seller's bank in the seller's country) to the credit. This means that the beneficiary of the irrevocable confirmed documentary credit (the seller) will be paid by the confirming bank once the terms and conditions of the credit have been met.

USES

A confirmed credit is used when the seller lacks full confidence that the buyer's bank can effectively guarantee payment. It is also used when the seller fears economic, political, or legal risk in the buyer's country.

ADVANTAGES/DISADVANTAGES

This is the most secure credit for the seller because it adds the guarantee of a second (and usually local) bank to that of the issuing bank.

Confirmation by a second bank is the equivalent of added insurance, and insurance costs money, so this form of credit is more costly.

KEY WORDING/ENGAGEMENT CLAUSE

The obligation of the issuing bank in an irrevocable confirmed documentary credit is typically stated in the credit itself with wording such as:

Confirmation instructions: With, Confirm, or Confirmed

and

This credit is subject to the Uniform Customs and Practice for Documentary Credits (1993 Revision), International Chamber of Commerce, Publication Number 500, and engages us in accordance with the terms thereof.

Silent Confirmation

If a documentary credit does not contain a confirmation request by the issuing bank, in certain circumstances the possibility exists of confirming the credit by silent confirmation (without the issuing bank's knowledge). In this case, the beneficiary and the advising bank make an independent agreement that adds the advising bank's confirmation to the credit for a fee.

SAMPLE IRREVOCABLE CONFIRMED DOCUMENTARY CREDIT

Turkish Export/Import Bank
Ankara, Turkey

To: The Trade Bank, 525 Market Street, 25th Floor, San Francisco, CA USA

We hereby issue our irrevocable documentary credit No. 3456789

Date of Issue: July 15, 2001
Date of expiry October 12,2001
Place of expiry: USA

Applicant:	*Beneficiary:*
Turkey Medical Equipment Importer	*American Medical Equipment Exporter*
Ankara, Turkey	*Houston, Texas, USA*

Amount: US$12,000, Twelve thousand US dollars

Credit available at sight with The Trade Bank, 525 Market Street, San Francisco, California USA, by payment.

Partial shipments: Allowed
Transhipments: Allowed
Shipment from any USA airport, for transportation to Esenboga Airport, Ankara Turkey by plane.

Latest day of shipment: September 20, 2001

Description of goods: Blood plasma machine per proforma invoice No. 123.

Quantity: 1 (one)

Unit price: US$12,000.00, Total price US$12,000.00.

Terms of price: FOB Texas

Documents required
1. Signed commercial invoice in original and 02 copies certifying that merchandise is in strict conformity with proforma invoice and indicating quality, quantity and unit price

2. Certificate of origin, legalized by local chamber of commerce in 02 copies indicating that the goods are of U.S.A. origin.

3. Copy of fax sent to us on shipment date about expedition details as description, value, loaded quantity of merchandise and characteristics of transport vehicle (flight no.) to our fax No.: 0-312-1234567.

4. Clean air waybill, in 03 copies consigned to Turkish Export/Import Bank and mark notify applicant and freight collect.

5. Beneficiary's written statement showing that 01 original invoice, 01 certificate of origin legalized by local chamber of commerce, 01 original clean air waybill have been sent together with the goods.

Additional conditions: Insurance will be covered by applicant
Original documents will be sent to us by courier "DHL"
All documents should bear our and the negotiating/presenting bank's reference numbers.

Charges: All charges outside Turkey are for beneficiary's account.

Period for presentation: Documents to be presented within 021 days after shipment date.

Confirmation instructions: Confirm.

Reinbursement bank: New York Bank, New York, NY USA.

If presented documents contain discrepancies, US$ 100. or equivalent in the documentary credit currency will be deducted from proceeds as additional processing fees.

Advise through bank: The Trade Bank, San Francisco, California USA

This credit is subject to the Uniform Customs and Practice for Documentary Credits (1993 Revision), International Chamber of Commerce, Publication Number 500, and engages us in accordance with the terms thereof.

Turkish Export/Import Bank

SAMPLE TRANSFERABLE DOCUMENTARY CREDIT

Swiss Bank Corporation
Schweizerischer Bankverein
Société de Banque Suisse
Società di Banca Svizzera

Notre
Unsere **Doc. Credit No**   173'896
Our

4002 Basle, 20th October 19..
Lieu/Date   Ort/Datum   Luogo/Data

Nous vous informons de l'ouverture du crédit documentaire irrévocable suivant
en votre faveur:

Wir benachrichtigen Sie von der Eröffnung des folgenden unwiderruflichen
Dokumentarkredites zu ihren Gunsten:

We inform you of the opening of the following irrevocable documentary credit
in your favour:

REGISTERED
TRANSITO LTD.
Rheinallee 183

4002 B a s e l

Montant / Betrag / Amount	Banque émettrice / Eröffnende Bank / Issuing bank
max. DM 386'000.--	Bank for Trade and Industry P.O. Box 1283
Validité / Gültigkeit / Validity	
15th January 19..	D-6000 Frankfurt 30
Donneur d'ordre / Auftraggeber / Applicant	No de réf. de notre correspondant / Ref.-Nr. unseres Korrespondenten / Ref. no of our correspondent — Ordre du / Auftrag vom / Order dated
Schmitt & Co. Ltd. Hinterlindenstrasse 47 Frankfurt 34	LC/539284 19.10.19..

Utilisable contre remise des documents suivants:
Benützbar gegen Einreichung folgender Dokumente:
Available against surrender of the following documents:

- invoice, 3 copies

- inspection certificate, evidencing that the goods are in accordance
  with the specifications mentioned below

- full set of clean shipped on board ocean bills of lading, made out
  to order and endorsed in blank

covering: 1'000 metric tons steel sheets DIN 456/243
             at DM 386.-- per mt, C & F Rotterdam

to be shipped from a Japanese seaport to Rotterdam
not later than 1st January 19..
Partial deliveries are permitted. Transshipment not allowed.
Documents to be presented not later than 15 days after date of
shipment.

This documentary credit is transferable.

We confirm this documentary credit to you as irrevocably valid until
15th January 19..

Yours faithfully

Swiss Bank Corporation

Jenny Boy

Ce crédit est soumis aux • Règles et usances uniformes relatives aux crédits documentaires • approuvées par la Chambre de Commerce internationale.
Dieser Kredit unterliegt den • Einheitlichen Richtlinien und Gebräuchen für Dokumenten-Akkreditive • wie sie von der Internationalen Handelskammer gutgeheissen worden sind.
This credit is subject to the • Uniform customs and practice for documentary credits • fixed by the International Chamber of Commerce.

F 6804N 1/8 2.82 10000

Discrepancies with Documents

Perhaps the greatest problem with documentary letters of credits is discrepancies with documents as they are prepared, presented, and reviewed by sellers, buyers, and the banks. All parties have the obligation to check the documentation to make certain it is in order and all parties are at risk for failing to do so properly.

The buyer can introduce problems to the process by specifying documents that are difficult or impossible to obtain. The seller can introduce problems by incorrectly preparing and presenting the document package to the bank.

Advising, confirming, and issuing banks can introduce problems by incorrectly reviewing (negotiating in bank language) the documents provided by the seller against the requirements of the documentary credit.

CONFORMITY WITH THE DOCUMENTARY CREDIT

The key issue is that the documents presented by the seller must be in conformity with the specifications of the letter of credit. Once again, banks deal in documents, not goods. The banks, therefore, are seeking conformity of the documentation to the wording of the credit and not of the goods to the documents.

BANK OPTIONS

Banks have up to seven banking days following the receipt of documents to examine and notify the party from which it received the documents of their acceptance or nonacceptance. If a bank involved in the transaction finds discrepancies in the documents, it has several options:

1. The advising or confirming bank can refuse to accept the documents and return them to the seller (beneficiary) so that they can be corrected or replaced.

2. The issuing bank, if it feels the discrepancy is not material to the transaction, can ask the buyer (applicant) for a waiver for the specific discrepancy, but must do so within seven banking days.

3. The advising or confirming bank can remit the documents under approval to the issuing bank for settlement.

4. The issuing or confirming bank can return the incorrect document(s) directly to the seller for correction or replacement and eventual return directly to the issuing or confirming bank.

5. The confirming bank can proceed with payment to the seller but require a guarantee from the seller for reimbursement if the issuing bank does not honor the documents as presented.

If there is a discrepancy, the buyer and seller must communicate directly and then inform the banks of their decision. In the case of serious discrepancies, an amendment to the credit may be necessary.

The seller may request the opening bank to present the documents to the buyer on a collection basis. However, the buyer may refuse to accept the documents/ merchandise.

Documentary Collections

A documentary collection is like an international COD (cash on delivery) transaction: the buyer pays for goods at delivery. A documentary collection, however, is distinguished from a typical COD in two ways: (1) instead of an individual, shipping company, or postal service collecting the payment, a bank handles the transaction, and (2) instead of cash on delivery for goods it is cash on delivery for documents, including a title document (negotiable bill of lading) that is used to claim the goods from the shipping company.

Banks, therefore, act as intermediaries to collect payment from the buyer in exchange for the transfer of documents that enable the holder to take possession of the goods. The procedure is easier than a documentary credit, and the bank charges are lower. The bank, however, does not act as surety of payment but rather only as collector of funds for documents.

Documentary Collections vs. Documentary Credits

In a documentary collection, the seller prepares and presents documents to the bank in much the same way as for a documentary letter of credit. However, there are two major differences between a collection and a letter of credit: (1) the draft involved is not drawn by the seller (the "drawer") upon a bank for payment, but rather on the buyer (the "drawee"), and (2) the seller's bank has no obligation to pay upon presentation but, more simply, acts as a collecting or remitting bank on behalf of the seller, thus earning a commission for its services.

The presenting (collecting) bank reviews the documents making certain they are in conformity with the collection order. Goods are transported, stored, and insured at the expense and risk of the seller until payment or acceptance occurs.

The Collection Order

The collection order is the key document prepared by the seller specifying the terms and conditions of the documentary collection. It must be prepared with care and precision because banks are permitted to act only upon the instructions given. Listed below are key provisions of the collection order.

1. The payment type and period as agreed with the buyer
2. The name and address of the buyer
3. The buyer's bank
4. Instructions, if any, about what to do with the accepted bill of exchange
5. Notation concerning payment of charges for the documentary collection
6. Instructions for the lodging of a protest in the event of nonacceptance or nonpayment
7. Instructions for notification of agent or representative in the buyer's country

SAMPLE COLLECTION ORDER

Sender:

Müller Ltd.
Tellstrase 26

4053 Basle

Documentary collection

Basle, 12th August 19..
Place / Date

Our Reference AK/83

We send you herewith the following documents for collection:

Registered

Swiss Bank Corporation
Schweizerischer Bankverein

Documentary collections
P.O. Box

4002 Basle

Amount	Maturity	Drawee (2)
US$ 14'300.--	90 days sight (1)	Maxwell Hammerton Inc. 12, Broadway New York, N.Y. 10014
		Drawee's bank: Commercial Credit Bank (3) New York

Draft/ Receipt	Invoice com-mercial	Invoice cust.-/ consul.	Insur.- Cert.	Certif. of Orig.	Weight/ Packing List	Bill of Lading	Waybill	Postal-/ Forw.- Receipt	other documents	
1 3/3		4	2		2				2	analysis certificates

Goods: 100 barrels "Chemical products - harmless"

by: s/s CAP SAN GIORGIO from: Le Havre to: New York on: 31.7.19..

Please follow the instructions marked «x»

	Documents/goods to be delivered against						Draft (4)		State the exact due-date		
	payment (1)	X	acceptance				to be sent back after acceptance		to be collected on due-date		
(5) X	Your charges for drawee's account; if refused					X	waive charges		do not deliver documents		
X	Your correspondent's charges are for drawee's account; if refused						waive charges	X	do not deliver documents		
(6) X	Protest in case of	X	non-payment		non-acceptance	X	Do not protest in case of		non-payment	X	non-acceptance
X	Advise	X	non-payment		non-acceptance		by airmail	X	by cable	X	giving reasons

Please credit the proceeds as follows:

☒ to our SFr account Nr. 10-326'791.0

☐ remit to

(7) Remarks:

In case of difficulties, the collecting bank is requested to inform our representatives: Messrs. Beach & Co. Inc., Broad Street 485, New York 34, who will be of assistance but who are not allowed to alter the above instructions.

Müller Ltd

Enclosures

Signature:

E 6851 N 1/2 4.80 5000

The execution of this order is subject to the «Uniform rules for collections» issued by the International Chamber of Commerce

Documents and Goods Movement in a Documentary Collection

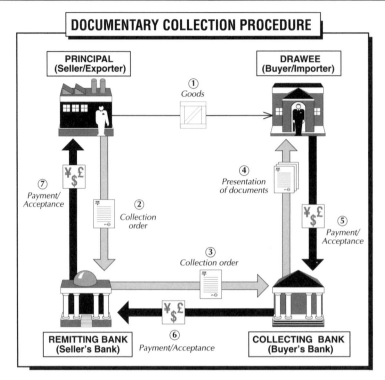

The buyer and seller agree on the terms of sale of goods.

1. The seller ships the goods to the buyer (drawee) and obtains a negotiable bill of lading from the shipping firm.

2. The seller prepares and presents (remits) a document package to the bank (the remitting bank) consisting of (a) a collection order specifying the terms and conditions under which the bank is to hand over documents to the buyer and receive payment, (b) the negotiable bill of lading, and (c) other documents as required by the buyer.

3. The remitting bank sends the documentation package by mail or courier to the designated collecting bank in the buyer's country with instructions to present them to the drawee (buyer) and collect payment.

4. The collecting bank (a) reviews the documents making certain they are in conformity with the collection order, (b) notifies the buyer (drawee) about the terms and conditions of the collection order, and (c) releases the documents once the payment conditions have been met.

5. The buyer (drawee) (a) makes a cash payment (signing the draft), or if the collection order allows, signs an acceptance (promise to pay at a future date) and (b) receives the documents and takes possession of the shipment.

6. The collecting bank pays the remitting bank either immediately or at the maturity date of the accepted bill of exchange.

7. The remitting bank then pays the seller (principal).

Important Principles Regarding the Role of Banks

Documentary letter of credit and documentary collection procedures are not infallible. Things can and do go wrong. Since banks act as intermediaries between buyers and sellers, both look to the banks as protectors of their interests. However, while banks have clear cut responsibilities, they are also shielded from certain problems deemed to be out of their control or responsibility.

1. In a documentary letter of credit, banks act upon specific instructions given by the applicant (buyer) in the documentary credit application. Buyer's instructions left out of the credit by mistake or omitted because "we've always done it that way" don't count. The buyer, therefore, should take great care in preparing the application so that it gives complete and clear instructions.

2. In a documentary collection, banks act upon specific instructions given by the principal (seller) in the collection order. Seller's instructions left out of the collection order by mistake or omitted because "we've always done it that way" don't count. The principal, therefore, should take great care in preparing the collection order so that it gives complete and clear instructions.

3. Banks are required to act in good faith and exercise reasonable care to verify that the documents submitted APPEAR to be as listed in the letter of credit or collection order. They are, however, under no obligation to confirm the authenticity of the documents submitted.

4. Banks are not liable for the acts of third parties. Third parties include freight forwarders, agents, customs authorities, insurance companies and other banks. They also are not responsible for delays or consequences resulting from Acts of God (floods, earthquakes, etc.), riots, wars, civil commotions, strikes, lockouts, or other causes beyond their control.

5. Banks also assume no liability or responsibility for loss arising out of delays or loss in transit of messages, letters, documents, etc.

6. Banks assume no responsibility regarding the quantity or quality of goods shipped. They are only concerned that documents presented appear on their face to be consistent with the instructions in the credit or collection order. Any dispute must be settled between the buyer and the seller.

7. Without explicit instructions, the banks take no steps to store or insure the goods. This can be a problem for both the seller and the buyer. A seller who has not received payment still has ownership and an insurable interest in the goods.

8. If a documentary collection remains unpaid or a bill of exchange is not accepted and the collecting bank receives no new instructions within 90 days, it may return the documents to the bank from which it received the collection order.

9. So long as the documents presented to the banks appear on their face to comply with the terms and conditions of a letter of credit, banks may accept them and initiate the payment process as stipulated in the credit.

If there are any conclusions to be made from the above they are: first, that the buyer and seller should know each other and have at least some basis of trust to be doing business in the first place, and second, that all parties to the transaction should take responsibility to follow carefully through on their obligations.

CHAPTER 9

Special Documents

THE SPECIAL DOCUMENTS COVERED in this chapter don't fall into the main categories, yet may be essential to the success of a transaction. These documents cover a wide range of requirements and may be classed into the following categories:

- Inspection Documents
- Insurance Documents
- Trade Agreement Documents

Inspection Documents

Inspection documents may be required by export and import authorities as well as by the importer/buyer prior to shipment. Some of these documents have been covered elsewhere, but are listed here for completeness.

INSPECTION CERTIFICATES AND DOCUMENTS

Document	Notes	Sample
Inspection Certificate (General)	A	-
Quality (Inspection) Certificate	B	-
Phytosanitary Certificate	C	-
Fumigation Certificate	D	-
Veterinary Certificate	E	-
Public Health Certificate	F	-

- A—INSPECTION CERTIFICATE (generally issued by a third-party independent testing company)
  This document offers independent proof of product quality, quantity or adherence to certain specifications. It is often required by the importer or the import authorities. It may also be required by certain nations as a means of controlling fraudulent transactions that circumvent exchange control regulations (i.e., overstated quantities or under-declared valuations). An import license may require a "clean report of findings" by an authorized inspection organization before the goods can clear customs or payment can be made.

- B—QUALITY CERTIFICATE (generally issued by third-party independent testing companies or government agencies)
  This document certifies that the products contained in the shipment meet the standards of the importing country. Most countries require that this certification be provided by the exporter and be approved and filed by the appropriate governmental control agency (i.e., the exporting country Department of Consumer Safety) prior to shipment.

- C—PHYTOSANITARY CERTIFICATE (generally issued by a third-party independent testing company or a government authority)
  This document certifies that a shipment of plants or plant products (i.e., seeds, bulbs, flowers, fruits, vegetables, etc.) is free from pests or disease. This certificate may require on-site inspection(s) during the growing season and is usually provided by the agricultural ministry of the country of export. In some instances, the certificate may be provided by an authorized private company.

- D—FUMIGATION CERTIFICATE (generally issued by a third-party independent testing company or a government authority)
  This document offers proof that wood-based packing materials, used clothing or packaging (i.e., coffee or cocoa bean bags), and certain other commodities have been fumigated or sterilized to kill any pests. These certificates are issued by private companies authorized to carry out these procedures and include details of the specific process, temperature range, chemicals and concentrations used.

- E—VETERINARY CERTIFICATE (generally issued by a third-party independent testing company or a government authority)
  This document certifies that a shipment of live animals or fresh, chilled or frozen meats (and sometimes canned meats) has been inspected for disease.

- F—PUBLIC HEALTH CERTIFICATE (generally issued by a third-party independent testing company or government authority)
  This document certifies that a shipment has been inspected for disease.

Insurance Documents

Insurance is a guarantee of financial protection against the risk of loss or damage with regard to a specified contingency or peril. There are a number of types of insurance used in international trade. These include coverage against risk of loss or damage to cargo, damage to foreign production facilities, and kidnapping and ransom insurance for foreign-based personnel. This section is devoted to insurance for international shipments of cargo.

BASIC PRINCIPLES OF INSURANCE

There are three basic principles which apply to export/import insurance:

- INSURABLE INTEREST A person may buy insurance on a shipment only if he or she will benefit directly by the safe arrival of the insured goods and will be economically harmed by any loss or damage. Different parties may have an insurable interest at any one time (i.e. the exporter, the importer, or a bank). Insurable interest may pass from party to party during a transaction depending upon the terms of sale. For instance, the terms of sale may require that ownership of the goods transfer from the exporter to the importer at the ship's rail.

- UTMOST GOOD FAITH When taking out an insurance policy, the insured must disclose any "material circumstance" that may influence the judgment of the insurer in establishing a rate (price) for a specific policy. The fact that a product is dangerous or fragile is an example of a material circumstance. Since the insurer does not usually inspect the goods or the specific vessel or airplane being used, this responsibility rests with the insured. Failure to disclose any material circumstance entitles the insurer to decline payment on a policy.

- **INDEMNITY AND SUBROGATION** Transport insurance is a contract of indemnity (security against loss or damage). This means that the insurer will undertake to compensate the insured for any financial loss the insured may have suffered due to loss or damage. Subrogation is the right of the insurer to collect damages from a negligent third party (i.e. the shipping company or ship's owners), and this right is automatically assigned to the insurer by the insured in the policy.

TYPES OF INSURANCE

There are a variety of different types of cargo insurance available, including:

- **GENERAL MARINE INSURANCE** Historically this was for risk of loss of ships and cargo carried on ships, but it is now a general term of insurance for any means of transport. Such coverage is often required when payment is by letter of credit. Different types of policies cover different levels of risk from Class A to Class C. "All Risk" insurance is Class A (but does not cover "all" risks).

  Specifically excluded from a Marine Insurance Policy (but often available as supplementary coverage) are losses due to delays, wars, strikes, riots and civil commotions, and unfitness of a vessel, container or conveyance.

  Cargo insurance is not available for loss due to misconduct of the insured, ordinary leakage or loss in weight, unsuitable or insufficient packaging, nuclear contamination, and inherent vice (loss due to the inherent nature of the goods such as natural evaporation of water-based products).

- **CUSTOMIZED CARGO POLICIES** This coverage may be secured when the nature of the goods excludes their protection under a standard (A, B, C) Marine Insurance Policy. Examples include insurance against product deterioration, refrigeration breakdown, or freezing, insurance for perishable items or time-sensitive items, and insurance for equipment that requires special handling.

- **SPECIAL RISK CARGO POLICIES** This coverage is for risk of loss or damage to high-risk cargoes (i.e. computer chips, laptop computers, fine arts, jewelry and antiques). Coverage is also available to high-risk destinations (i.e. the interiors of Russia or the Sudan) and/or for political risk coverage against expropriation, nationalization or confiscation.

- **OPEN CARGO POLICIES** These policies are written to cover a number of shipments within a specific time period. This coverage is also carried by freight forwarders and customs brokers and is made available (for a fee) to their customers for shipments they handle.

- **EXPORT CREDIT RISK POLICIES** These policies cover loss due to nonpayment by the importer/buyer. They are often required by the exporter/seller's lender in open account and problematic country of destination transactions. This insurance is often offered by a government or quasi-governmental agency in countries (i.e. India) whose economic and foreign policy is aligned with the encouragement of exports.

INSURANCE DOCUMENTS

Document	Notes	Sample
Marine Insurance Document	A	page 42
Insurance Certificate	B	page 104
Beneficiary Certificate	C	-
Customs Bond	D	-
ATA Carnet	E	-

- **A—MARINE INSURANCE POLICY DOCUMENT** This serves as proof that an insurance policy has been issued to cover a particular shipment and includes all the specific information for the shipment (i.e., vessel, sailing dates, container numbers, etc.). It also includes the name of the party to whom the loss is payable and is a negotiable instrument, which the insured may sign over to another. The marine insurance policy is almost always required on exports paid for with a letter of credit and the inclusion of this document must be indicated in the exporter's shipping instructions and/or bill of lading. Certain countries (i.e., Saudi Arabia, Nigeria) require that insurance be provided by companies with offices or agents within their borders while others (i.e., China) require that insurance be purchased from the state's own underwriting company.

- **B—INSURANCE CERTIFICATE** This document indicates the type and amount of insurance coverage in force on a particular shipment under the exporter's open policy. It may also be used for an insurance bordereau, which is insurance coverage for multiple shipments made within a specific time (usually one month). It offers assurances to the consignee that any loss or damage to the cargo in transit will be covered (less the prescribed deductible indicated in the policy). These certificates are usually used for import, not export, shipments.

- **C—BENEFICIARY CERTIFICATE**
  This document indicates that the beneficiary of an insurance policy is someone other than the purchaser of the policy. It may be required to be included in the document packet in certain letter of credit payment situations.

- **D—CUSTOMS BOND**
  A bond is a contractual obligation of an insurance company to insure performance of a principal's obligation as imposed by law or regulation. For example, a US Customs Bond is required by the US Customs Service to ensure payment of all duties associated with an import shipment.

- **E—The ATA CARNET** (issued by national chambers of commerce affiliated with the Paris-based International Chamber of Commerce (ICC))
  This is an international customs document that may be used for the temporary duty-free admission of certain goods into a country (e.g., samples for a trade show, cars for an automobile race, musical instruments for a music concert, etc.) in lieu of the usual customs documents. Technically, an ATA Carnet is a form of insurance or bond. The ATA Carnet guarantees that import duties and fees will be paid if the goods are not re-exported within a stated time.

Insurance Document (or Certificate)

DEFINITION

A document indicating the type and amount of insurance coverage in force on a particular shipment. It is used to assure the consignee that insurance is provided to cover loss of or damage to cargo while in transit.

ISSUED BY

The insurance document is issued by an insurance company or its agent, which may include a carrier, freight forwarder, customs broker or logistics firm.

✔ KEY ELEMENTS

In documentary letter of credit transactions, the insurance document includes the following elements:

1. Appears on its face to be issued and signed by an insurance carrier, underwriter or agent for same
2. Covers the risks specified in the documentary letter of credit
3. Indicates that the coverage is effective at the latest from the date of loading of the goods on board a transport vessel or the taking in charge of the goods by the carrier, as indicated by the transport document (bill of lading, etc.)
4. Specifies coverage for at least 110 percent of either: (a) the CIF or CIP value of the shipment, if such can be determined from the various documents on their face, otherwise, (b) the amount of the payment, acceptance or negotiation specified in the documentary credit, or (c) the gross amount of the commercial invoice
5. Is presented as the sole original, or if issued in more than one original, all originals
6. The insurance currency should be consistent with the currency of the letter of credit

! CAUTIONS & NOTES

Documentary credit transactions indicating CIF (Cost Insurance Freight) or CIP (Carriage and Insurance Paid) pricing should list an insurance document in their required documentation.

"Cover notes" issued by insurance brokers (as opposed to insurance companies, underwriters, or their agents) are not accepted in letter of credit transactions unless authorized specifically by the credit.

IN CASE OF LOSS OR SHORTFALL

The consignee should always note on the delivery document any damage or shortfall prior to signing for receipt of goods. The consignee has the responsibility to make reasonable efforts to minimize loss, including steps to prevent further damage to the shipment. Expenses incurred in such efforts are almost universally collectible under the insurance policy. Prompt notice of loss is essential.

Copies of documents necessary to support an insurance claim include the insurance policy or certificate, bill of lading, invoice, packing list, and a survey report (usually prepared by a claims agent).

SAMPLE CERTIFICATE OF MARINE INSURANCE

$ _____
(sum insured)

CERTIFICATE OF MARINE INSURANCE

No. 473301

WASHINGTON INTERNATIONAL INSURANCE COMPANY
300 PARK BOULEVARD, SUITE 500, ITASCA, IL 60143-2625

This is to Certify, *That on the* _____ day of _____ 19___ , *this Company*

insured under Policy No. _____ made for _____

for the sum of _____ Dollars,

on _____

Valued at sum insured. Shipped on board the S/S or M/S _____ and/or following steamer or steamers

at and from _____ , via _____
(Initial Point of Shipment)   (Port of Shipment)

to _____
(Port or Place of Destination)

and it is understood and agreed, that in case of loss, the same

is payable to the order of _____ on surrender of this Certificate which conveys the right of collecting any such loss as fully as if the property were covered by a special policy direct to the holder hereof, and free from any liability for unpaid premiums. This certificate is subject to all the terms of the open policy, provided however, that the rights of a bona fide holder of this certificate for value shall not be prejudiced by any terms of the open policy which are in conflict with the terms of this certificate.

SPECIAL CONDITIONS

NEW MERCHANDISE shipped subject to an UNDER DECK bill of lading insured–
Against all risks of physical loss or damage from any external cause, irrespective of percentage, excepting those excluded by the F.C. & S., Nuclear Exclusion and S.R. & C.C. Warranties, arising during transportation between the points of shipment and of destination named herein.
The above conditions apply only to New Approved Commodities, properly packed for export, as listed in the Master Policy to which this Certificate is made a part of. Commodities such as, but not limited to, Automobiles, Household Goods and Personal Effects, Wines, Liquors, Beer and Similar Spirits, are subject to further conditions and/or warranties of the policy.
Non-approved commodities are subject to the F.P.A. conditions of the Master Policy unless broader conditions have been approved by these underwriters prior to attachment of risk and so endorsed thereon.

MARKS & NUMBERS

USED MERCHANDISE AND/OR ON DECK SHIPMENTS insured–
Warranted free of particular average unless caused by the vessel being stranded, sunk, burnt, on fire or in collision, but including risk of jettison and/or washing overboard, irrespective of percentage

DEDUCTIBLE	COUNTRY CODE

TERMS AND CONDITIONS–SEE ALSO BACK HEREOF

WAREHOUSE TO WAREHOUSE: This insurance attaches from the time the goods leave the Warehouse and/or Store at the place named in the Policy for the commencement of the transit and continues during the ordinary course of transit, including customary transhipment if any, until the goods are discharged overside from the overseas vessel at the final port. Thereafter the insurance continues whilst the goods are in transit and/or awaiting transit until delivered to final warehouse at the destination named in the Policy or until the expiry of 15 days (or 30 days if the destination to which the goods are insured is outside the limits of the port) whichever shall first occur. The time herein referred to above to be reckoned from midnight of the day on which the discharge overside of the goods hereby insured from the overseas vessel is completed. Held covered at a premium to be arranged in the event of transhipment, if any, other than as above and/or in the event of delay in excess of the above time limits arising from circumstances beyond the control of the Assured.
NOTE–IT IS NECESSARY FOR THE ASSURED TO GIVE PROMPT NOTICE TO THESE ASSURERS WHEN THEY BECOME AWARE OF AN EVENT FOR WHICH THEY ARE "HELD COVERED" UNDER THIS POLICY AND THE RIGHT TO SUCH COVER IS DEPENDENT ON COMPLIANCE WITH THIS OBLIGATION.
PERILS CLAUSE: Touching the adventures and perils which this Assurer is contented to bear and takes upon itself, they are of the seas, fires, assailing thieves, jettisons, barratry of the masters and mariners, and all other like perils, losses and misfortunes that have or shall come to the hurt, detriment or damage of the said goods and merchandise, or any part thereof, except as may be otherwise provided for herein or endorsed hereon.
SHORE CLAUSE: Where this insurance by its terms covers while on docks, wharves or elsewhere on shore, and/or during land transportation, it shall include the risks of collision, derailment, overturning or other accident to the conveyance, fire, lightning, sprinkler leakage, cyclones, hurricanes, earthquakes, floods (meaning the rising of navigable waters), and/or collapse or subsidence of docks or wharves, even though the insurance be otherwise F.P.A.
BOTH TO BLAME CLAUSE: Where goods are shipped under a Bill of Lading containing the so-called "Both to Blame Collision" Clause, these Assurers agree as to all losses covered by this insurance, to indemnify the Assured for this Policy's proportion of any amount (not exceeding the amount insured) which the Assured may be legally bound to pay to the shipowners under such clause. In the event that such liability is asserted the Assured agrees to notify these Assurers who shall have the right at their own cost and expense to defend the Assured against such claim.
MACHINERY CLAUSE: When the property insured under this Policy includes a machine consisting when complete for sale or use of several parts, then in case of loss or damage covered by this insurance to any part of such machine, these Assurers shall be liable only for the proportion of the insured value of the part lost or damaged, or at the Assured's option, for the cost and expense including labor and forwarding charges, of replacing or repairing the lost or damaged part; but in no event shall these Assurers be liable for more than the insured value of the complete machine.
LABELS CLAUSE: In case of damage affecting labels, capsules or wrappers, these Assurers, if liable therefor under the terms of this policy, shall not be liable for more than an amount sufficient to pay the cost of new labels, capsules or wrappers, and the cost of reconditioning the goods, but in no event shall these Assurers be liable for more than the insured value of the damaged merchandise.
DELAY CLAUSE: Warranted free of claim for loss of market or inherent vice or nature of the subject matter insured or for loss, damage or deterioration arising from delay, whether caused by a peril insured against or otherwise.
AMERICAN INSTITUTE CLAUSES: This insurance, in addition to the foregoing, is also subject to the following American Institute Cargo Clauses, current forms:

1. MARINE EXTENSION CLAUSES	4. CARRIER	7. INCHMAREE	10. SOUTH AMERICA 60 DAY CLAUSE
2. DEVIATION	5. BILL OF LADING, ETC.	8. CONSTRUCTIVE TOTAL LOSS	11. S.R. & C.C. ENDORSEMENT
3. CRAFT, ETC.	6. EXPLOSION	9. GENERAL AVERAGE	12. WAR RISK INSURANCE

PARAMOUNT WARRANTIES: THE FOLLOWING WARRANTIES SHALL BE PARAMOUNT AND SHALL NOT BE MODIFIED OR SUPERSEDED BY ANY OTHER PROVISION INCLUDED HEREIN OR STAMPED OR ENDORSED HEREON UNLESS SUCH OTHER PROVISION REFERS SPECIFICALLY TO THE RISKS EXCLUDED BY THESE WARRANTIES AND EXPRESSLY ASSUMES THE SAID RISKS:
F.C. & S.: Notwithstanding anything herein contained to the contrary, this insurance is warranted free from capture, seizure, arrest, restraint, detainment, confiscation, preemption, requisition or nationalization, and the consequences thereof or any attempt thereat, whether in time of peace or war and whether lawful or otherwise; also warranted free, whether in time of peace or war, from all loss, damage or expense caused by any weapon of war employing atomic or nuclear fission and/or fusion or other reaction or radioactive force or matter or by any mine or torpedo, also warranted free from all consequences of hostilities or warlike operations (whether there be a declaration of war or not), but this warranty shall not exclude collision or contact with aircraft, rockets or similar missiles or with any fixed or floating object (other than a mine or torpedo), stranding, heavy weather, fire or explosion unless caused directly (and independently of the nature of the voyage or service which the vessel concerned or, in the case of a collision, any other vessel involved therein, is performing) by a hostile act by or against a belligerent power; and for the purposes of this warranty 'power' includes any authority maintaining naval, military or air forces in association with a power.
Further warranted free from the consequences of civil war, revolution, rebellion, insurrection, or civil strife arising therefrom, or piracy.
NUCLEAR EXCLUSION: Notwithstanding anything to the contrary herein, it is hereby understood and agreed that this Policy shall not apply to any loss, damage or expense due to or arising out of, whether directly or indirectly, nuclear reaction, radiation, or radioactive contamination, regardless of how it was caused. However, subject to all provisions of this Policy, if this Policy insures against fire, then direct physical damage to the property insured located within the United States or Puerto Rico by fire directly caused by the above excluded perils, is insured, provided that the nuclear reaction, radiation, or radioactive contamination was not caused, whether directly or indirectly, by any of the perils excluded by the F.C. & S. Warranty of this Policy.
Nothing in this clause shall be construed to cover any loss, damage, liability or expense caused by nuclear reaction, radiation or radioactive contamination arising directly or indirectly from the fire mentioned above.
S.R. & C.C. Warranted free of loss or damage caused by or resulting from:
(a) strikes, lockouts, labor disturbances, riots, civil commotions, or the acts of any person or persons taking part in any such occurrences or disorders.
(b) vandalism, sabotage or malicious act, which shall be deemed also to encompass the act or acts of one or more persons, whether or not agents of a sovereign power, carried out for political, terroristic or ideological purposes and whether any loss, damage or expense resulting therefrom is accidental or intentional.
TIME FOR SUIT: No suit or action against this Assurer for the recovery of any claim by virtue of this insurance shall be sustained in any Court of Law or Equity unless commenced within one (1) year from the time loss occurred or, if such limitation is not valid by the law of the place where the policy is issued, within the shortest contractual period of limitation permitted by such law.

This Certificate is issued in Original and Duplicate, one of which being accomplished the other to stand null and void.   To support a claim local Revenue Laws may require this certificate to be stamped.

Not transferable unless countersigned

Countersigned _____

ADDITIONAL CONDITIONS AND
INSTRUCTIONS TO CLAIMANTS ON REVERSE SIDE

Paul D. Amstutz
President

James P. Sheehy
Assistant Treasurer

ORIGINAL

W-13FF 6/97

Trade Agreement and Trade Preference Documents

Many countries have special trade agreements with other nations. Bilateral agreements often have an historic and/or common language basis (e.g.,the UK and South Africa) while others are politically based (e.g., the USA and Israel). Multi-lateral agreements are most often based upon geography and are often referred to as regional trade agreements (RTA). Some countries have also granted special trade preferences to underdeveloped nations (e.g., the Generalized System of Preferences (GSP) program). Countries that are party to a trade agreement agree to reduce or eliminate tariffs and to streamline import/export procedures between their members. There are two types of documents in this category:

1. Import/export declarations standardized among all member nations.

2. Certificates of Origin standardized among all member nations.

TRADE AGREEMENT DOCUMENTS

Document	Notes	Sample
Certificate of Origin	A	page 109
Import/Export Declaration	B	page 111

■ A—CERTIFICATE OF ORIGIN (issued by the exporter)
This document is for goods originating in and sent to another trade pact member country. This certificate allows eligible goods to qualify for reduced or eliminated tariffs when imported into another member nation.

■ B—IMPORT/EXPORT DECLARATION (issued by the exporter)
This document is used as an export declaration when exporting from any trade pact member country to a non-member country and as both an import and export declaration when transporting goods across country borders within the trade pact.

NOTE: The following forms are illustrative of regional trade forms. Others may be required when exporting/importing goods between nations that are members of other trade pacts.

Certificate of Origin

DEFINITION

A document stating the country of origin of the goods in a particular shipment. If a shipment is made between countries that are members of a trade pact, this document will attest that the goods originated in a member country.

ISSUED BY

A certificate of origin can be issued by the exporter, a governmental agency of the country of export, a chamber of commerce or a trade association. In some cases, the importer may require that the certificate of origin be issued or certified by a specific agency or organization.

✔ KEY ELEMENTS

A certificate of origin should include the following elements:

1. Name and address of exporter
2. Name and address of importer
3. Description of goods
4. Harmonized System tariff classification number of the goods
5. Indication of whether the exporter is the producer of the goods
6. Regional Value Content indication (when applicable)
7. Country of origin of goods
8. The name, signature and/or stamp or seal of the certifying authority

! CAUTIONS & NOTES

REQUEST FOR CERTIFICATE The certificate of origin is typically required by the import authority of the country of destination. If you are the importer/buyer and your country requires such documentation make sure that you specify in your request to the exporter/seller the documentation (in form and content) as specified by your country's customs authority.

STANDARD FORMS A certificate or origin can be the key document required for obtaining special (reduced) tariff rates for imports from countries listed as beneficiaries to programs such as the GSP (Generalized Systems of Preferences) or as members to trade pacts such as NAFTA (North American Free Trade Agreement). In some cases, a specific form must be used for this purpose (e.g., the NAFTA CERTIFICATE OF ORIGIN).

IDENTIFICATION OF CERTIFYING AUTHORITY Buyers should avoid the use of such terms as "first class," "well-known," "qualified," "independent," "official," "competent," or "local" when referring to the certifying authority. It is preferable to specifically name the required certifying authority. In letter of credit transactions, the use of such vague terminology will result in the bank's acceptance of any relevant document that appears "on its face" to be in compliance with the documentary credit, so long as it was not issued (signed) by the beneficiary (seller).

SAMPLE CERTIFICATE OF ORIGIN

Exporteur / Exportateur / Esportatore / Exporter	Nr. / No. 201884
MUELLER AG Birsstrasse 26 4132 Muttenz / Switzerland	**URSPRUNGSZEUGNIS** **CERTIFICAT D'ORIGINE** **CERTIFICATO D'ORIGINE** **CERTIFICATE OF ORIGIN**

Empfänger / Destinataire / Destinatario / Consignee

ADILMA TRADING CORPORATION
27, Nihonbashi, Chiyoda-Ku

TOKYO 125 / Japan

SCHWEIZERISCHE EIDGENOSSENSCHAFT
CONFÉDÉRATION SUISSE
CONFEDERAZIONE SVIZZERA
SWISS CONFEDERATION

Ursprungsstaat
Pays d'origine
Paese d'origine   SWITZERLAND
Country of origin

Angaben über die Beförderung (Ausfüllung freigestellt)
Informations relatives au transport (mention facultative)
Informazioni riguardanti il trasporto (indicazione facoltativa)
Particulars of transport (optional declaration)

Bemerkungen
Observations
Osservazioni
Observations

LETTER OF CREDIT NR. 064204

Zeichen, Nummern, Anzahl und Art der Packstücke; Warenbezeichnung
Marques, numéros, nombre et nature des colis; désignation des marchandises
Marche, numeri, numero e natura dei colli; designazione delle merci
Marks, numbers, number and kind of packages; description of the goods

Nettogewicht
Poids net
Peso netto
Net weight
kg, l, m³
etc./ecc.

ADILMA TRADING	6 cases	CYLINDER- PRESS COMPLETELY ASSEMBLED	12'140,0 kg
VIA TOKYO			
NR. 1-6			
ORDER 0-535/1			

Bruttogewicht
Poids brut
Peso lordo
Gross weight

12'860,0 kg

Die unterzeichnete Handelskammer bescheinigt den Ursprung oben bezeichneter Ware
La Chambre de commerce soussignée certifie l'origine des marchandises désignées ci-dessus
La sottoscritta Camera di commercio certifica l'origine delle merci summenzionate
The undersigned Chamber of commerce certifies the origin of the above mentioned goods

Basel, 2 6. 04.

Basler Handelskammer
Chambre de Commerce de Bâle
Camera di Commercio di Basilea
Basle Chamber of Commerce

SAMPLE NAFTA CERTIFICATE OF ORIGIN

DEPARTMENT OF THE TREASURY
UNITED STATES CUSTOMS SERVICE

Aproved through 12/31/96
OMB No. 1515-0204
See back of form for Paper-
work Reduction Act Notice.

NORTH AMERICAN FREE TRADE AGREEMENT
CERTIFICATE OF ORIGIN

Please print or type   19 CFR 181.11, 181.22

1. EXPORTER NAME AND ADDRESS	2. BLANKET PERIOD *(DD/MM/YY)*
	FROM
	TO
TAX IDENTIFICATION NUMBER:	

3. PRODUCER NAME AND ADDRESS	4. IMPORTER NAME AND ADDRESS
TAX IDENTIFICATION NUMBER:	TAX IDENTIFICATION NUMBER:

5. DESCRIPTION OF GOOD(S)	6. HS TARIFF CLASSIFICATION NUMBER	7. PREFERENCE CRITERION	8. PRODUCER	9. NET COST	10. COUNTRY OF ORIGIN

I CERTIFY THAT:

• THE INFORMATION ON THIS DOCUMENT IS TRUE AND ACCURATE AND I ASSUME THE RESPONSIBILITY FOR PROVING SUCH REP-
RESENTATIONS. I UNDERSTAND THAT I AM LIABLE FOR ANY FALSE STATEMENTS OR MATERIAL OMISSIONS MADE ON OR IN CON-
NECTION WITH THIS DOCUMENT;

• I AGREE TO MAINTAIN, AND PRESENT UPON REQUEST, DOCUMENTATION NECESSARY TO SUPPORT THIS CERTIFICATE, AND TO
INFORM, IN WRITING, ALL PERSONS TO WHOM THE CERTIFICATE WAS GIVEN OF ANY CHANGES THAT COULD AFFECT THE ACCU-
RACY OR VALIDITY OF THIS CERTIFICATE;

• THE GOODS ORIGINATED IN THE TERRITORY OF ONE OR MORE OF THE PARTIES, AND COMPLY WITH THE ORIGIN REQUIREMENTS
SPECIFIED FOR THOSE GOODS IN THE NORTH AMERICAN FREE TRADE AGREEMENT, AND UNLESS SPECIFICALLY EXEMPTED IN
ARTICLE 411 OR ANNEX 401, THERE HAS BEEN NO FURTHER PRODUCTION OR ANY OTHER OPERATION OUTSIDE THE TERRITORIES
OF THE PARTIES; AND

• THIS CERTIFICATE CONSISTS OF _____ PAGES, INCLUDING ALL ATTACHMENTS.

11.	11a. AUTHORIZED SIGNATURE	11b. COMPANY	
	11c. NAME *(Print or Type)*	11d. TITLE	
	11e. DATE *(DD/MM/YY)*	11f. TELEPHONE NUMBER	*(Voice)* *(Facsimile)*

Customs Form 434 (121793)

Regional Trade Pact Import/Export Declaration

DEFINITION

A standardized export/import document used in common by members of a regional trade group containing compliance, administrative and statistical information.

ISSUED BY

This document is typically issued by the exporter/seller.

✔ KEY ELEMENTS

The typical trade pact import/export declaration contains the following elements:

1. Name and address of exporter/seller/consignor

2. Name and address of importer/buyer/consignee

3. Description and value of the goods

4. A statement of origin of the goods

5. Country of destination of the goods

6. Carrier and means of transport

7. Other compliance, administrative and statistical information

! CAUTIONS & NOTES

This document is used as an export declaration when exporting from any trade pact member country to a non-member country and as both an import and export declaration when transporting goods across country borders within the trade group.

Because of its standardized format, this document is often linked to a computer system for the electronic transfer of information to export and import authorities within the trade group.

THE EU (EUROPEAN UNION) SAD (SINGLE ADMINISTRATIVE DOCUMENT)

This document is a prime example of a regional trade pact import/export declaration. It was established by the European Community Council in 1988 with the goal of standardizing customs documentation and simplifying international transactions.

This particular document is used as an import/export declaration and also for the declaration of goods in transit within EU and EFTA (European Free Trade Area) countries. It may be submitted by computer directly to the customs authorities in all the 15 EU member nations.

Countries outside of the EU have shown interest in using the SAD and some have already adopted the format for their import documentation (e.g., Bulgaria).

SAMPLE EU SAD (SINGLE ADMINISTRATIVE DOCUMENT)

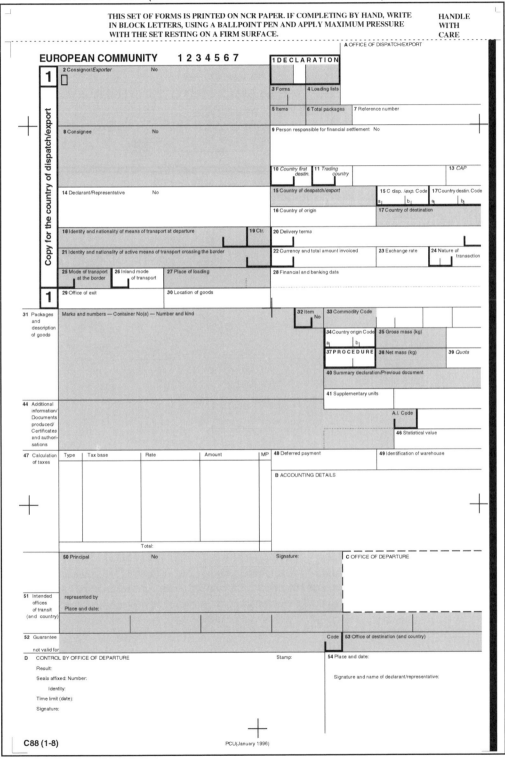

Inspection Certificate

DEFINITION

A document issued by an authority to indicate that goods have been inspected prior to shipment (typically according to a set of industry, customer, government, or carrier specifications) and a statement of the results of the inspection.

ISSUED BY

The inspection certificate is generally issued by a neutral, independent third-party inspection service or a government agency. For certain countries and certain commodities, the inspection certificate must be issued by a special government entity.

✔ KEY ELEMENTS

An inspection certificate should include the following elements:

1. Name and address of consignor

2. Name and address of consignee

3. Description of goods

4. Date of the inspection

5. Statement of sampling methodology

6. Statement of the results of the inspection

7. The name, signature and/or stamp or seal of the inspecting entity

! CAUTIONS & NOTES

IDENTIFICATION OF CERTIFYING AUTHORITY Buyers should avoid the use of such terms as "first class," "well-known," "qualified," "independent," "official," "competent," or "local" when referring to an acceptable inspection authority. It is preferable that the parties agree beforehand as to a specific inspection organization or entity and for the buyer to name the required certifying organization or entity in the documentary credit (when used). In letter of credit transactions, the use of such vague terminology will result in the bank's acceptance of any relevant document that appears "on its face" to be in compliance with the documentary credit, so long as it was not issued by the beneficiary (seller).

SAMPLE INSPECTION CERTIFICATE

•SGS•SGS•SGS•SGS•SGS•SGS•SGS•SGS•SGS•SGS•SGS•SGS•SGS•SGS•SGS•SGS•SGS•SGS•SGS•SGS•SGS•SGS•

 **SGS Supervise (Suisse) S.A.**

May 10, 19..

Hardstrasse 1
Postfach 4149
CH-4002 Basel
Tel. (+41-61) 271 36 11
Fax (+41-61) 271 40 48
Telex : 962 457 SGS

Certificate No 1407/ 012488

BUYER	:	TA PING CO. LTD. YACHT BUILDING
		18-5, HARBOUR STREET, TAIPEI, TAIWAN
SELLER	:	SWISS EXPORT LTD. AIRFREIGHT DIVISION
		8008 ZUERICH,SWITZERLAND
LETTER OF CREDIT NBR.	:	FB-03-45786-9
GOODS	:	MACHINERY PARTS, as designated below
CONTRACT NBR.	:	FA12345WO79PE
IMPORT PERMIT NUMBER	:	TW-2395-497-0006, as declared
SERVICES REQUIRED	:	FINAL PRE-SHIPMENT INSPECTION

This is to certify that, at buyers' request and based on the specifications submitted to us, we have inspected the following goods:

1. MATERIAL DESIGNATION
    1 LOT ACCESSORIES AND SPARE PARTS FOR FOOD PROCESSING MACHINERY, as detailed in seller's commercial invoice and corresponding packing list both dated April 29, 19

2. INSPECTIONS PERFORMED AND FINDINGS
    - 2.1.   Material identification for conformity with the specifications submitted to us.
    - 2.2.   Visual inspection on workmanship, finish and condition.
    - 2.3.   Quantitative and completeness checks.
    - 2.4.   Dimensional checks at random, where applicable.
    - 2.5.   Packing inspection: The packing, consisting of 5 plywood cases, is considered adequate to ship the goods by air to Taipei under normal conditions of transport and handling.
    - 2.6.   Marking inspection: The shipping marks include: **SWISS EXPORT 0405/1-5**
    - 2.7.   Loading details as per Air Waybill No. BSL 122077 issued by PANALPINA LTD BASLE-AIRPORT on 4 MAY ..

3. INSPECTION RESULTS AND CONCLUSION
    Based on the inspections performed, we certify the goods to be new, of good workmanship and finish, free from apparent damage or defect, and that the shipment is fully in compliance with the contract requirements in specification, quantity, quality, proper packing and marking.

5. DATE AND PLACE OF INSPECTION
    April 30, 19.. on seller's premises in Zurich, Switzerland with subsequent review of loading details.

This certificate is evidence of and reports on our findings at the time and place of inspection. It does not release buyers or sellers from their contractual obligations.

SGS SUPERVISE (SUISSE) SA
BASLE OFFICE, SWITZERLAND

As Member of SOCIETE GENERALE
DE SURVEILLANCE S.A. (SGS)
Geneva, Switzerland

The issuance of this Certificate does not exonerate buyers or sellers from exercising all their rights and discharging all their liabilities under the Contract of Sale. Stipulations to the contrary are not binding on us. – The present inspection has been carried out to the best of our knowledge and ability, and our responsibility is limited to the exercise of reasonable care.

•SGS•SGS•SGS•SGS•SGS•SGS•SGS•SGS•SGS•SGS•SGS•SGS•SGS•SGS•SGS•SGS•SGS•SGS•SGS•SGS•SGS•SGS•

CHAPTER 10

Electronic Documents

ELECTRONIC COMMERCE HAS HAD A REVOLUTIONARY EFFECT on exporters, importers, export and import authorities, as well as the many service providers to the international trade community. Until as recently as five years ago, the processes for handling documentation were firmly entrenched in the nineteenth century. Each country had its own unique sets of regulations and documentation requirements, which were interpreted and enforced by the thousands of bureaucrats whose livelihoods depended upon the proliferation of red tape.

Paper was the key. Copies were king. Some countries (e.g., Columbia) required from 24 to 36 copies of certain import documents so that each of the agencies, bureaus and commissions within the government would have their own set for their files.

The advent of international airfreight, faxes, PCs, the Internet and wireless communication has coincided with political and social shifts towards regionalization and globalization forcing traditionally slow-to-change governments, customs authorities and businesses into the 21st century. For the savvy international exporter and importer, several of these changes (most notably, the electronic filing of standardized export/import documents) should result in significant reductions in paperwork and savings of time and money. But this changeover to "paperless" documents is in its early stages and there are some cautions that must be observed:

1. Electronic filing systems are not "customer based." They have been implemented to meet the data and revenue collection needs of nations or regional trading pacts, rarely the needs of exporters and importers.

2. Systems and documentation are often incompatible from one nation to another.

3. Some bureaucrats (and even nations) will continue to require paper documents as "backups" for the electronic ones into the foreseeable future.

4. The legal status of "electronic originals" with signatures, notary seals, and other authorizations or validations, is unresolved. Therefore, hard copies of many documents (including the all-important "negotiable bill of lading") still must accompany export and import shipments.

Future Trends in Electronic Documentation

Recent approaches taken by specific countries to address the four issues listed above are enlightening in that they project trends for the near future. According to a survey of customs reform and modernization trends conducted by the World Customs Organization (WCO), nearly 90 percent of customs administrations are planning on extending their use of technology to include such items as artificial intelligence, bar coding and document imaging. Their goal is to establish "optimized electronic communication links between customs and business" that will eventually lead to a "seamless data flow" or, as it is sometimes described, an "integrated data transaction." As noted earlier, these changes are being implemented because of the tangible benefits for the nations involved, and generally not for the convenience of the exporter and importer. For example, every one of the developed countries in the WCO survey indicated that upgrading electronic data systems was prompted by the "need to combat trans-national crimes such as money laundering." In addition, many cited the strategic advantage offered by "the timely insight of current and emerging trends, threats to public safety and avenues for change to policies, strategies and legislation."

The ideals of electronic processing have been well-stated by the Philippines Bureau of Customs, which wants to generate maximum revenue for the government while "its role for national development and international trade facilitation shall be imbued in the hearts and minds of every Customs official and staff as the Bureau moves forward in its other roles of promoting National Security, Justice, Health and other objectives." Exporters and importers will be glad to learn that these noble goals will be aided by the Customs Bureau's ability to "process all documents electronically within minutes and...release goods in a matter of hours as its computerization moves forward to an advanced state of electronic commerce."

"User-Friendly" Customs Systems and Personnel

What is new to this equation is that many countries now realize the economic and regulatory advantages that occur when there is increased co-operation between the customs agencies and the business sectors. Finland was one of the first nations to encourage partnerships between the customs department and the international business community. It is rightfully proud of establishing "co-operation networks...in the following spheres of activities: control of international transport systems, co-operation with police authorities in criminal investigation, sharing of databases of Customs administration and agricultural authorities, data interchange between shipping companies, haulers, harbor operators, forwarding agents, importers exporters and the Customs administration." The New Zealand Customs Service has even instigated a multiphased program (including a Public Relations segment) program to "put the service back in Customs Service."

Customs Personnel Slow to Change

Customs agencies are aware that changes are not always implemented smoothly. When Algeria began its ten-year customs modernization plan in 1993, a great deal of time and effort was wisely directed towards re-educating and retraining personnel to lessen "the risk of resistance to change." WCO members are fully aware that computer literacy will be essential for customs officers as information technology becomes an integral part of customs administration and most of the day-to-day operation shifts to dependency on computer-based systems. At the same time, globalization dictates that these officers have enhanced language skills.

Incompatible Systems

In addition to problems from the "human element," there are problems with hardware and software systems. The transition from a paper-based system to an electronic one is being implemented on varying time lines using different, often incompatible systems. Like other "new" technologies, a universal standard does not currently exist for customs documentation. Think of it like old-time railroads that ran on tracks of different widths; or electrical services that used different voltages, outlets and plugs; or VCRs that use different kinds and sizes of tapes. We don't know yet if an "adaptor" will be developed so that electronic documentation systems will work together or if certain systems will simply be abandoned.

Legality of E-Documents

As must be clear by now, there are many different documents required for international trade transactions. Before paper documents are replaced by e-documents, however, two major issues will need to be resolved on both the national and international level:

1. LEGAL STATUS That electronically transmitted contracts, testaments, and declarations (including, for example, bills of lading and bank letters of credit) have the same legal status as ones on paper.
2. AUTHENTICITY That the authenticity (signatures, seals etc.) of electronically transmitted documents have the same legal status as ones on paper.

The need for clarification is obvious. Virtually every jurisdiction has laws that require numerous kinds of documents be "signed" or "in writing" with an implied requirement that there be a physical document or hand-written signature. Legislative attempts to legalize e-documents and signatures are slow and inconsistent. A report by the Internet Law and Policy Forum (ILPF) has identified seven countries that have recently enacted legislation specifically relating to electronic authentication (Argentina, Germany, Italy, Malaysia, Russia, Singapore and the USA). Other nations are in the process of adopting such proposals (Australia, Austria, Belgium, Columbia, Denmark, Hong Kong, South Korea, and the UK), and other countries have prepared legislative reports on the subject (Canada, Finland, France, Ireland, Japan, the Netherlands and New Zealand).

The ILPF report notes that these unilateral approaches to legalizing e-documents may in fact hinder the adoption of international legislation on the same issue. As the report notes "Divergent national standards...uncertainty concerning the legal effect of electronic signatures, conflicting licensing regimes, conflicting operational and technical requirements for Certificate Authorities (CAs), uncertain liability exposure—all of these factors are likely to impede the cross-border use of electronic signatures. Several initiatives are underway to develop international standards to overcome these obstacles."

Regional and international trends to watch include:

- The EU's draft directive on electronic signatures currently obligates all 15 members of the EU to enact legislation implementing harmonized requirements.

- The United Nations Commission on International Trade Law (UNCITRAL) adopted a general framework for paperless transactions in December 1996 and is now developing uniform rules that relate more specifically to electronic signatures and the operation of CAs.

- The United States has circulated a draft for comments of a proposed international convention that will bind signatories to recognize the principles and requirements it contains. Similar in most respects to the United State's recently enacted "E-signatures in Global and National Commerce Act," this initiative has received favorable response from a dozen or more countries.

- The Organization for Economic Cooperation and Development (OECD) has adopted a Declaration on Authentication for Electronic Commerce, which encourages electronic authentication policies that minimize government regulation, support technological neutrality and recognize national autonomy. One interesting phrase in the declaration is the encouragement of member countries (Australia, Austria, Belgium, Canada, Czech Republic, Denmark, Finland, France, Germany, Greece, Hungary, Iceland, Ireland, Italy, Japan, Korea, Luxembourg, Mexico, Netherlands, New Zealand, Norway, Poland, Portugal, Spain, Sweden, Switzerland, Turkey, UK, US) to "take a non-discriminatory approach to electronic authentication from other countries."

The summation of all these factors is that the specific document requirements for exporting and importing are constantly changing.

Perhaps the easiest way to understand what electronic documentation means to the exporter and importer is to look at specific examples of the current status of electronic documentation through different systems and note the advantages and disadvantages they offer.

The USA's AES and ACS

The prime example of a single country's automated documentation system is the one in place in the United States. For exporters, there is the Automated Export System (AES), while importers use the Automated Commercial System (ACS). From the point of view of the exporter and importer the systems are operationally separate, but to the US Customs Service and the other governmental departments and agencies concerned with what comes in and goes out of the country, the data bases are linked.

Exporting from the USA Through the (AES)

In order for exports to leave the United States, a Shipper's Export Declaration (SED) is required. In a 1996 attempt at modernizing this procedure, the Census Bureau and Customs Service allowed exporters to submit a signed facsimile of the SED. But copy illegibility and the increased person hours required to verify data caused Customs to stop accepting fax submissions in May, 2000. Customs completely revamped their computer systems to make them Y2K (year 2000) compliant and so, in addition to the original paper SEDs, the exporter can now file the form electronically through the Automated Export System (AES) or via the Internet with AESDirect. There are currently four different options for filing the required SED and export manifest documents.

OPTION #1 This requires the predeparture filling of paper forms.

OPTION #2 This is the basic way most export shipments are currently handled-with full predeparture transmission of complete information through the AES.

OPTION #3 This allows partial information to be reported predeparture and then complete information within five days of export. No pre-approval is required.

OPTION #4 This is only available to certain pre-approved exporters and allows them to send shipments without predeparture notification to the AES. These exporters must submit their forms within ten working days after departure.

PROCEDURES

Exporters must file a letter of intent (LOI) and obtain approval to become part of the AES system. For options #2 and #3, exporters can file the LOI on line at AESDirect. Those requesting option #4 must still provide a paper LOI.

Even with e-documentation it is obvious that bureaucracy still flourishes. But at the new consumer-friendly US Customs Service, there is a wealth of easily accessible information regarding the AES on the Customs website and some of it is even quite humorous. In response to a question about how many blanks need to be filled in on the AES form, Customs made the following answer: "Most conventional export shipments require about 20 data elements." But, "if you are trying to export a used vehicle powered by a nuclear reactor and containing a Cray super-computer which will transit two countries before it is delivered to the buyer in Libya, then you would come close to needing to report all 71 possible elements."

This humor is welcome but it also points to an important benefit of the AES —the regulatory data needs for most of the following extensive list of agencies is already incorporated into the single AES form:

- The Department of Agriculture (DOE)
- The US Arms Control and Disarmament Agency (ACD)*
- The Bureau of Alcohol, Tobacco and Firearms*
- The Army Corps of Engineers (ACE)
- The Federal Aviation Administration (FAA)*
- The Bureau of Labor Statistics (BLS)
- The Census Bureau (Census)
- The Center for Disease Control (CDC)*
- The US Coast Guard (Coast Guard)*
- The Commerce Department (Commerce)
- The Consumer Product Safety Commission (CPS)*
- The Defense Department (DOD)*
- The Drug Enforcement Administration (DEA)*
- The Energy Department (DOE)
- The Environmental Protection Agency (EPA)*

- The Federal Maritime Commission (FMC)
- The US Fish and Wildlife Service (FWS)
- The National Highway Safety Administration (HSA)
- The Internal Revenue Service (IRS)
- The International Trade Commission (ITC)
- The Department of Justice (Justice)
- The Nuclear Regulatory Commission (NRC)
- The Small Business Administration (SBA)
- The State Department (State)
- The Department of Transportation (DOT)
- The Treasury Department (Treasury)*

*Indicates agencies which still require paper documentation in addition to the AES.

Now multiply these 26 different agencies and their required forms by the hundreds of countries in the world and you will quickly understand how confusing exporting and importing was before customs agencies began consolidating information into single forms like the AES Export Declaration or the European Union's Single Administrative Document (SAD).

Importing into the USA Through the (ACS)

The Automated Commercial System (ACS) was established by US Customs to facilitate the process of importing merchandise, cut costs and reduce paperwork requirements for both customs and the trade community. The ACS is used to track, control and process all commercial goods imported into United States.

A voluntary program called the Automated Broker Interface (ABI) permits qualified participants (importers, brokers, carriers, port authorities and independent service centers), to file import data electronically with Customs. There are numerous cost-saving benefits in the ACS/ABI, most of which have an acronym attached.

- THE AUTOMATED CLEARINGHOUSE (ACH) is an electronic payment option that allows ABI filers who have established a draw-down account to pay Customs fees, duties and taxes with one electronic transaction.

- THE OTHER GOVERNMENT AGENCIES (OGA) INTERFACE eliminates the need for paper copies of other agency forms that would otherwise be required upon entry. Entry and summary data flow electronically to the U.S. Department of Transportation (DOT), Bureau of the Census (Census), Food and Drug Administration (FDA), and the Fish and Wildlife Service (FWS) and the plethora of other agencies listed in the AES section above.

- THE AUTOMATED MANIFEST SYSTEM (AMS) is a cargo inventory control and release notification system. The AMS allows faster identification and release of low-risk shipments, speeds the flow of cargo and entry processing and provides importers or their agents with the electronic authorization for cargo release before the cargo arrives. The AMS program allows for imports using different types of carriers.

- **AMS SEA** allows participants to transmit manifest data electronically prior to vessel arrival. Customs can then determine in advance whether the merchandise "merits examination or immediate release." The system also allows the importer the opportunity to arrange for examination, release and distribution of the merchandise before the vessel even reaches port. AMS Air and AMS Rail offer similar services to merchandise arriving by other means of transport.

- **THE NATIONAL IN-BOND** system is incorporated into the AMS and tracks cargo en route in the US from the point of unloading to the port of entry or export.

- **THE PAPERLESS MASTER IN-BOND (PMIB)** program is for shipments by sea that utilize Automated Bills of Lading (ABOL). Since all the information that would normally appear on paper copies is already available in AMS, such documents are not required for PMIB shipments from the carrier's custody at the port of unloading to the same carrier's custody at the port of destination.

The European Union's SAD

The European Union (EU) is a regional trade agreement (RTA) between 15 member nations and is slated to include an additional 9 nations in the next few years. The EU's Single Administrative Document (SAD) was implemented in 1988 with the purpose of establishing a standardized customs document for all its members, harmonizing codification and simplifying the procedures for international trading. The SAD immediately replaced most of the customs declaration forms that were previously required and also came to be used for transit procedures with the four European Free Trade Area (EFTA) countries. The SAD is used as an export, import or transit declaration for any consignment moving within the EU and contains all necessary information, standardized and expressed in harmonized WCO codes. By linking through the Belgian SADBEL system, any firm or customs broker can make a declaration directly to customs.

Since the EU system is not currently Internet-based, this means that for the exporter or importer to take advantage of e-document filing, their computer system must be compatible with EU Customs and Excise IBM AS/400 systems. The other choice is to utilize the services of a shipper, customs broker or logistics firm that already has such links.

ASYCUDA-A Globalized System

Exporters and importers who trade with over 70 of the world's underdeveloped nations are probably unaware that they are tied into a United Nations Customs network called the Automated System for Customs Data Management (ASYCUDA). This system began in 1981 (well before the use of personal computers in the business world) when the Economic Community of Western African States (ECOWAS) approached the UN for assistance in compiling foreign trade statistics in their member states. It was quickly realized that this could only be done if both the Customs clearance offices and procedures were "modernized." The first system developed utilized computers that were extremely limited by today's standards, but as technology improved, so did the system. The latest version (ASYCUDA2) has repeatedly proven to be very stable and reliable even when faced with challenging physical and social environments.

The adaptability and reliability of the system is a major reason that it now is the trans-global computerized customs management system that covers most foreign trade procedures. ASYCUDA uses the international codes and harmonized standards established by the International Organization for Standardization (ISO), the World Customs Organization (WCO), and the United Nations (UN). The system handles manifests and customs declarations, accounting procedures, transit and suspense procedures, and it generates data for use in statistical economic analysis. Because of the system's flexibility, it can be configured to suit the national characteristics of individual Customs regimes, national tariffs, laws and regulations.

ASYCUDA was developed in Geneva, Switzerland by the United Nations Conference on Trade and Development (UNCTAD) to assist least-developed countries boost their economy through viable trading options. Since Customs duties are the main source of public revenue in developing countries, the reinforcement of customs control and the collection of customs duties was (and still is) one of ASYCUDA's primary goals. Another major focus is the establishment of trade links between developing and industrialized countries.

The ASYCUDA was established and is in place for the benefit of customs agencies and governments and as such, is not currently accessible to the trade community but this will change soon. The next version of ASYCUDA is being developed specifically to allow for Electronic Data Interchange (EDI) between traders and customs and the electronic filing of export and import documents.

E-Documents in a Closed Environment

To summarize, only a limited number of national or regional systems exist by which exporters and importers can directly utilize e-documentation for their shipments.

In contrast, e-documents for exports and imports are widely accepted and used by shippers, brokers and logistical firms. This is because these firms have established a legal relationship with each of their customers in what is referred to as a "closed" system (or environment).

In a closed system, all of the relevant parties have agreed in advance on their respective rights and duties. The closed environment that is already familiar to many businesses is the Secure Electronic Transaction (SET) system developed and used by Visa, Mastercard, American Express and other members of the credit card community. With SET, each of the parties to a secure electronic transaction—the cardholder, merchant, and member banks that process the transaction—has a digital signature that establishes its identity within the system. The parties rights and obligations are established by a series of contracts. Shippers, customs brokers and logistics firms that use e-commerce systems with their customers do so in a similar, contractually based, closed environment.

CHAPTER 11

50 Country Document Requirements

THIS CHAPTER OFFERS A LOOK AT DOCUMENTATION REQUIREMENTS on a country-by-country basis. In the pages that follow are tables and notes for basic and special documents for importing to the world's top 50 trading nations. The information provided is not comprehensive. Every country has specialized requirements and documentation that cannot be fully described in a book of this size. The information provided, however, will give the international trader an idea of the range of country document requirements in an easy to understand format for comparison.

BASIC IMPORT DOCUMENTS

The reader will immediately notice, as was stated earlier in this book, that there is a great deal of similarity from country-to-country in import documentation requirements. For example, virtually every country requires presentation of a commercial invoice, bill of lading and certificate of origin. There are many exceptions, however, with countries adding documents to their "basic" list.

SPECIAL IMPORT DOCUMENTS

The reader will also note that additional documentation is almost always required for the importation of specialized commodities and products. At the least, these include animals, plants, food products, alcohol, drugs, and other goods that affect health, safety and national security.

SAMPLE FORMS

For most transactions, import authorities will accept industry standard forms of the commercial invoice, bill of lading and certificate of origin. Whenever possible, we refer you to generic sample forms in other parts of this book.

Many other documents (in form, content and language) are country-specific. Reproducing samples of the thousands of these forms is beyond the scope of this book.

FOR FURTHER INFORMATION

The research for this chapter was a monumental job and we intend it to be a good representation of the documentation requirements for the countries listed. However, as with such data, requirements change rapidly and the nature of your transaction may not fit into a simplistic formula.

For these reasons, we highly recommend that you consult with a freight-forwarder, logistic professional, or a customs broker for up-to-the-minute requirements. This is true especially if you are importing a regulated good such as animals, plants, drugs, food products, alcohol, textiles, textile products, motor vehicles, medical devices, toys, chemicals, cultural relics, arms and armaments, radioactive materials, high technology products (including hardware and software), biological vectors, or aerospace products.

Argentina's Import Document Requirements

BASIC DOCUMENTS

Document	Originals	Copies	Notes	Sample
Bill of Lading (or Airway Bill)	1	2	-	page 40
Commercial Invoice	-	3	A	page 36
Packing List	1	2	B	page 53
Preshipment Inspection Required	1	0	C	-
Shipper's Export Declaration	1	2	D	page 66

SPECIAL DOCUMENTS (WHEN REQUIRED)

Document	Originals	Copies	Notes	Sample
Analysis Certificate	1	1	E	-
Certificate of Origin	1	1	F	page 107
Free Sale Certificate	1	1	G	-
Sanitary Certificate	1	1	H	-

COUNTRY NOTES

1. Argentina is a MERCOSUR member and enjoys free trade arrangements with Bolivia, Brazil, Chile, Paraguay and Uruguay. Special documents are required for shipments between these member countries.
2. To expedite procedures, all documents should be in Spanish as well as the exporter's language.

DOCUMENT NOTES

A-Must be in Spanish. All copies must be signed in ink by the exporter/agent (with name an title printed beneath) and registered with the Argentine Consulate. The invoice must have the following declaration:
"DECLARO BAJO JURAMENTO QUE LOS PRECIOS CONSIGNADOS EN ESTA FACTURA COMERCIAL SON LOS REALMENTE PAGADOS O A PAGARSE, Y QUE NO EXISTE CONVENIO ALGUNO QUE PERMITA SU ALTERACION, Y QUE TODOS LOS DATOS REFERENTES AL LA CALIDAD, CANTIDAD,VALOR,PRECIOS, ETC., Y DESCRIPCION DE LA MERCADERIA CONCURERDAN EN TODAS SU PARTES CON LO DECLARADO EN LA CORRESPONDIENTE SHIPPER'S EXPORT DECLARATION." (Unofficial translation: I swear that the prices on this commercial invoice are those really paid or to be paid, and that no agreement exists that permits their modification, and that all data pertaining to quality, quantity, value, prices, etc., and description of the merchandise agree in all their parts with what was declared in the corresponding Shipper's Export declaration.")
B-Not required but strongly suggested.
C-All material valued at $800.00 (US) or more requires preshipment inspection by authorized inspection services such as Bureau Veritas, Inspectorate America or Intertek.
D-The Shippers Export Declaration (SED) must be on an appropriate form from the exporter's country.
E-For livestock, plants and plant products, seeds, grains, bulbs, cuttings, rhizomes, tubers, etc.
F-Only required for certain classifications of goods such as textiles and footwear.
G-For certain specified medicines, medicinal preparations, and pharmaceuticals.
H-For all plants and plant products seeds, grains, and livestock.

Australia's Import Document Requirements

BASIC DOCUMENTS

Document	Originals	Copies	Notes	Sample
Bill of Lading (or Airway Bill)	1	2	-	page 40
Commercial Invoice	-	3	A	page 36
Packing List	1	2	B	page 53

SPECIAL DOCUMENTS (WHEN REQUIRED)

Document	Originals	Copies	Notes	Sample
Australian Content Certificate	1	1	C	-
Certificate of Origin	1	1	D	page 107
Health Certificate	1	1	E	-
Proforma Invoice	1	3	F	-
Phytosanitary Certificate	1	1	G	-

COUNTRY NOTES

Australia is a member of the Closer Economic Relations Trade Agreement (CER), which allows for tariff-free exchange of goods with New Zealand.

DOCUMENT NOTES

A - This provides a clear and precise description of the products, terms of sale and any and all other information needed to establish the cost, insurance and freight prices. FOB and CIF prices should be in Australian dollars.

B - Not required but strongly suggested.

C - Footwear, clothing, and cut and uncut fabric are only allowed to be imported if they contain Australian made materials. Tariffs are assessed on the foreign content of the products.

D - When required by customer.

E - For meat and poultry products.

F - When requested by importer.

G - For all produce.

Austria's Import Document Requirements

BASIC DOCUMENTS

Document	Originals	Copies	Notes	Sample
Bill of Lading (or Airway Bill)	1	3	-	page 40
Commercial Invoice	1	4	A	page 36
Packing List	1	2	B	page 53
SAD Customs Declaration	1	2	C, D	page 106

SPECIAL DOCUMENTS (WHEN REQUIRED)

Document	Originals	Copies	Notes	Sample
Certificate of Origin	1	4	E	page 107
Import License	1	2	F	-
Inspection Certificate	1	1	G	-
Insurance Certificate	1	1	H	page 104
Phytosanitary Certificate	1	1	I	-
Proforma Invoice	1	2	J	-
Sanitary Certificate	1	1	K	-
Special Certificates	1	1	L	-
Wine Certificate	1	1	M	-

COUNTRY NOTES

Austria is a member of the European Union (EU). The above requirements are for imports from non-EU countries.

DOCUMENT NOTES

A—This provides a clear and precise description of the product(s), terms of sale and any and all other information needed to establish the cost, insurance and freight prices.

B—Not required but strongly suggested.

C— Replacing the Summary Declaration Form, the "new model" for written customs declarations within Austria and all other EU countries is the Single Administrative Document (SAD). Easily processed by electronic means, the SAD is used when importing or transporting any goods in the EU and contains the necessary information standardized and expressed in EU codes. It can be submitted by computer directly to Austrian Customs.

D—The SAD must be declared by a resident of the EU.

E—When requested by importer or required for certain controlled goods.

F—EU import quotas are maintained through these licenses covering agricultural produce and products, war materials, and certain protected consumer goods such as shoes.

G—For processed foods.

H—If required by importer or shipper.

I—Indicates plants and/or plant products are free from disease.

J—If requested by customer.

K—Indicates live animals and/or animal products are healthy and disease free.

L—For imports of textiles, iron and steel, fishmeal, milk, eggs, fowl, lard, meat by-products, animal glands, heads and skins, precious metals and stones, weapons, vehicles of all types, timber, textiles, alcoholic beverages.

M—For some wines, sparkling wines, vermouth.

Belgium's Import Document Requirements

BASIC DOCUMENTS

Document	Originals	Copies	Notes	Sample
Bill of Lading (or Airway Bill)	1	2	A	page 40
Commercial Invoice	1	3	B	page 36
Packing List	1	2	C	page 53
SAD Customs Declaration	1	2	D,E	page 106

SPECIAL DOCUMENTS (WHEN REQUIRED)

Document	Originals	Copies	Notes	Sample
Certificate of Origin	1	1	F	page 107
Import License	1	2	G	-
Inspection Certificate	1	1	H	-
Insurance Certificate	1	1	I	page 104
Phytosanitary Certificate	1	1	J	-
Proforma Invoice	1	2	K	-
Sanitary Certificate	1	1	L	-
Special Certificates	1	1	M	-
Wine Certificate	1	1	N	-

COUNTRY NOTES

Belgium is a member of the European Union (EU). The above requirements are for imports from non-EU countries.

DOCUMENT NOTES

A-"To Order" bills are acceptable.

B-This is the standard transaction document. It helps if the HTS code (Harmonized Tariff Schedule) is used.

C-Not required but strongly suggested.

D- Replacing the Summary Declaration Form, the "new model" for written customs declarations within Belgium and all other EU countries is the Single Administrative Document (SAD). Easily processed by electronic means, the SAD is used when importing or transporting any goods in the EU and contains the necessary information standardized and expressed in EU codes. It can be submitted by computer directly to Belgian Customs.

E-The SAD must be declared by a resident of the EU.

F-Only required for stipulated goods. The importers instruct their suppliers regarding the circumstances when these must be issued and certified by a local Chamber of Commerce.

G-EU import quotas are maintained through these licenses covering agricultural produce and products, war materials, and certain protected consumer goods such as shoes. Applications for licenses must be made with the Belgian Office of Quotas and Licenses. No problems if the importer is Belgian.

H-For processed foods.

I-If required by importer or shipper.

J-Indicates plants and/or plant products are free from disease.

K-If requested by customer.

L-Indicates live animals and/or animal products are healthy and disease free.

M.-For imports of textiles, iron and steel, fishmeal, milk, eggs, fowl, lard, meat by-products, animal glands, heads and skins, precious metals and stones, weapons, vehicles of all types, timber, textiles, alcoholic beverages

N-For some wines, sparkling wines, vermouth.

Brazil's Import Document Requirements

BASIC DOCUMENTS

Document	Originals	Copies	Notes	Sample
Bill of Lading (or Airway Bill)	1	5	A	page 40
Commercial Invoice	1	5	B	page 36
Import Permit	0	1	C	-
Packing List	1	2	D	page 53

SPECIAL DOCUMENTS (WHEN REQUIRED)

Document	Originals	Copies	Notes	Sample
Certificate of Origin	1	4	E	page 107
Health Certificate	1	1	F	-
Inspection Certificate	1	1	G	-
Insurance Certificate	1	1	H	page 104
Proforma Invoice	1	1	I	-
Pro-vitamin A Certificate	1	1	J	-
Sanitary Certificate	1	1	K	-

COUNTRY NOTES

1. Brazil is a MERCOSUR member and enjoys free trade arrangements with Argentina, Bolivia, Chile, Paraguay and Uruguay. Special documents are required for shipments between these member countries.
2. To expedite procedures, all documents should be in Spanish as well as the exporter's language and all documents must comply with the information and standards of the Brazilian Government Agency for Foreign Trade (SECEX).

DOCUMENT NOTES

A-Must include the SECEX import permit number, date of expiration and freight charges.

B-Called the "fatura commercial," this must be on company letterhead and include the full addresses of the shipper, seller and consignee, the import permit number, other reference numbers, date of the order, shipping date, delivery and payment terms, a complete description of the merchandise, export markings, terms of sale and any and all other information needed to establish the cost, insurance and freight prices. Must be signed in blue ink.

C-Called "Guia de Importacao," this is the essential document for importing to Brazil. Issued by SECEX in advance of shipment, the validity of the permit is for 60, 90, or 120 days after which the permit expires.

D-Not required but strongly suggested to streamline customs procedures.

E-A declaration of origin combined with a declaration of correct prices may be made on the commercial invoice provided it is certified by the foreign exporter or local chamber of commerce and contains the following notarized declaration: "I (name and title) hereby swear that the prices stated in this invoice are the correct market price for any country for the merchandise described herein, and the origin of these goods is (name of country) and I accept full responsibility for any inaccuracies or errors herein."

F-For live animals and animal products.

G-For used merchandise, machinery and equipment.

H-If required by importer or shipper.

I-If requested by importer.

J-Needs statement that this product is 400,00 to 500,00 units of provitamin-A for animal use only.

K-For live animals and/or animal products and by-products, live plants and parts thereof, fruit, vegetables, seeds, potatoes, raw cotton, and cotton strips and combing.

Canada's Import Document Requirements

BASIC DOCUMENTS

Document	Originals	Copies	Notes	Sample
Bill of Lading (or Airway Bill)	1	3	-	page 40
Commercial Invoice	1	3	A	page 36
Packing List	1	3	B	page 53

SPECIAL DOCUMENTS (WHEN REQUIRED)

Document	Originals	Copies	Notes	Sample
Canadian Customs Invoice	1	3	C	pg ###
Certificate of Origin	1	2	D	page 107
Inspection Certificate	1	2	E	-
Insurance Certificate	1	1	F	page 104
NAFTA Certificate of Origin	1	2	G	page 108
Phytosanitary Quarantine Certificate	1	2	H	-
Proforma Invoice	1	1	I	-
Sanitary Certificate	1	2	J	-

COUNTRY NOTES

Canada is a member of the North American Free Trade Agreement (NAFTA), which allows for tariff-free exchange of goods within Canada, Mexico and the USA.

DOCUMENT NOTES

A-Must be an accurate description of goods itemizing FOB and CIF values signed in ink by an exporting official attesting to the accuracy of the information provided. May be used in lieu of Canadian Customs Invoice (CCI) if valued less than $1,600 (Canadian), or if all information needed for CCI is included.

B-Not required but strongly advised.

C-Not needed on shipments valued below $1,600 (Canadian) or if all required information is included on the exporter's commercial invoice.

D-If requested by customer for non-NAFTA countries.

E-For food, animals, dairy products, meats, fats, raw fur, honeybees, blueberries, vegetables, seeds, forest products, nursery stock, feed stuffs, used bags, used vehicles, farm equipment, pharmaceuticals, tires, steel, firearms, ammunition, flammable products, hazardous materials, chlorofluorocarbons and pharmaceuticals.

F- If required by importer or shipper.

G-Follows NAFTA's Rules of Origin and indicates where products/goods originated. Certificate to be sent to importer who must possess it at time of accountability. "Blanket Certificates" can cover more than one shipment over a twelve month period.

H-For plants and plant products.

I-If requested by importer or shipper.

J-For fresh fruits and vegetables, seeds, and certain live animals.

Chile's Import Document Requirements

BASIC DOCUMENTS

Document	Originals	Copies	Notes	Sample
Bill of Lading (or Airway Bill)	1	2	-	page 40
Commercial Invoice	1	4	A	page 36
Packing List	1	1	B	page 53
Proforma Invoice	1	2	C	-

SPECIAL DOCUMENTS (WHEN REQUIRED)

Document	Originals	Copies	Notes	Sample
Analysis Certificate	1	1	E	-
Certificate of Origin	1	1	F	page 107
Import License	1	1	G	-
Insurance Certificate	1	1	H	page 104
Phytosanitary Certificate	1	1	I	-
Sanitary/ Veterinary Certificate	1	1	J	-

COUNTRY NOTES

1. Chile is a MERCOSUR member and enjoys free trade arrangements with Argentina, Bolivia, Brazil, Paraguay and Uruguay. Special documents are required for shipments between these member countries.
2. To expedite procedures, all documents should be in Spanish as well as the exporter's language.

DOCUMENT NOTES

A-Should show FOB, or FAS and/or CIF itemized values. Invoice must include the following certification: "Under oath we declare that we are the owners (or shippers) of the above-mentioned merchandise, that the prices and other details are exact, that the said merchandise is a product of the soil or industry of (the country of origin) and that we accept the legal consequences which might arise through any inexactitude contained in this invoice." Signature(s) and title(s) should be provided.

B-Not required but strongly suggested.

C-Required to register imports. Must include all cost components, price, insurance and other costs to derive total CIF price.

D-For spirituous beverages.

E-For foodstuffs.

F-If requested by importer.

G-Required for all shipments over $3,000.00 (US). An Informe de Importacion must be issued by the Central Bank in Chile (which can usually be processed through the importer's local bank). This approval must be granted prior to shipment of goods.

H-If required by importer or shipper.

I-For plants, plant cuttings, bark, root stocks, flowers, stems, fruits, wood or any part of a plant in its natural state or process capable of harboring plant pests or of being a pest in itself as well as commodities dangerous to plants (including plant products, living organisms, containers and soils), also fragile objects (glass, porcelain etc.) packed in straw jackets and/or straw packing material. Must include proof of sterilization.

J-Required for all animal imports. A veterinarian or other competent authority in the country of origin must certify that the animals are in good health and free of contagious diseases.

China Import Document Requirements

BASIC DOCUMENTS

Document	Originals	Copies	Notes	Sample
Bill of Lading (or Airway Bill)	1	3	A	page 40
Commercial Invoice	1	2	B	page 36
Insurance Certificate	1	2	C	page 104
Packing List	1	2	-	page 53
Sales Contract	1	2	D	-

SPECIAL DOCUMENTS (WHEN REQUIRED)

Document	Originals	Copies	Notes	Sample
Certificate of Origin	1	3	E	page 107
Import License	1	2	F	-
Import Commodity Inspection Certificate	1	2	G	-
Import Quota Certificate	1	2	H	-
Import Safety/Quality Inspection Certificate	1	2	I	-
Phytosanitary Quarantine Certificate	1	2	J	-
Veterinary Quarantine Certificate	1	2	K	-
Wood Packaging Certificates	1	0	L	-

DOCUMENT NOTES

A-The name of the People's Republic of China (PRC) should appear in French on the waybill. ("Republique Populaire de Chine").

B-Must be an accurate description of goods itemizing FOB and CIF values signed by an exporting official attesting to the accuracy of the information provided.

C-Policy must be issued by the People's Insurance Company of China (PICC), a state-owned agency.

D-Must specify importer's authorized contact names and numbers in the PRC. Contract must also specify requirements for inspection and any necessary quarantine certificates required under China's law.

E-May be required by importer or bank or letter of credit. Must be notarized by a Notary Public and certified by exporter's local Chamber of Commerce, which will require their own notarized copy. Documents must also be legalized at Chinese Government Offices where rules are subject to change. Follow current rules.

F-An import license issued by MOFERT and a license from a local foreign trade bureau is required for most commodities.

G-Inspection prior to shipment is required for all items appearing on a published Inspection List.

H- Quota certificates are necessary on certain steel, polyester, plastic and cotton products/materials.

I-Obtained from the local China Commodity Inspection Bureau for the following goods: autos, motorcycles, motorcycle engines, refrigerators/freezers, air conditioners, compressors, television sets, and movies. Certain electrical products also require inspection certificates from the State Technical Supervision Bureau.

J-Application for import must be submitted in advance and health of plants, plant products and seeds must be certified by local testing company or lab. Quarantine may be required.

K-Application for import must be submitted in advance and health of animals must be certified by local veterinarian. Quarantine may be required.

L-All wood packing materials must have been certified by local Department of Agriculture to have undergone heat treatment or other pest control processes. The following statements must be used on the Commercial Invoice and Bill of Lading:" THIS SHIPMENT CONTAINS NO SOLID WOOD PACKING MATERIAL" or "SOLID WOOD PACKING MATERIAL IN THIS SHIPMENT IS NOT CONIFEROUS WOOD."

Colombia's Import Document Requirements

BASIC DOCUMENTS

Document	Originals	Copies	Notes	Sample
Bill of Lading (or Airway Bill)	3	2	-	page 40
Commercial Invoice	-	3	A	page 36
Import License	1	2	B	-
Packing List	1	2	C	page 53
Preshipment Inspection Required	1	0	D	-
Proforma Invoice	1	3	E	-

SPECIAL DOCUMENTS (WHEN REQUIRED)

Document	Originals	Copies	Notes	Sample
Certificate of Origin	1	4	F	page 107
Disinfection Certificate	1	1	G	-
Insurance Certificate	1	2	H	page 104
Manufacturer's Certificate	1	1	I	-
Phytosanitary Certificate	1	1	J	-
Purity Certificate	1	1	K	-
Sanitary Certificate	1	1	L	-

COUNTRY NOTES

1. Colombia is an ALADI member and enjoys special reduced tariff arrangements with Argentina, Bolivia, Brazil, Chile, Cuba, Ecuador, Mexico, Paraguay, Peru, Uruguay and Venezuela. Special documents are required for shipments between these member countries.
2. To expedite procedures, all documents should be in Spanish as well as the exporter's language.

DOCUMENT NOTES

A-Must be in Spanish or have a Spanish translation and include this declaration "DECLARAMOS BAJO JURAMENTO QUE LOS PRECIOS DE ESTA FACTURA SON FOB EN EL PUERTO DE EMBARQUE, QUE SON LOS MISMOS QUE CARAGMOS AL CLIENTE Y QUE LA MERCANCIA A QUE ELLA SE REFIERE ES ORIGINARIA DE (country of origin). Y EN FE DE LO EXPUESTO FIRMANOS LA PRESENTE DECLARACION EN (city, state, country), EL (date) DE (year).
B-All shipments must be registered with the Colombian foreign trade Institute (INCOMEX) and the original registration form or license is required for Customs clearance.
C-Not required but strongly suggested.
D-All material valued at $2000 (US) or more requires preshipment inspection by authorized inspection services such as Bureau Veritas or Inchcape.
E-For registration purposes, the importer may request this be provided, signed by the exporter or agent, certified by a Chamber of Commerce and legalized by a Colombian consulate.
F-May be required for Letter of Credit, or the import license. Must be notarized, certified by a Chamber of Commerce and legalized by the Colombian Consulate.
G-For shipment where used (coffee) sacks are utilized. Legalization by Colombian Consulate is required.
H-Must be from Colombian insurance company.
I-Certifying that alcoholic beverages comply with laws of the country of origin as well as Colombian laws.
J-For fruits and vegetables.
K-For food oils, lard, confectionery, baked goods, liquor essence, canned goods. Issued by exporter and legalized by government agency.
L-For products of animal and/or vegetable origin including canned meat and milk.

Czech Republic's Import Document Requirements

BASIC DOCUMENTS

Document	Originals	Copies	Notes	Sample
Bill of Lading (or Airway Bill)	1	1	-	page 40
Commercial Invoice	1	2	A	page 36
Inspection/Insurance Certificate	1	2	B	page 104

SPECIAL DOCUMENTS (WHEN REQUIRED)

Document	Originals	Copies	Notes	Sample
Certificate of Origin	1	2	C	page 107
Health Certificate	1	2	D	-
Special Certificate	1	2	E	-
Packing List	1	1	F	page 53
Proforma Invoice	1	1	G	-

DOCUMENT NOTES

A-This provides a clear and precise description of the product(s), terms of sale and any and all other information needed to establish the cost, insurance and freight prices. Should have a signature, name and title.

B- Insurance must be obtained from Czech State Insurance Company.

C-May be requested by customer.

D-For animal and animal by-products, animal raw materials, fruits, live plants and their parts.

E-For toys, electrical home appliances, cosmetics and fireworks.

F-Not required but strongly suggested.

G-If requested by customer.

Egypt's Import Document Requirements

BASIC DOCUMENTS

Document	Originals	Copies	Notes	Sample
Bill of Lading (or Airway Bill)	1	2	A, B	page 40
Commercial Invoice	1	1	A, C	page 36
Packing List	1	1	D	page 53
Proforma Invoice	1	4	E	-

SPECIAL DOCUMENTS (WHEN REQUIRED)

Document	Originals	Copies	Notes	Sample
Age Certificate	1	1	F	-
Certificate of Origin	1	5	A, G	page 107
Chemical Certificate	1	1	H	-
Consular Customs Invoice	1	5	A, I	-
Disinfection Certificate	1	1	J	-
Free Sale Certificate	1	1	K	-
Insurance Certificate	1	1	L	page 104
Radiation Certificate	1	1	M	-
Sanitary Certificate	1	1	N	-

COUNTRY NOTES
Egypt is a member of the Arab League Free Trade Zone (AFTZ).

DOCUMENT NOTES
A -Signed documents must be authenticated by exporter and certified in the following order:
1. Notarized by a Notary Public and certified by exporter's Chamber of Commerce.
2. Certified by nearest Egyptian Cooperation Foundation (ECF).
3. Legalized by the Egyptian Embassy or any Egyptian Consulate.
B-Bill of lading must contain the terms "Consignee" and "Notify Party."
C-Egyptian Customs insist on accurate description of goods, prices, costs, etc.
D-This document is required by Egyptian Customs.
E-Should include: country of origin, name of importer, kind of commodity, customs tariff item, the unit, the quantity, price per unit, the basis of contract, the amount in foreign currency.
F-For whiskey.
G-Certificate of Origin must include the name and address of the Egyptian importer.
H-For food additives and other food processing materials. Certificate must be issued by an inspection authority, list the chemical composition of the commodity, and state that it is authorized "safe for use" in the country of origin.
I-One copy is kept by the ECF and one by the Consulate.
J-For shaving brushes and bristles. Certificate must state these items have been sterilized.
K-Foodstuffs, pharmaceuticals, and wood products may require a certificate stating these items are in free circulation in the country of origin.
L-When requested by importer or shipper. Insurers must have an agent or representative in Egypt.
M-Many agricultural products are subject to random Geiger counter inspection to verify that they are not contaminated by radioactivity.
N-For fresh and canned meats, plants and plant products.

Finland's Import Document Requirements

BASIC DOCUMENTS

Document	Originals	Copies	Notes	Sample
Bill of Lading (or Airway Bill)	1	1	-	page 40
Commercial Invoice	1	5	A	page 36
Packing List	1	1	B	page 53
SAD Customs Declaration	1	2	C, D	page 106

SPECIAL DOCUMENTS (WHEN REQUIRED)

Document	Originals	Copies	Notes	Sample
Certificate of Origin	1	5	E	page 107
Import License	1	2	F	-
Inspection Certificate	1	1	G	-
Insurance Certificate	1	1	H	page 104
Phytosanitary Certificate	1	1	I	-
Proforma Invoice	1	5	J	-
Sanitary Certificate	1	1	K	-
Special Certificates	1	1	L	-
Wine Certificate	1	1	M	-

COUNTRY NOTES

Finland is a member of the European Union (EU). The above requirements are for imports from non-EU countries.

DOCUMENT NOTES

A-This provides a clear and precise description of the product(s), terms of sale and any and all other information needed to establish the cost, insurance and freight prices.

B-Not required but strongly suggested.

C- Replacing the Summary Declaration Form, the "new model" for written customs declarations within Finland and all other EU countries is the Single Administrative Document (SAD). Easily processed by electronic means, the SAD is used when importing or transporting any goods in the EU and contains the necessary information standardized and expressed in EU codes. It can be submitted by computer directly to Finnish Customs.

D-The SAD must be declared by a resident of the EU.

E-When requested by importer or required for certain controlled goods.

F-EU import quotas are maintained through these licenses covering agricultural produce and products, war materials, and certain protected consumer goods such as shoes.

G-For processed foods.

H-If required by importer or shipper.

I-Indicates plants and/or plant products are free from disease.

J-If requested by customer.

K-Indicates live animals and/or animal products are healthy and disease free.

L-For imports of textiles, iron and steel, fishmeal, milk, eggs, fowl, lard, meat by-products, animal glands, heads and skins, precious metals and stones, weapons, vehicles of all types, timber, textiles, alcoholic beverages

M-For some wines, sparkling wines, vermouth.

France's Import Document Requirements

BASIC DOCUMENTS

Document	Originals	Copies	Notes	Sample
Bill of Lading (or Airway Bill)	1	1	-	page 40
Commercial Invoice	1	5	A	page 36
Packing List	1	2	B	page 53
SAD Customs Declaration	1	2	C, D	page 106

SPECIAL DOCUMENTS (WHEN REQUIRED)

Document	Originals	Copies	Notes	Sample
Certificate of Origin	1	5	E	page 107
Import License	1	2	F	-
Inspection Certificate	1	1	G	-
Insurance Certificate	1	1	H	page 104
Phytosanitary Certificate	1	1	I	-
Proforma Invoice	1	2	J	-
Sanitary Certificate	1	1	K	-
Special Certificates	1	1	L	-
Wine Certificate	1	1	M	-

COUNTRY NOTES

France is a member of the European Union (EU). The above requirements are for imports from non-EU countries.

DOCUMENT NOTES

A-This provides a clear and precise description of the product(s), terms of sale and any and all other information needed to establish the cost, insurance and freight prices. Wise if provided in both French and English.

B-Not required but strongly suggested.

C- Replacing the Summary Declaration Form, the "new model" for written customs declarations within France and all other EU countries is the Single Administrative Document (SAD). Easily processed by electronic means, the SAD is used when importing or transporting any goods in the EU and contains the necessary information standardized and expressed in EU codes. It can be submitted by computer directly to French Customs.

D-The SAD must be declared by a resident of the EU.

E-Notarized document is needed when requested by importer or required for certain controlled goods.

F-EU import quotas are maintained through these licenses covering agricultural produce and products, war materials, and certain protected consumer goods such as shoes.

G-For processed foods.

H-If required by importer or shipper.

I-Indicates plants and/or plant products are free from disease.

J-If requested by customer.

K-Indicates live animals and/or animal products are healthy and disease free.

L.-There are a series of special inspection certificates that apply to certain categories of goods. These include: Compliance Certificate for electronics and machinery, Lumber Certificate for logs and lumber, Purity Certificate for plant seeds and a Salubrity Certificate for fishing products.

M-For some wines, sparkling wines, vermouth.

Germany's Import Document Requirements

BASIC DOCUMENTS

Document	Originals	Copies	Notes	Sample
Bill of Lading (or Airway Bill)	1	1	-	page 40
Commercial Invoice	1	5	A	page 36
Packing List	1	1	B	page 53
SAD Customs Declaration	1	2	C, D	page 106

SPECIAL DOCUMENTS (WHEN REQUIRED)

Document	Originals	Copies	Notes	Sample
Certificate of Origin	1	5	E	page 107
Import License	1	2	F	-
Inspection Certificate	1	1	G	-
Insurance Certificate	1	1	H	page 104
Phytosanitary Certificate	1	1	I	-
Proforma Invoice	1	2	J	-
Sanitary Certificate	1	1	K	-
Special Certificates	1	1	L	-
Wine Certificate	1	1	M	-

COUNTRY NOTES

Germany is a member of the European Union (EU). The above requirements are for imports from non-EU countries.

DOCUMENT NOTES

A—This provides a clear and precise description of the product(s), terms of sale and any and all other information needed to establish the cost, insurance and freight prices. Should have a signature, name and title.

B—Not required but strongly suggested.

C— Replacing the Summary Declaration Form, the "new mode" for written customs declarations within Germany and all other EU countries is the Single Administrative Document (SAD). Easily processed by electronic means, the SAD is used when importing or transporting any goods in the EU and contains the necessary information standardized and expressed in EU codes. It can be submitted by computer directly to German Customs.

D—The SAD must be declared by a resident of the EU.

E—When requested by importer or required for certain controlled goods.

F—EU import quotas are maintained through these licenses covering agricultural produce and products, war materials, and certain protected consumer goods such as shoes.

G—For processed foods and lard.

H—If required by importer or shipper.

I—Indicates plants and/or plant products are free from disease. Special attention is paid to potatoes.

J—If requested by customer.

K—Indicates live animals and/or animal products are healthy and disease free. Special attention is paid to eggs and poultry.

L.—For imports of textiles, iron and steel, fishmeal, milk, eggs, fowl, lard, meat by-products, animal glands, heads and skins, precious metals and stones, weapons, vehicles of all types, timber, textiles, alcoholic beverages.

M—For some wines, sparkling wines, vermouth.

Greece's Import Document Requirements

BASIC DOCUMENTS

Document	Originals	Copies	Notes	Sample
Bill of Lading (or Airway Bill)	1	2	-	page 40
Commercial Invoice	1	6	A	page 36
Packing List	1	1	B	page 53
SAD Customs Declaration	1	2	C, D	page 106

SPECIAL DOCUMENTS (WHEN REQUIRED)

Document	Originals	Copies	Notes	Sample
Certificate of Origin	1	3	E	page 107
Composition Certificate	1	1	F	-
Disinfection Certificate	1	1	G	-
Health Certificate	1	1	H	-
Import License	1	1	I	-
Import Permit	1	1	J	-
Insurance Certificate	1	1	K	page 104
Phytosanitary Certificate	1	1	L	-
Proforma Invoice	1	2	M	-
Sanitary Certificate	1	1	N	-
Special Certificates	1	1	O	-

COUNTRY NOTES

Greece is a member of the European Union (EU). The above requirements are for imports from non-EU countries.

DOCUMENT NOTES

A-This is the key transaction document and must contain all information necessary to establish the cost, insurance and freight prices. Should have a signature, name and title.

B-Not required but strongly suggested.

C- Replacing the Summary Declaration Form, the "new model" for written customs declarations within Greece and all other EU countries is the Single Administrative Document (SAD) (see sample page ### D-The SAD must be declared by a resident of the EU.

E-When requested by importer or required for certain controlled goods.

F-For pharmaceuticals, medicines, hospital supplies, dietary products, cosmetics, insecticides, pesticides, and man-made mineral water.

G-For used goods and clothing.

H-For poultry, plants and plant products, seeds and vegetables.

I-EU import quotas are maintained through these licenses covering agricultural produce and products, war materials, and certain protected consumer goods such as shoes.

J-For dairy products, meat, poultry and their by-products, seeds and fruits.

K-If required by importer or shipper.

L-Indicates plants and/or plant products are free from disease. Special attention is paid to potatoes.

M-If requested by customer.

N-Indicates live animals and/or animal products are healthy and disease free.

O-For imports of textiles, iron and steel, fishmeal, milk, eggs, fowl, lard, meat by-products, animal glands, heads and skins, precious metals and stones, weapons, vehicles of all types, timber, textiles, alcoholic beverages.

Hong Kong Import Document Requirements

BASIC DOCUMENTS

Document	Originals	Copies	Notes	Sample
Bill of Lading (or Airway Bill)	1	2	-	page 40
Commercial Invoice	1	2	A	page 36
Packing List	1	1	B	page 53

SPECIAL DOCUMENTS (WHEN REQUIRED)

Document	Originals	Copies	Notes	Sample
Analysis Certificate	1	1	C	-
Certificate of Origin	1	2	D	page 107
Consular Invoice	1	1	E	-
Health Certificate	1	1	F	-
Import License	1	1	G	-
Insurance Certificate	1	1	H	page 104
Phytosanitary Quarantine Certificate	1	2	I	-
Proforma Invoice	1	1	J	-
Special Regulations	1	1	K	-

DOCUMENT NOTES

A-Must be an accurate description of goods itemizing FOB and CIF values signed in ink by an exporting official attesting to the accuracy of the information provided. Photostats are not accepted.

B-Not required but strongly advised.

C-For all dutiable goods and food products when required.

D-If requested by customer.

E-For all dutiable commodities. Contact importer for details.

F-For animals, poultry, meats and meat by-products. Certificate must attest compliance with all sanitary packing procedures both before and after slaughter. Certificate must contain the words "Not Fit For Human Consumption."

G-For textiles, fresh and frozen meat and poultry, pesticides, biological and chemical weapons material, radioactive materials, medicines and pharmaceuticals, substances that deplete the ozone layer, computers and some communications technologies.

H- If required by importer or shipper.

I-For plants, plant products and seeds.

J-If required by importer or shipper.

K-Contact importer for special restrictions on milk, frozen confections, and prepackaged foods.

Hungary's Import Document Requirements

BASIC DOCUMENTS

Document	Originals	Copies	Notes	Sample
Bill of Lading (or Airway Bill)	3	3	-	page 40
Commercial Invoice	1	3	A	page 36

SPECIAL DOCUMENTS (WHEN REQUIRED)

Document	Originals	Copies	Notes	Sample
Certificate of Origin	1	3	B	page 107
Import License	1	1	C	-
Insurance Certificate	1	1	D	page 104
Packing List	1	1	E	page 53
Pharmaceutical Certificate	1	1	F	-
Phytosanitary Certificate	1	1	G	-
Proforma Invoice	1	1	H	-
Veterinary Certificate	1	1	I	-

DOCUMENT NOTES

A-This provides a clear and precise description of the product(s), terms of sale and any and all other information needed to establish the cost, insurance and freight prices. Must have exporter's signature, name and title.

B-When requested by customer or when country of origin is not evident. Certification by authorized Chamber of Commerce is required.

C-Hungary's Ministry of International Economic Relations means of imposing quotas.

D-Must be from an Hungarian insurance company.

E-Facilitates customs clearance

F-Pharmaceutical products must be registered and approved by the National Hungarian Institute for Pharmacy.

G-For plants and plant products. Must include the statement "The consignment is free from the quarantine and harmful pest and diseases listed in the Ministerial Directive 4/1794/Mem.E.Z."

H-When requested by customer.

I-For live animals, meat, meat products and meat derived products.

India's Import Document Requirements

BASIC DOCUMENTS

Document	Originals	Copies	Notes	Sample
Bill of Lading (or Airway Bill)	1	1	-	page 40
Commercial Invoice	1	3	A	page 36
Import License	1	3	B	-

SPECIAL DOCUMENTS (WHEN REQUIRED)

Document	Originals	Copies	Notes	Sample
Certificate of Origin	1	2	C	page 107
Cleanliness Certificate	1	1	D	-
Health Certificate	1	1	E	-
Packing List	1	1	F	page 53
Phytosanitary Certificate	1	1	G	-
Proforma Invoice	1	3	H	-
Sanitary Certificate	1	2	I	-

COUNTRY NOTES

India is a member of the South Asian Preferential Trading Agreement (SAARC), which allows for tariff reduced exchange of goods within 7 nations in South Asia.

DOCUMENT NOTES

A-Must be in metric units. This provides a clear and precise description of the product(s), terms of sale and any and all other information needed to establish the cost, insurance and freight prices.

B-Obtained from Director General of Foreign Trade. Must have importer/exporter number from the appropriate Regional Licensing Authority.

C-At customer's request and then must be certified by Indian Chamber of Commerce.

D-Must be signed by doctor with the initial "M.D." following name and include the shipping country of origin.

E-For all livestock.

F-Although not required, shipments through the ports of Calcutta, Madras and Mumbai are always facilitated when a packing list is attached to the other required documents.

G-For all plants and plant products.

H-When requested by customer. Also needed when applying for Import License. A published price list may be required from the exporter.

I-For tobacco.

Indonesia's Import Document Requirements

BASIC DOCUMENTS

Document	Originals	Copies	Notes	Sample
Bill of Lading (or Airway Bill)	4	6	-	page 40
Certificate of Origin	1	6	A	page 107
Commercial Invoice	1	3	B	page 36
Packing List	1	6	C	page 53
Proforma Invoice	1	1	D	-

SPECIAL DOCUMENTS (WHEN REQUIRED)

Document	Originals	Copies	Notes	Sample
Health Certificate	1	1	E	-
Insurance Certificate	1	1	F	page 104
Phytosanitary Certificate	1	1	G	-
Steamship Certificate	1	1	H	-

COUNTRY NOTES

1. Indonesia is a member of the Association for Southeast Asian Nations (ASEAN), which allows for tariff-free exchange of goods within 10 nations in Southeast Asia.
2. Indonesian customs law requires importers to notify the customs office by submitting import documents on "standard form computer diskette."
3. Video tapes and discs must be reviewed by the censor board. All printed material in Chinese languages, Bahasa Indonesian and other Indonesian dialects is banned from importation.
4. The US Dept. of State has suspended all licenses and approvals to export any USA origin defense material and services to Indonesia even by third party exporters.

DOCUMENT NOTES

A-Required for all products. Narcotics and certain drugs get extra scrutiny.
B-This provides a clear and precise description of the product(s), terms of sale and any and all other information needed to establish the cost, insurance and freight prices.
C-Required for bales and cases and containers.
D-Accompanies Commercial invoice.
E-Fruits, potatoes and seeds require certificate from country of origin but will also be inspected in Indonesia.
F-Not required but strongly suggested.
G-For plants, plant products, and seeds.
H-May be required. Follow importer's instructions.

Ireland's Import Document Requirements

BASIC DOCUMENTS

Document	Originals	Copies	Notes	Sample
Bill of Lading (or Airway Bill)	1	2	-	page 40
Commercial Invoice	1	6	A	page 36
Packing List	1	1	B	page 53
SAD Customs Declaration	1	2	C, D	page 106

SPECIAL DOCUMENTS (WHEN REQUIRED)

Document	Originals	Copies	Notes	Sample
Certificate of Origin	1	3	E	page 107
Import License	1	1	F	-
Insurance Certificate	1	1	G	page 104
Phytosanitary Certificate	1	1	H	-
Proforma Invoice	1	2	I	-
Special Certificates	1	1	J	-

COUNTRY NOTES

Ireland is a member of the European Union (EU). The above requirements are for imports from non-EU countries.

DOCUMENT NOTES

A-This provides a clear and precise description of the product(s), terms of sale and any and all other information needed to establish the cost, insurance and freight prices. Should have a signature, name and title.

B-Not required but strongly suggested.

C- Replacing the Summary Declaration Form, the "new model" for written customs declarations within Ireland and all other EU countries is the Single Administrative Document (SAD). Easily processed by electronic means, the SAD is used when importing or transporting any goods in the EU and contains the necessary information standardized and expressed in EU codes. It can be submitted by computer directly to Irish Customs.

D-The SAD must be declared by a resident of the EU.

E-When requested by importer or required for certain controlled goods including port and Madeira wines, seafood and certain textile products.

F-EU import quotas are maintained through these licenses covering agricultural produce and products, war materials, and certain protected consumer goods such as shoes.

G-If required by importer or shipper.

H-Indicates plants and/or plant products are free from disease. Special attention is paid to potatoes.

I-If requested by customer.

J-For imports of specific wood products.

Israel's Import Document Requirements

BASIC DOCUMENTS

Document	Originals	Copies	Notes	Sample
Bill of Lading (or Airway Bill)	1	2	A, B	page 40
Certificate of Origin	1	2	C	page 107
Commercial Invoice	1	6	D	page 36
Insurance Certificate	1	1	E	page 104
Packing List	1	1	F	page 53

SPECIAL DOCUMENTS (WHEN REQUIRED)

Document	Originals	Copies	Notes	Sample
Aged Certificate	1	1	G	-
Health Certificate	1	1	H	-
Import License	1	3	I	-
Kosher Certificate	1	2	J	-
Phytosanitary Certificate	1	1	K	-
Proforma Invoice	1	7	L	-
Sanitary Certificate	1	1	M	-

COUNTRY NOTES

Israel has bilateral trade agreements with Canada and the USA. To qualify for preferences an official certificate of origin form must be obtained from and certified by Canadian-Israeli and/or American-Israel Chambers of Commerce which both sell and certify the forms.

DOCUMENT NOTES

A -Goods bound for the Palestinian Territories must comply with Israeli Customs regulations.

B-All ocean bills of lading must include the clause "This vessel is not to call at or enter the territorial waters of any Yemeni, Jordanian, Saudi Arabian, Iraqi, Lebanese, Syrian, Sudanese, Libyan or other Arab port (except Egypt) prior to unloading in Israel unless the ship is in distress or subject to force majeure."

C-Must use approved Israeli Certificate of Origin form.

D-Approved Israeli Commercial Invoice form is preferred.

E-When required by importer of shipper. Insurers must have an agent or representative in Israel

F-Not required but facilitates Customs process

G-Required for liquors and whiskey.

H-Obtained from signed by exporter's Department of Agriculture for foodstuffs, cattle, meat, hides and skins, fruits, vegetables, hay and straw, seeds and grains and bees.

I-Exemptions from licenses have recently been issued for several countries--check with Israel Customs.

J-Food and all contents of food products may require a Kosher certification.

K-For fruits, vegetables, flowers, plants and plant products, logs and lumber.

L-If requested by customer.

M-For refrigerated and frozen meats, hides and animal parts.

Italy's Import Document Requirements

BASIC DOCUMENTS

Document	Originals	Copies	Notes	Sample
Bill of Lading (or Airway Bill)	1	1	-	page 40
Commercial Invoice	1	1	A, E	page 36
Packing List	1	2	B	page 53
SAD Customs Declaration	1	2	C, D	page 106

SPECIAL DOCUMENTS (WHEN REQUIRED)

Document	Originals	Copies	Notes	Sample
Certificate of Origin	1	4	E	page 107
Import License	1	2	F	-
Insurance Certificate	1	1	G	page 104
Phytosanitary Certificate	1	1	H	-
Health Certificate	1	1	I	-
Proforma Invoice	1	2	J	-

COUNTRY NOTES

Italy is a member of the European Union (EU). The above requirements are for imports from non-EU countries.

DOCUMENT NOTES

A-This provides a clear and precise description of the product(s), terms of sale and any and all other information needed to establish the cost, insurance and freight prices.

B-Not required but strongly suggested.

C- Replacing the Summary Declaration Form, the "new model" for written customs declarations within Italy and all other EU countries is the Single Administrative Document (SAD). Easily processed by electronic means, the SAD is used when importing or transporting any goods in the EU and contains the necessary information standardized and expressed in EU codes. It can be submitted by computer directly to Italian Customs.

D-The SAD must be declared by a resident of the EU.

E-When requested by importer or required for certain controlled goods such as textiles and apparel. For all else, a statement as to a product's origin on the commercial invoice is permissible as long as this statement is certified by the exporter's Chamber of Commerce and signed by the exporter with name and title.

F-EU import quotas are maintained through these licenses covering agricultural produce and products, war materials, and certain protected consumer goods such as shoes and textiles.

G-If required by importer or shipper.

H-Indicates plants and/or plant products are free from disease.

I-For live fish and edible fish.

J-If requested by customer.

Japan's Import Document Requirements

BASIC DOCUMENTS

Document	Originals	Copies	Notes	Sample
Bill of Lading (or Airway Bill)	1	2	-	page 40
Commercial Invoice	1	2	A	page 36
Packing List	1	2	B	page 53

SPECIAL DOCUMENTS (WHEN REQUIRED)

Document	Originals	Copies	Notes	Sample
Certificate of Quality	1	2	C	-
Certificate of Origin	1	2	D	page 107
Food Permit	1	2	E	-
Health Certificate	1	2	F	-
Import License	1	3	G	-
Inspection Certificate	1	2	H	-
Phytosanitary Certificate	1	2	I	-

COUNTRY NOTES

Additional documents may be required to make sure that imports comply with relevant Japanese laws and regulations at the time of import.

DOCUMENT NOTES

A-Should be on company letterhead and signed by authorized person. This provides a clear and precise description of the product(s), terms of sale and any and all other information needed to establish the cost, insurance and freight prices.

B-Must be in metric units.

C-For frozen food and vegetables.

D-Per customer's request.

E-For all foodstuffs.

F-For textiles and wool clothing.

G-For items under quotas such as leather, rice, wheat and rice flour.

H-For poultry, eggs, meat, blood, bones, hooves, horns, skin, and selected plants, seeds and plant products.

I-For all agricultural products, plants, plant materials, soil, animals, meat and meat products.

Korea's Import Document Requirements

BASIC DOCUMENTS

Document	Originals	Copies	Notes	Sample
Bill of Lading (or Airway Bill)	1	2	A	page 40
Commercial Invoice	1	4	B	page 36
Import License	1	2	C	-
Packing List	1	2	D	page 53
Proforma Invoice	1	2	E	-

SPECIAL DOCUMENTS (WHEN REQUIRED)

Document	Originals	Copies	Notes	Sample
Certificate of Inspection	1	2	F	-
Certificate of Origin	1	2	F	page 107
Sanitary Certificate	1	4	G	-

COUNTRY NOTES
Korea has an electronic Data Interchange (EDI) for paperless import clearance. Also, tariff quotas can change seasonally.

DOCUMENT NOTES
A-Must be signed by the exporter.
B-Per customer's request. Attach to Commercial Invoice at customs.
C-Required for all transactions and to open a Letter of Credit.
D-Required.
E-Required by importer on all Letter of Credit transactions. Must be notarized and then legalized by a Korean consulate.
F-For pharmaceutical, medical equipment/instruments, sanitary (hospital) supplies, cosmetics.
G-For plant and plant products.

Malaysia's Import Document Requirements

BASIC DOCUMENTS

Document	Originals	Copies	Notes	Sample
Bill of Lading (or Airway Bill)	1	2	-	page 40
Commercial Invoice	1	3	A	page 36

SPECIAL DOCUMENTS (WHEN REQUIRED)

Document	Originals	Copies	Notes	Sample
Certificate of Origin	1	2	B	page 107
Import License/Permit	1	0	C	-
Insurance Certificate	1	1	D	page 104
Meat Inspection Certificate	1	3	E	-
Packing List	1	2	F	page 53
Proforma Invoice	1	2	G	-
Sanitary Certificate	1	2	H	-
Whisky Certificate	1	3	I	

COUNTRY NOTES

1. Malaysia is a member of the Association for Southeast Asian Nations (ASEAN), which allows for tariff-free exchange of goods within 10 nations in Southeast Asia.
2. All imported consumer goods are required to be labeled with the identity of the importer. Stickers may be used. All labels must be in English or Bahasa Malaysia.
3. Documents must be in English or Bahasa Malaysian or English and the exporter's language.

DOCUMENT NOTES

A-This provides a clear and precise description of the product(s), terms of sale and any and all other information needed to establish the cost, insurance and freight prices. Must be signed in ink by company official.

B-If requested by customer.

C-Required for arms, munitions, motor vehicles, certain dangerous drugs and chemicals, plants, foodstuffs, ores.

D-If required by customer or shipper.

E-For meat and meat products. Pork and pork products require additional certification.

F-Not required but suggested.

G-If requested by customer.

H-For meats and meat products.

I-Required for selected alcoholic beverages, brandy and whisky. For political reasons, the importation of alcoholic beverages is periodically banned.

Mexico's Import Document Requirements

BASIC DOCUMENT

Document	Originals	Copies	Notes	Sample
Bill of Lading (or Airway Bill)	1	2	-	page 40
Commercial Invoice	1	6	A	page 36
Packing List	1	3	B	page 53

SPECIAL DOCUMENTS (WHEN REQUIRED)

Document	Originals	Copies	Notes	Sample
Certificate of Origin	1	12	C	page 107
Certificate of Quality	1	6	D	-
Free Sale Certificate	1	6	E	-
Health Certificate	1	6	F	-
Insurance Certificate	1	1	G	page 104
Microbiological Analysis	1	2	H	-
NAFTA Certificate of Origin	1	2	I	page 108
Phytosanitary Certificate	1	2	J	-
Preshipment Inspection	1	1	K	-
Proforma Invoice	1	1	L	-
Textile and Footwear Origin Certificate	1	6	M	-

COUNTRY NOTES

Mexico is a member of the North American Free Trade Agreement (NAFTA) which allows for tariff-free exchange of goods within Canada, Mexico and the USA.

DOCUMENT NOTES

A-Must be an accurate description of goods itemizing FOB and CIF values signed in ink by an exporting official attesting to the accuracy of the information provided. May be used in lieu of Canadian Customs Invoice (CCI) if valued less than $1,600 (Canadian), or if all information needed for CCI is included.

B-Required in triplicate.

C-In Spanish. Authorized by exporter's Chamber of Commerce for shipments from non-NAFTA countries on medical products, pharmaceuticals, cosmetics, toiletries, alcoholic beverages, fertilizers, pesticides, and any materials containing toxic substances.

D-For selected items that need a laboratory certification of compliance with Mexican standards.

E-Certification that product or materials are consumed or used freely in the country of origin.

F-For live animals and animal products

G-If required by importer or shipper.

H-Analysis document from laboratory or authorized organization for products which contain micro-organisms.

I-Follows NAFTA Rules of Origin and indicates where products/goods originated. Certificate to be sent to importer who must have it in his/her possession at time of accountability. "Blanket Certificates" can cover more than one shipment over a twelve month period.

J-For plants and plant products.

K-Importer may request inspection by Bureau Veritas, ITS, SGS or similar company.

L-If requested by importer or shipper.

L-Textiles and footwear require special certificates of origin.

Netherlands' Import Document Requirements

BASIC DOCUMENTS

Document	Originals	Copies	Notes	Sample
Bill of Lading (or Airway Bill)	1	3	-	page 40
Commercial Invoice	1	5	A	page 36
Packing List	1	5	B	page 53
SAD Customs Declaration	1	2	C, D	page 106

SPECIAL DOCUMENTS (WHEN REQUIRED)

Document	Originals	Copies	Notes	Sample
Certificate of Inoculation	1	0	E	-
Certificate of Origin	1	5	F	page 107
Import License	1	2	G	-
Insurance Certificate	1	1	H	page 104
Health Certificate	1	5	I	-
Phytosanitary Certificate	1	5	J	-
Proforma Invoice	1	5	K	-
Veterinary Certificate	1	5	L	-

COUNTRY NOTES

The Netherlands is a member of the European Union (EU). The above requirements are for imports from non-EU countries.

DOCUMENT NOTES

A-This provides a clear and precise description of the product(s), terms of sale and any and all other information needed to establish the cost, insurance and freight prices.

B-Not required but strongly suggested.

C- Replacing the Summary Declaration Form, the "new model" for written customs declarations within the Netherlands and all other EU countries is the Single Administrative Document (SAD). Easily processed by electronic means, the SAD is used when importing or transporting any goods in the EU and contains the necessary information standardized and expressed in EU codes. It can be submitted by computer directly to Dutch Customs.

D-The SAD must be declared by a resident of the EU.

E-For dogs and cats.

F-For letter of credit shipment, import license applications or when requested by importer. May be required for certain controlled goods such as food and agricultural items, fuels and textiles. Must be certified by the exporter's Chamber of Commerce.

G-EU import quotas are maintained through these licenses covering agricultural produce and products, war materials, and certain protected consumer goods such as shoes.

H-If required by importer or shipper.

I-For live animals, animal products and fertilizer from animals.

J-Indicates potatoes and other plants and/or plant products are free from disease.

K-If requested by customer.

K-Indicates live animals and/or animal products are healthy and disease free.

L.-For blood meal, bone and fish meal.

New Zealand's Import Document Requirements

BASIC DOCUMENTS

Document	Originals	Copies	Notes	Sample
Bill of Lading (or Airway Bill)	1	2	-	page 40
Commercial Invoice	-	3	A	page 36
Packing List	1	2	B	page 53

SPECIAL DOCUMENTS (WHEN REQUIRED)

Document	Originals	Copies	Notes	Sample
Certificate of Origin	1	1	C	page 107
Health Certificate	1	3	D	-
Proforma Invoice	1	1	E	-
Phytosanitary Certificate	1	1	F	-
Wood Products Certificate	1	1	G	-

COUNTRY NOTES

New Zealand is a member of the Closer Economic Relations Trade Agreement (CER), which allows for tariff-free exchange of goods with Australia.

DOCUMENT NOTES

A -This provides a clear and precise description of the products, terms of sale and any and all other information needed to establish the cost, insurance and freight prices. FOB and CIF prices should be in Australian dollars.
B-Not required but strongly suggested.
C-When required by customer.
D-For fruits and vegetables, live plants and seeds.
E-When requested by customer.
F-When requested by customer.
G-All wood products and wood packing materials, including shavings and sawdust, must be treated or fumigated prior to import.

Nigeria's Import Document Requirements

BASIC DOCUMENTS

Document	Originals	Copies	Notes	Sample
Bill of Lading (or Airway Bill)	1	6	-	page 40
Commercial Invoice/Certificate of Origin	1	8	A	-
Insurance Certificate	1	6	B	page 104
Packing List	1	6	C	page 53

SPECIAL DOCUMENTS (WHEN REQUIRED)

Document	Originals	Copies	Notes	Sample
Certificate of Analysis	1	6	D	-
Certificate of Manufacture and Free Sale	1	6	E	-
Certificate of Value	1	6	F	-
Import Duty Report	1	1	G	-
Preshipment Inspection	1	1	H	-
Proforma Invoice	1	2	I	-
Sanitary Certificate	1	6	J	-

COUNTRY NOTES

-Nigeria is a member of the Economic Community of West African States (ECOWAS), which allows for tariff-free exchange of goods within 16 West African countries.

-International exporters should be aware that warnings have been issued by several countries that fraudulent business activity is common in Nigeria. Shipments should be made only after the issuance of an irrevocable letter of credit confirmed by a bank in the exporter's country.

DOCUMENT NOTES

A- Must use the Nigerian Invoice Form, which includes a Certificate of Origin. This provides a clear and precise description of the product(s), terms of sale and any and all information needed to establish the cost, insurance and freight prices. Invoice must be signed by exporter and certified by an authorized Chamber of Commerce and legalized at the Nigerian Consulate.

B-All imports must be insured by a Nigerian company or agency.

C-Must show full detail.

D- For food, drugs, cosmetics, pesticides and toxic substances.

E-A statement signed by authorized party of exporter indicating that the product is sold freely in the country of origin.

F-Form signed by exporter or authorized employee in support of invoiced value.

G-Although not required now, some delay may take place if this form is not included.

H-Pre-inspection was abolished in 1999. Even so, some customers still want the piece of mind that accompanies such a certification and request this service.

I-If requested by customer.

J-For certain animals and animal products, plant and plant products, seeds, soil and used merchandise.

Norway's Import Document Requirements

BASIC DOCUMENTS

Document	Originals	Copies	Notes	Sample
Bill of Lading (or Airway Bill)	1	4	-	page 40
Commercial Invoice	1	4	A	page 36
Packing List	1	4	B	page 53

SPECIAL DOCUMENTS (WHEN REQUIRED)

Document	Originals	Copies	Notes	Sample
Certificate of Origin	1	4	C	page 107
Health Certificate	1	4	D	-
Insurance Certificate	1	2	E	page 104
Phytosanitary Certificate	1	2	F	-
Proforma Invoice	1	4	G	-
Sanitary Certificate	1	2	H	-

COUNTRY NOTES

Norway is a member of the European Free Trade Association (EFTA), which allows for tariff-free exchange of goods within Iceland, Liechtenstein, Norway and Switzerland.

DOCUMENT NOTES

A-This provides a clear and precise description of the product(s), terms of sale and any and all other information needed to establish the cost, insurance and freight prices.

B-Not required but strongly suggested.

C-When requested by importer or required for certain controlled goods.

D-For pickled meat, issued by a veterinarian and signed by the Norwegian consulate.

E-If required by importer or shipper.

F-Indicates lumber, plants and/or plant products are free from disease.

G-If requested by customer.

H-For live animals meat, (not tinned or pickled), animal products, meat products, milk products, eggs, honey, vegetables, live plants and plant products, selected seeds and selected food products.

Pakistan's Import Document Requirements

BASIC DOCUMENTS

Document	Originals	Copies	Notes	Sample
Bill of Lading (or Airway Bill)	1	3	-	page 40
Commercial Invoice	1	3	A	page 36

SPECIAL DOCUMENTS (WHEN REQUIRED)

Document	Originals	Copies	Notes	Sample
Certificate of Cleanliness	1	2	B	-
Certificate of Origin	1	2	C	page 107
Insurance Certificate	1	3	D	page 104
Meat Certificate	1	3	E	-
Packing List	1	1	F	page 53
Phytosanitary Certificate	1	1	G	-
Preshipment Inspection	1	3	H	-
Proforma Invoice	1	3	I	-
Producer's Certificate	1	3	J	-

COUNTRY NOTES

Pakistan is a member of the South Asian Preferential Trading Agreement (SAARC), which allows for tariff reduced exchange of goods within 7 nations in South Asia.

DOCUMENT NOTES

A-Signed by exporter and all costs itemized in CIF. This provides a clear and precise description of the product(s), terms of sale and any and all other information needed to establish the cost, insurance and freight prices.

B-For used clothing.

C-When requested by customer or required for letter of credit.

D-When required by importer or shipper. Must be issued by a Pakistani insurance company.

E-Meat and meat products must have a certificate stating that no pig, swine hog or boar products are included.

F-Not required but facilitates customs entry.

G-For all plants and plant products. Leaf tobacco needs an additional certificate.

H-For goods valued at more than $3000 (US).

I-When requested by customer.

J-For iron and steel.

Peru's Import Document Requirements

BASIC DOCUMENTS

Document	Originals	Copies	Notes	Sample
Bill of Lading (or Airway Bill)	3	2	-	page 40
Commercial Invoice	-	3	A	page 36
Preshipment Inspection Required	1	0	B	-

SPECIAL DOCUMENTS (WHEN REQUIRED)

Document	Originals	Copies	Notes	Sample
Certificate of Origin	1	3	C	page 107
Packing List	1	2	D	page 53
Phytosanitary Certificate	1	3	E	-
Purity Certificate	1	3	F	-
Sanitary Certificate	1	3	G	-
Sanitary & Purity Certificate	1	3	H	-

COUNTRY NOTES

1. Peru is an ALADI member and enjoys special reduced tariff arrangements with Argentina, Bolivia, Brazil, Chile, Colombia, Cuba, Ecuador, Mexico, Paraguay, Uruguay and Venezuela. Special documents are required for shipments between these member countries.
2. To expedite procedures, all documents should be in Spanish as well as the exporter's language.
3. Restrictions are in place for animal and food products from the Belgium, Ecuador. France, Holland, Ireland, Luxembourg, Portugal, Switzerland, and the UK.

DOCUMENT NOTES

A-Must be in Spanish or have a Spanish translation. Certain pesticides, radioactive waste, fireworks, used clothing and footwear, and used vehicles are prohibited.

B-All new products valued at $5000 (US) or more and used goods valued at $2000 (US) or more requires preshipment inspection by authorized inspection services such as Bureau Veritas or Cotechna.

C-If requested by customer.

D-Not required but strongly suggested since it may expedite customs clearance.

E-For seeds. grains, plants and plant products.

F-For flour, butter, milk and non-bovine lard.

G-For hides and all animal products both edible and non-edible.

H-For all animals and animal products, fish, plants and plant products, seeds, fresh fruit.

Philippines' Import Document Requirements

BASIC DOCUMENTS

Document	Originals	Copies	Notes	Sample
Bill of Lading (or Airway Bill)	1	5	-	page 40
Commercial Invoice	1	4	A	page 36
Packing List	1	3	B	page 53

SPECIAL DOCUMENTS (WHEN REQUIRED)

Document	Originals	Copies	Notes	Sample
Certificate of Origin	1	2	C	page 107
Import Permit	1	2	D	-
Insurance Certificate	1	1	E	page 104
Preshipment Inspection	1	2	F	-
Proforma Invoice	1	1	G	-

COUNTRY NOTES

1. The Philippines is a member of the Association for Southeast Asian Nations (ASEAN), which allows for tariff-free exchange of goods within 10 nations in Southeast Asia.
2. The Philippine Bureau of Food and Drug (BFAD) requires that all imported packaged food products be registered with the BFAD and include the name and address of the importer on the package. Unlabeled and/or unregistered items will be confiscated.
3. Only the Government's National Food authority can import rice.

DOCUMENT NOTES

A-This provides a clear and precise description of the product(s), terms of sale and any and all other information needed to establish the cost, insurance and freight prices. Must be signed in ink by company official and include the statement: "I (name, title, company) hereby swear that the prices stated in this invoice are the current export market prices and that the origin of the goods described herein is (country) and assume full responsibility for any inaccuracies or errors therein."
B-Must be certified.
C-If requested by customer.
D-The Bureau of Plant Industry issues permits for fresh produce, seeds and plants. The Bureau of animal Industry issues permits for meat and live animals. Sanitary Certificates, Health Certificates and Veterinary Certificates may be required for these permits.
E-If required by customer or shipper.
F-Preshipment inspection is required for improperly declared shipments, goods requiring laboratory analysis, second quality or waste goods and materials, shipments designated by customs as "high risk," and shipments that wish to take advantage of quick release processing in ports.
G-If requested by buyer.

Poland's Import Document Requirements

BASIC DOCUMENTS

Document	Originals	Copies	Notes	Sample
Bill of Lading (or Airway Bill)	1	2	-	page 40
Certificate of Origin	1	4	A	page 107
Commercial Invoice	1	4	B	page 36

SPECIAL DOCUMENTS (WHEN REQUIRED)

Document	Originals	Copies	Notes	Sample
Import License	1	4	C	-
Packing List	1	2	D	page 53
Phytosanitary Certificate	1	4	E	-
Proforma Invoice	1	3	E	-
Sanitary Certificate	1	0	F	-

COUNTRY NOTES
Documents may be in English, French, German or Polish.

DOCUMENT NOTES
A—Required.

B—This provides a clear and precise description of the product(s), terms of sale and any and all other information needed to establish the cost, insurance and freight prices. Should have a signature, name and title.

C—For all military goods, radioactive materials, alcoholic beverages, milk, cheese, milk products, tobacco products, engines, automotive products and certain agriculture products.

D— For live plants and plant products, fresh fruit and vegetables.

E—If requested by customer.

F—For all animals and animal products.

Portugal's Import Document Requirements

BASIC DOCUMENTS

Document	Originals	Copies	Notes	Sample
Bill of Lading (or Airway Bill)	1	4	-	page 40
Commercial Invoice	1	4	A	page 36
Packing List	1	2	B	page 53
SAD Customs Declaration	1	2	C, D	page 106

SPECIAL DOCUMENTS (WHEN REQUIRED)

Document	Originals	Copies	Notes	Sample
Certificate of Authenticity	1	4	E	-
Certificate of Origin	1	4	F	page 107
Import License	1	2	G	-
Health Certificate	1	4	H	-
Insurance Certificate	1	1	I	page 104
Phytosanitary Certificate	1	1	J	-
Proforma Invoice	1	2	K	-
Sanitary Certificate	1	1	L	-

COUNTRY NOTES

Portugal is a member of the European Union (EU). The above requirements are for imports from non-EU countries.

DOCUMENT NOTES

A-This provides a clear and precise description of the product(s), terms of sale and any and all other information needed to establish the cost, insurance and freight prices. Original should be in Portuguese, certified by Chamber of Commerce and signed in ink.

B-Not required but strongly suggested.

C- Replacing the Summary Declaration Form, the "new model" for written customs declarations within Portugal and all other EU countries is the Single Administrative Document (SAD). Easily processed by electronic means, the SAD is used when importing or transporting any goods in the EU and contains the necessary information standardized and expressed in EU codes. It can be submitted by computer directly to Portuguese Customs.

D-The SAD must be declared by a resident of the EU.

E-For alcohol, tobacco, and grapes.

F-When requested by importer or required for certain controlled goods.

G-EU import quotas are maintained through these licenses covering agricultural produce and products, war materials, and certain protected consumer goods such as shoes.

H-For all foodstuffs including processed foods.

I-If required by importer or shipper.

J-Indicates plants and/or plant products are free from disease.

K-If requested by customer.

L-For potatoes and all seeds.

Romania's Import Document Requirements

BASIC DOCUMENTS

Document	Originals	Copies	Notes	Sample
Bill of Lading (or Airway Bill)	1	4	-	page 40
Commercial Invoice	1	4	A	page 36
Packing List	1	2	B	page 53

SPECIAL DOCUMENTS (WHEN REQUIRED)

Document	Originals	Copies	Notes	Sample
Certificate of Origin	1	4	C	page 107
Phytosanitary Certificate	1	4	D	-
Proforma Invoice	1	4	E	-

COUNTRY NOTES

Documents may be in English, French or German.

DOCUMENT NOTES

A-This provides a clear and precise description of the product(s), terms of sale and any and all other information needed to establish the cost, insurance and freight prices. Should have a signature, name and title.
B-Required.
C-May be requested by customer.
D-For all plants and plant products.
E-If requested by customer.

Russia's Import Document Requirements

BASIC DOCUMENTS

Document	Originals	Copies	Notes	Sample
Bill of Lading (or Airway Bill)	1	4	-	page 40
Certificate of Origin	1	4	A	page 107
Commercial Invoice	1	4	B	page 36
Packing List	1	2	C	page 53

SPECIAL DOCUMENTS (WHEN REQUIRED)

Document	Originals	Copies	Notes	Sample
Import License	1	4	D	-
Phytosanitary Certificate	1	4	E	-
Proforma Invoice	1	4	F	-
Veterinary Certificate	1	4	G	-

COUNTRY NOTES;

1. Documents should be in Russian or in Russian and the exporter's language.
2. Conditions in Russia remain inconsistent. Exporters should expect variations in document requirements and be prepared by having a duplicate set of validated documents available.
3. Since 1997, Russian ports and the railroad have been subject to strikes, government and customs inconsistency, reforms and rail tariff growth. Although the Russian government has uniform customs levels for all products, some individuals and companies in Western Russia get customs privileges and exporters find that customs tariffs may be lower through ports of arrival in Western Russia.

DOCUMENT NOTES

A-Must be certified by Chamber of Commerce.

B-This provides a clear and precise description of the product(s), terms of sale and any and all other information needed to establish the cost, insurance and freight prices. Must have a signature, name and title and be certified by Chamber of Commerce. Should have Russian license number, bank contact.

C-Facilitates customs clearance.

D-For selected commodities. The list is subject to frequent changes.

E-For all plants and plant products, animals and animal products.

F-If requested by customer.

G-For meat and meat products.

Saudi Arabia's Import Document Requirements

BASIC DOCUMENTS

Document	Originals	Copies	Notes	Sample
Bill of Lading (or Airway Bill)	1	2	-	page 40
Certificate of Origin	1	1	A, B	page 107
Commercial Invoice	1	1	A, C	page 36
Export Information Sheet (EIS)	1	2	D	-
Insurance Certificate	1	1	E	-
Packing List	1	1	-	page 53
Steamship (or Airline) Company Certificate	1	1	F	-

SPECIAL DOCUMENTS (WHEN REQUIRED)

Document	Originals	Copies	Notes	Sample
Food Manufacturer's Ingredients Certificates	1	1	G	-
Consumer Protection Certificate	1	1	H	-
Price List	1	1	I	-
"Halal" meat (and poultry) Certificate	1	1	J	-
Official Health Certificate	1	1	K	-
Seed and Grain Certificate of Inspection	1	1	L	-
Phytosanitary Certificate	1	1	M	-
Seed Analysis Certificate	1	1	N	-
Certificate of Weight	1	1	O	-
Certificate of Free Sale	1	1	P	-
Certificate of Conformity	1	1	Q	-
Other Certificates	1	1	R	-

COUNTRY NOTES

Saudi Arabia is a member of the Arab League Free Trade Zone (AFTZ).

DOCUMENT NOTES

A -Signed documents must be authenticated by exporter and certified in the following order:
    1. Notarized by a Notary Public and certified by exporter's Chamber of Commerce.
    2. Certified at the nearest Saudi Arabian Business Council. Copies must be marked "Council Copies."
    3. Legalized by the Saudi Embassy or any Saudi Consulate.

B-Certificate of Origin must include the name and address of the Saudi Importer.

C-Saudi Customs insist on accurate description of goods (including the 6-digit HSN) plus a notarized declaration signed by an exporting official attesting to the accuracy of the information provided.

D-EIS does not need to be authenticated, but one copy is kept by the Business Council and one by the Consulate.

E-Insurers must have an agent or representative in Saudi Arabia.

F-Issued by shipper to identify vessel or plane and ports of call. Must be notarized.

G-Obtained from and signed by exporter's local Health Department.

H-Obtained from and signed by exporter's Department of Agriculture.

I-On exporter's letterhead.

J-Must be legalized by a recognized Islamic Center.

K-Licensed veterinarian's certification.

L-Certified by seed inspection specialist.

M-Disease-free certificate from exporter's Dept. of Agriculture for vegetables, fruits, plants and grains.

N-From exporter's Department of Agriculture

O-Information provided by the exporter and verified by the shipper.

P-For pharmaceuticals, medicines, animal feeds, etc. Certificates must come from the authenticating office of the exporter's Department of State as well as being authenticated by a Saudi Arabian Consulate.

Q-Stamped copy of a previously approved Saudi Arabian Standards Organization document for electrical appliances, equipment and accessories, toys, motor vehicles.

R-Special certificates and/or permission are necessary for importation of livestock, pets, horses, motor vehicles, carpets, items made with hair, used clothing, sport or hunting firearms, and some books and electronic media materials.

Singapore's Import Document Requirements

BASIC DOCUMENTS

Document	Originals	Copies	Notes	Sample
Bill of Lading (or Airway Bill)	1	3	-	page 40
Commercial Invoice	1	2	A	page 36
Packing List	1	2	B	page 53

SPECIAL DOCUMENTS (WHEN REQUIRED)

Document	Originals	Copies	Notes	Sample
Alcoholic Beverages & Animal Fat	1	2	C	-
Certificate of Origin	1	2	D	page 107
Inspection Certificate	1	2	E	-
Phytosanitary Certificate	1	2	F	-
Veterinary Certificate	1	2	G	-

COUNTRY NOTES

Singapore is a member of the Association of South East Nations Free Trade Area (ASEAN-AFTA) and enjoys tariff free exchange of goods between the 10 members countries.

DOCUMENT NOTES

A-This provides a clear and precise description of the product(s), terms of sale and any and all other information needed to establish the cost, insurance and freight prices. Should include ASEAN Harmonized Tariff Numbers and CIF value.

B-Required for customs clearance.

C-The specific certificate required is determined upon receipt of contract.

D-Per request. Required for Letter of Credit transactions. Must be certified.

E-For all animals, birds, plants and plant products.

F-For live plants and plant parts.

G-For items under quotas such as leather, rice, wheat and rice flour.

H-For animals, birds, meat and meat products.

South Africa's Import Document Requirements

BASIC DOCUMENTS

Document	Originals	Copies	Notes	Sample
Bill of Entry	1	1	A	-
Bill of Lading (or Airway Bill)	1	2	B	page 40
Commercial Invoice	1	1	C	page 36
Customs Worksheet	1	1	D	-

SPECIAL DOCUMENTS (WHEN REQUIRED)

Document	Originals	Copies	Notes	Sample
Certificate of Origin	1	1	E	page 107
Dangerous Goods Documents	1	1	F	-
Fumigation Certificate	1	1	G	-
Import Permit	1	2	H	-
Inspection Certificate	1	1	I	-
Phytosanitary Certificate	1	1	M	-
Quality Certificate	1	1	N	-
South African Bureau of Standards Certificate	1	1	O	-
Veterinary Health Certificate	1	1	P	-

COUNTRY NOTES

South Africa is a member of the Southern African Development Community (SADC).

DOCUMENT NOTES

A -South African Customs form DA500 is required.

B-Requires customs stamp on entry.

C-Must match relevant transport documents.

D-Translates other currency values into South African Rands.

E-For certain strategic commodities and goods facing anti-dumping charges.

F-A number of special "red chevroned" forms are required for firearms, radioactive materials, etc.

G-Proof that goods and their packing material are free of pests.

H-For certain goods under the jurisdiction of the South African Departments of: Agriculture, Water Affairs, Sea Fisheries, Trade and Industry, Mineral Affairs, Health.

M-Proof that all plants and plant products (seeds, flowers, etc.) are free from pests and disease.

N-Proof of inspection prior to import of fresh and processed fruit and vegetables.

O-Prior certification that specified consumer products meet testing standards.

P-Copy of import permit specifying conditions of treatment of animals is required before obtaining this certificate. South Africa has many different agreements with different countries regarding the conditions in which food products must be traded (i.e. meat only from approved slaughterhouses etc.).

Spain's Import Document Requirements

BASIC DOCUMENTS

Document	Originals	Copies	Notes	Sample
Bill of Lading (or Airway Bill)	1	2	-	page 40
Commercial Invoice	1	4	A	page 36
Packing List	1	2	B	page 53
SAD Customs Declaration	1	2	C, D	page 106

SPECIAL DOCUMENTS (WHEN REQUIRED)

Document	Originals	Copies	Notes	Sample
Certificate of Origin	1	4	E	page 107
Import License	1	2	F	-
Insurance Certificate	1	1	G	page 104
Pharmaceutical Certificate	1	2	H	-
Proforma Invoice	1	2	I	-
Sanitary Certificate	1	1	J	-
Special Certificates	1	1	K	-

COUNTRY NOTES

Spain is a member of the European Union (EU). The above requirements are for imports from non-EU countries.

DOCUMENT NOTES

A-This provides a clear and precise description of the product(s), terms of sale and any and all other information needed to establish the cost, insurance and freight prices.

B-Not required but strongly suggested.

C- Replacing the Summary Declaration Form, the "new model" for written customs declarations within Spain and all other EU countries is the Single Administrative Document (SAD). Easily processed by electronic means, the SAD is used when importing or transporting any goods in the EU and contains the necessary information standardized and expressed in EU codes. It can be submitted by computer directly to Spanish Customs.

D-The SAD must be declared by a resident of the EU.

E-When requested by importer or required for certain controlled goods.

F-EU import quotas are maintained through these licenses covering agricultural produce and products, war materials, and certain protected consumer goods such as shoes.

G-If required by importer or shipper.

H-For drugs and sanitary (hospital) supplies.

I-If requested by customer.

J-Indicates plants and/or plant products are free from disease.

K-Sea vessels require a certificate of compliance from the Marine Authority of the Spanish Ministry of Transportation.

Sweden's Import Document Requirements

BASIC DOCUMENTS

Document	Originals	Copies	Notes	Sample
Bill of Lading (or Airway Bill)	1	2	-	page 40
Commercial Invoice	1	5	A	page 36
Packing List	1	2	B	page 53
SAD Customs Declaration	1	2	C, D	page 106

SPECIAL DOCUMENTS (WHEN REQUIRED)

Document	Originals	Copies	Notes	Sample
Certificate of Origin	1	5	E	page 107
Import License	1	2	F	-
Insurance Certificate	1	1	G	page 104
Phytosanitary Certificate	1	3	H	-
Proforma Invoice	1	2	I	-
Sanitary Certificate	1	5	J	-

COUNTRY NOTES

Sweden is a member of the European Union (EU). The above requirements are for imports from non-EU countries.

DOCUMENT NOTES

A-This provides a clear and precise description of the product(s), terms of sale and any and all other information needed to establish the cost, insurance and freight prices.

B-Not required but strongly suggested.

C- Replacing the Summary Declaration Form, the "new model" for written customs declarations within Sweden and all other EU countries is the Single Administrative Document (SAD). Easily processed by electronic means, the SAD is used when importing or transporting any goods in the EU and contains the necessary information standardized and expressed in EU codes. It can be submitted by computer directly to Swedish Customs.

D-The SAD must be declared by a resident of the EU.

E-When requested by importer or required for certain controlled goods such as textiles.

F-EU import quotas are maintained through these licenses covering agricultural produce and products, war materials, and certain protected consumer goods such as shoes.

G-If required by importer or shipper.

H-Indicates potatoes, plants and/or plant products are free from disease.

I-If requested by customer.

J-For live animals and/or animal products. cheese and fats, live plants, seeds, vegetables and plant products, animal feeds, dairy equipment and all alcohol products. Must be legalized by Swedish Consul or an official in the country of export.

Switzerland's Import Document Requirements

BASIC DOCUMENTS

Document	Originals	Copies	Notes	Sample
Bill of Lading (or Airway Bill)	1	1	-	page 40
Commercial Invoice	1	5	A	page 36

SPECIAL DOCUMENTS (WHEN REQUIRED)

Document	Originals	Copies	Notes	Sample
Brandy Certificate	1	2	B	-
Certificate of Age	1	2	C	-
Certificate of Origin	1	5	D	page 107
Health Certificate	1	2	E	-
Import License	1	2	F	-
Inspection Certificate	1	1	G	-
Insurance Certificate	1	1	H	page 104
Packing List	1	1	I	page 53
Phytopathological Certificate	1	1	J	-
Proforma Invoice	1	2	K	-

COUNTRY NOTES

Switzerland is a member of the European Free Trade Area (EFTA), which allows for tariff-free exchange of goods within Iceland, Liechtenstein, Norway and Switzerland.

DOCUMENT NOTES

A-This provides a clear and precise description of the product(s), terms of sale and any and all other information needed to establish the cost, insurance and freight prices. Should have a signature, name and title.
B- Certifies that Brandy is made from wine.
C-Certifies that whiskey has been aged in wood for a minimum of three years.
D-When requested by customer.
E-For farm animals, fish, seafood, game, selected pets, bees, honeycombs and beeswax, meat and meat products.
F-For items under state control and those that may affect agricultural production.
G-For meat and meat products.
H-If required by importer or shipper.
I-Not required but strongly suggested.
J-For live plants, fresh fruit and vegetables, seeds, trees, shrubs and cuttings.
K-If requested by customer.

Taiwan's Import Document Requirements

BASIC DOCUMENTS

Document	Originals	Copies	Notes	Sample
Bill of Lading (or Airway Bill)	1	2	-	page 40
Commercial Invoice	1	3	A	page 36
Packing List	1	2	B	page 53

SPECIAL DOCUMENTS (WHEN REQUIRED)

Document	Originals	Copies	Notes	Sample
Import License	1	2	C	-
Inspection Certificate	1	2	D	-
Insurance Certificate	1	1	E	page 104
Proforma Invoice	1	1	F	-

COUNTRY NOTES

Narcotics, arms, munitions, and several important agricultural products including rice, animal offal, sugar and selected dairy products are banned outright. There is also a defacto ban on pickup trucks and fishing boats.

DOCUMENT NOTES

A-This provides a clear and precise description of the product(s), terms of sale and any and all other information needed to establish the cost, insurance and freight prices.

B-Required.

C-Licenses are required for specific goods from specific countries or regions. The decisions about which country or commodity is on the list are often politically based and therefore the list changes frequently.

D-For certain live plants and plant products, animals and animal products.

E-If required by customer or shipper.

F-If requested by customer.

Thailand's Import Document Requirements

BASIC DOCUMENTS

Document	Originals	Copies	Notes	Sample
Bill of Lading (or Airway Bill)	1	3	-	page 40
Commercial Invoice	1	3	A	page 36
Packing List	1	3	B	page 53

SPECIAL DOCUMENTS (WHEN REQUIRED)

Document	Originals	Copies	Notes	Sample
Certificate of Free Sale	1	2	C	-
Certificate of Origin	1	2	D	page 107
Import License	1	3	E	-
Phytosanitary Certificate	1	2	F	-
Sanitary Certificate	1	2	G	-

COUNTRY NOTES

Thailand is a member of the Association for Southeast Asian Nations (ASEAN) which allows for tariff-free exchange of goods within 10 nations in Southeast Asia.

DOCUMENT NOTES

A-This provides a clear and precise description of the product(s), terms of sale and any and all other information needed to establish the cost, insurance and freight prices. Should be signed in blue ink with name and title. Must have "True and Correct" clause. Attach packing list at customs.

B-Per customer's request. Attach to Commercial Invoice at customs.

C-For all medical equipment.

D-At customer's request.

E-For 43 categories of goods including petroleum products, textiles, industrial and agricultural products.

F-For all plants and plant products.

G-For live animals, fruit and seeds.

Turkey's Import Document Requirements

BASIC DOCUMENTS

Document	Originals	Copies	Notes	Sample
Bill of Lading (or Airway Bill)	1	2	-	page 40
Certificate of Origin	1	5	A	page 107
Commercial Invoice	1	4	B	page 36
Packing List	1	3	C	page 53

SPECIAL DOCUMENTS (WHEN REQUIRED)

Document	Originals	Copies	Notes	Sample
Import License/Permit	1	5	D	-
Health Certificate	1	4	E	-
Phytosanitary Certificate	1	4	F	-
Proforma Invoice	1	2	G	-

COUNTRY NOTES

Turkey formed a customs union with the European Union EU, which allows for special tariff structure with the 15 countries in the EU.

DOCUMENT NOTES

A—Must be notarized and signed by the Turkish consul.

B—Must be certified by the Turkish consulate. Must include the following statement "We hereby certify that this is the first and original copy of our invoice, the only one issued by our firm for the goods herein mentioned." Exporter should sign in blue ink with name and title.

C—Required. Attach to Commercial Invoice at customs.

D—For medicines, medical products, chemicals, vaccines, hormones, organic chemicals, live animals, plants and seeds.

E—For plants and plant products, fresh fruit and vegetables.

G—At request.

United Arab Emirates' Import Document Requirements

BASIC DOCUMENTS

Document	Originals	Copies	Notes	Sample
Bill of Lading (or Airway Bill)	1	2	-	page 40
Certificate of Origin	1	5	A, B	page 107
Commercial Invoice	1	4	A, C	page 36
Insurance Certificate	1	0	D	page 104
Steamship (or Airline) Company Certificate	1	4	E	-

SPECIAL DOCUMENTS (WHEN REQUIRED)

Document	Originals	Copies	Notes	Sample
Certificate of Inspection	1	5	F	-
Food Manufacturer's Ingredients Certificates	1	4	G	-
"Halal" meat (and poultry) Certificate	1	5	H	-
Health Certificate	1	4	I	-
Import License	1	5	J	-
Packing List	1	4	K	page 53
Certificate of Free Sale	1	4	L	-

COUNTRY NOTES
1. The United Arab Emirates (UAE) is a member of the Arab League Free Trade Zone (AFTZ).
2. All documents must be in Arabic or in Arabic and the exporter's language.

DOCUMENT NOTES

A —Signed documents must be authenticated by exporter, signed in blue ink, and certified in the following order:
   1. Certified by Arab Chamber of Commerce.
   2. Legalized by the UAE Embassy or Consulate
B—Certificate of Origin must include the name and address of the UAE importer and a "true and correct" statement signed in blue ink.
C—UAE Customs insist on accurate description of goods plus a declaration signed by an exporting official attesting to the accuracy of the information provided.
D—Insurers must have an agent or representative in UAE.
E—Issued by shipper to identify vessel or plane and ports of call. Must be notarized.
G—For all seeds and grains.
H—Must be legalized by a recognized Islamic Center.
I—Obtained from and signed by exporter's Health Department for all meat, meat products, livestock, fruits, vegetables.
J—For all beef and poultry. Must include animal's country of origin.
K—Not required but strongly suggested.
L—For pharmaceuticals, medical supplies and equipment.

United Kingdom's Import Document Requirements

BASIC DOCUMENTS

Document	Originals	Copies	Notes	Sample
Bill of Lading (or Airway Bill)	1	3	-	page 40
Commercial Invoice	1	5	A	page 36
Packing List	1	2	B	page 53
SAD Customs Declaration	1	2	C, D	page 106

SPECIAL DOCUMENTS (WHEN REQUIRED)

Document	Originals	Copies	Notes	Sample
Certificate of Origin	1	5	E	page 107
Import License	1	2	F	-
Insurance Certificate	1	1	G	page 104
Phytosanitary Certificate	1	2	H	-
Proforma Invoice	1	2	I	-
Sanitary Certificate	1	2	J	-
Wood Products Certificate	1	2	K	-

COUNTRY NOTES

The United Kingdom is a member of the European Union (EU). The above requirements are for imports from non-EU countries.

DOCUMENT NOTES

A-This provides a clear and precise description of the product(s), terms of sale and any and all other information needed to establish the cost, insurance and freight prices.

B-Not required but strongly suggested.

C- Replacing the Summary Declaration Form, the "new model" for written customs declarations within the United Kingdom (UK) and all other EU countries is the Single Administrative Document (SAD). Easily processed by electronic means, the SAD is used when importing or transporting any goods in the EU and contains the necessary information standardized and expressed in EU codes. It can be submitted by computer directly to UK Customs.

D-The SAD must be declared by a resident of the EU.

E-When requested by importer or required for certain controlled goods such as textiles. Must be notarized.

F-EU import quotas are maintained through these licenses covering agricultural produce and products, war materials, and certain protected consumer goods such as shoes. Currently, firearms and explosives, specified military equipment and drugs need an import license from the UK Department of Trade and Industry.

G-If required by importer or shipper.

H-Indicates potatoes, plants and/or plant products are free from disease.

I-If requested by customer.

J- UK Animal and Plant Sanitary Regulations must be complied with and documented.

K-Specific wood products have special UK documentation requirements.

United States of America's Import Document Requirements

BASIC DOCUMENTS

Document	Originals	Copies	Notes	Sample
Bill of Lading (or Airway Bill)	1	3	-	page 40
Commercial Invoice	1	3	A	page 36
Entry Manifest	1	3	B	-
Packing List	1	3	C	page 53

SPECIAL DOCUMENTS(WHEN REQUIRED)

Document	Originals	Copies	Notes	Sample
Certificate of Origin	1	2	D	page 107
Insurance Certificate	1	1	E	page 104
NAFTA Certificate of Origin	1	2	F	page 108
Licenses	1	2	G	-
Phytosanitary Certificate	1	2	H	-
Proforma Invoice	1	1	I	-
Sanitary Certificate	1	2	J	-

COUNTRY NOTES

The United States is a member of the North American Free Trade Agreement (NAFTA), which allows for tariff-free exchange of goods within Canada, Mexico and the USA.

DOCUMENT NOTES

A-Must be an accurate description of goods itemizing FOB and CIF values signed in ink by an exporting official attesting to the accuracy of the information provided.

B-Use either Entry Manifest (Customs form 7533) or entry/Immediate Delivery (Customs form 3461).

C-Not required but strongly advised.

D-If requested by customer for non-NAFTA countries.

E- If required by importer or shipper.

F-Follows NAFTA's Rules of Origin and indicates where products/goods originated. Certificate to be sent to importer who must possess it at time of accountability. "Blanket Certificates" can cover more than one shipment over a twelve month period.

G-A license or permit from the responsible US agency is necessary to import:

Bureau of Alcohol Tobacco and Firearms-alcoholic beverages, tobacco products, firearms and ammunition.

Animal and Plant Health Inspection Service-animals, animal products, plants and plant products.

Agricultural Marketing Service-fruits, vegetables and specialty nuts.

U.S. Fish and Wildlife Service-fish, seafood, game animals, forest products, petroleum products.

Food and Drug Administration- certain drugs, cosmetics, trademarked articles.

H-For plants and plant products.

I-If requested by importer or shipper.

J-For fresh fruits and vegetables, seeds, and certain live animals.

Vietnam's Import Document Requirements

BASIC DOCUMENTS

Document	Originals	Copies	Notes	Sample
Bill of Lading (or Airway Bill)	1	3	-	page 40
Commercial Invoice	1	2	A	page 36
Entry Manifest	1	3	B	
Packing List	1	2	C	page 53

SPECIAL DOCUMENTS (WHEN REQUIRED)

Document	Originals	Copies	Notes	Sample
Certificate of Origin	1	2	D	page 107
Insurance Certificate	1	2	E	page 104
Phytosanitary Certificate	1	2	F	-
Proforma Invoice	1	2	G	
Special Permits	1	2	H	
Veterinary Certificate	1	2	I	

DOCUMENT NOTES

A—This provides a clear and precise description of the product(s), terms of sale and any and all other information needed to establish the cost, insurance and freight prices.

B—Only certain government approved enterprises may import goods into Vietnam. Firms who do not have approval must import through approved agents/brokers and pay a fee to do so.

C—Required for customs clearance.

D—Per request. Required for Letter of Credit transactions. Must be certified.

E—Required by import agent/broker

F—For for live plants and plant parts or products.

G—Required by Import agent/broker

H—For items placed under quotas by Ministry decree—agricultural and food products, construction products, pharmaceuticals, motorcycles automobiles, auto parts. The government will occasionally suspend all imports of certain commodities (i.e. sheet steel, paper products) in competition with state-owned enterprises.

I—For animals, birds, meat and meat products.

CHAPTER 12

Checklists for Key Documents

THE FOLLOWING IS a series of checklists for document preparation and examination by the buyer, seller, and advising and issuing banks. These checklists cover the most common documents and have an emphasis on document consistency in documentary collection and documentary letter of credit payment situations. The issues covered in these checklists, however, apply for document preparation in all payment and transaction situations.

EXPORTER/SELLER/BENEFICIARY (OF THE LETTER OF CREDIT)

The exporter/seller/beneficiary has the responsibility of preparing and presenting documents in accordance with the terms of the contract for the sale of goods, the documentary collection or documentary letter of credit. If the documents are incorrect or inconsistent there is a risk of having them refused, wasting time and money, and possibly imperiling the transaction itself.

IMPORTER/BUYER/APPLICANT (OF THE LETTER OF CREDIT)

The importer/buyer/applicant initially has the responsibility of listing and clearly communicating to the seller which documents are required. Once the document package is received, either directly from the seller, or indirectly from the seller through the banks, the buyer examines the documents for consistency and accuracy. Problems with documents can lead to receiving unwanted or incorrect goods, problems securing goods from the shipping company or clearing a shipment through customs.

ISSUING (BUYER'S) BANK

In letter of credit payment situations, the issuing (buyer's) bank has the responsibility of examining the documents presented by the seller to make certain they are consistent with the credit.

ADVISING BANK

The advising bank (often the confirming bank as well) has the responsibility of examining the documents presented by the issuing bank to determine if they are consistent with the requirements of the documentary credit.

General Consistency Checklist

 SELLER BUYER ADVISING BANK ISSUING BANK

The following is a list of general points of consistency the seller, buyer, and banks should be aware of when preparing or examining documents. Does information on all the documents agree as to the following:

1. Name and address of seller/shipper/exporter/beneficiary?   ❑
2. Name and address of buyer/consignee/importer?   ❑
3. Issuer name and address?   ❑
4. Quantities and description of the goods?   ❑
5. Country of origin of the goods?   ❑
6. Country of destination of the goods?   ❑
7. Invoice numbers, documentary credit numbers?   ❑
8. Certifications?   ❑
9. Legalizations?   ❑
10. Shipping marks and numbers?   ❑
11. Net weight, gross weight, volume?   ❑
12. Number of crates, cartons, or containers?   ❑
13. Documents that so require are legally certified or legalized?   ❑
14. All documents are in complete sets and of the number specified?   ❑

The Draft

 SELLER BUYER   ADVISING BANK ISSUING BANK

1. Is the name of the drawee correct?   ❑
2. Is the name of the payee correct?   ❑
3. Does the draft contain the "to the order of" notation?   ❑
4. Does the draft contain an expiration date?   ❑
5. Does the draft contain an unconditional instruction to pay?   ❑
6. Are the amounts in words and figures identical?   ❑
7. Is the draft drawn on the party named in the documentary credit?   ❑
8. If the draft is made out to own order (ourselves), is it endorsed?   ❑
9. Does the draft contain any and all notations as stipulated in the letter of credit? (i.e., drawn under credit number _____)?   ❑
10. Does the draft name the place and date of issue?   ❑
11. Does the draft bear the signature of the issuer?   ❑
12. Are the values of the draft, invoices, and the credit consistent?   ❑

The Commercial Invoice

 SELLER BUYER ADVISING BANK ISSUING BANK

1. Is the invoice issued by the seller as named in the contract, documentary collection or documentary letter of credit? ❏

2. Is the invoice issued to the buyer as named in the contract, documentary collection or documentary letter of credit? ❏

3. Is the invoice issued to the correct address of the buyer as stated in the contract, documentary collection or documentary letter of credit? ❏

4. Does the description of the goods in the invoice correspond exactly to their description in the contract, documentary collection or documentary letter of credit? ❏

5. Does the quantity of the goods in the invoice correspond exactly to the quantities specified in the contract, documentary collection or documentary letter of credit? ❏

6. Does the value of the goods (unit price and total price) correspond exactly to the values specified in the contract, documentary collection or documentary letter of credit? ❏

7. Does the invoice amount not exceed the amount of the contract, documentary collection or documentary letter of credit? ❏

8. Is the invoice free of any unauthorized charges? ❏

9. Does the currency used in pricing in the invoice match that of the contract, documentary collection or documentary letter of credit? ❏

10. Does the invoice state the delivery terms (e.g., CIF, EXW)? ❏

11. Do the delivery terms stated in the invoice match those specified in the contract, documentary collection or documentary letter of credit? ❏

12. If required by the contract, documentary collection or documentary letter of credit, is the invoice signed? ❏

13. If required by the contract or documentary letter of credit, does the invoice bear proper certifications, authorizations, or legalizations? ❏

14. If required by the contract or documentary letter of credit, does the invoice contain any special marks, numbers, or other notations? ❏

The Transport Document

 SELLER BUYER ADVISING BANK ISSUING BANK

1. Does the transport document contain the correct consignee name and address as specified in the credit? ❑

2. Does the transport document contain an "on board" notation? ❑

3. Does the transport document contain a notation naming the vessel? ❑

4. Does the transport document contain a notation of the on board date? ❑

5. Does the transport document name the correct port of loading and port of destination as stipulated in the documentary credit? ❑

6. Is the transport document "clean" (without notations for shortage, loss, or damage)? ❑

7. If the transport document states "on deck" stowage, it is allowed by the credit? ❑

8. If required by the documentary credit, is the "notify address" listed? ❑

9. Was the transport document issued within the period specified in the documentary credit? ❑

10. Is the full set of originals being presented? ❑

11. Is the transport document *not* a charter party document, *unless* authorized by the documentary credit? ❑

12. Is the transport document *not* a forwarder's transport document, *unless* authorized by the documentary credit? ❑

13. Is the quantity and description of the goods consistent with that contained in the documentary credit? ❑

14. Are the marks and numbers on the transport document consistent with those on other documents? ❑

15. Are the freight payments terms consistent with those stipulated in the documentary credit? ❑

16. Does the transport document meet the stipulations of the documentary credit with regard to transshipment? ❑

17. Does the transport document meet all other stipulations of the documentary credit? ❑

Checklist for the Seller

SELLER (IN DOCUMENTARY LETTER OF CREDIT PAYMENT TRANSACTIONS)

BANK DOCUMENT CHECKLIST PRIOR TO SUBMISSION TO THE BANK

1. Do all the documents refer to the same order and the same credit? ❑
2. Are the documents present in the correct number and in complete sets? ❑
3. Is the name and address of the shipper correct? ❑
4. Is the name and address of the buyer/consignee correct? ❑
5. Is the issuer name and address correct? ❑
6. Does the description of the goods, unit price, and total price match the description in the credit? ❑
7. Is the description of the goods, unit price, and total price consistent from document to document? ❑
8. Does the invoice total not exceed the amount available in the credit? ❑
9. Is the country of origin of the goods listed and as specified in the documentary credit? ❑
10. Is the country of destination of the goods listed and as specified in the documentary credit? ❑
11. Do all the dimensions, weights, number of units, and markings agree on all documents? ❑
12. Have all the necessary documents been certified or legalized? ❑
13. Are the invoice numbers and documentary credit numbers correct and listed in the proper places? ❑
14. Is the bill of exchange legally signed? ❑
15. Does the bill of exchange have to be endorsed? ❑
16. Does the insurance document cover all the risks specified in the credit? ❑
17. Has the insurance document been properly endorsed? ❑
18. Are the documents being presented within the validity period? ❑
19. Is the bill of lading "clean," without notations? ❑
20. If the bill of lading has an "on deck" notation, does the credit allow for it? ❑
21. If the bill of lading is a charter party bill, does the credit allow for it? ❑
22. Is the notify address in the bill of lading correct? ❑
23. Is the bill of lading endorsed? ❑
24. Are corrections properly initialed by their originator? ❑

Inspection Certificate

 SELLER BUYER ADVISING BANK ISSUING BANK

1. Does the inspection certificate contain key details of the consignor, consignee, and inspection entity? ❑
2. Does the inspection certificate contain a description of the goods that is consistent with the description of goods in the credit? ❑
3. Does the inspection certificate contain the date of the inspection? ❑
4. Does the inspection certificate contain a statement of the sampling methodology? ❑
5. Does the certificate contain a statement of the inspection results? ❑
6. Does the inspection certificate contain the name, signature, and/or stamp or seal of the inspecting entity? ❑

Insurance Document

 SELLER BUYER ADVISING BANK ISSUING BANK

1. Was the insurance document issued as either a policy or as a certificate as stipulated in the credit? ❑
2. Is the insurance document issued and signed by an insurance carrier, underwriter, or their agent (*not* by a broker)? ❑
3. Does the insurance document cover all the risks specified in the credit? ❑
4. Does the insurance document cover the risks resulting from a) the particular mode of shipment, b) the transport route, or c) reloading or "on deck" storage, etc.? ❑
5. Does the insurance document indicate that cover is effective at the latest from the date of loading of the goods on board or the taking in charge of the goods by the carrier, as indicated by the transport document? ❑
6. Is the information in the insurance document concerning mode of transport and transport route consistent with the documentary credit? ❑
7. Does the document specify coverage for at least 110 percent of either a) the CIF or CIP value of the shipment, or, if that information is not provided, b) the amount of the payment, acceptance or negotiation specified in the documentary credit, or c) the gross amount of the invoice? ❑
8. Is the currency of the insurance document consistent with the credit? ❑
9. Have all issued originals of the document been presented? ❑
10. If endorsement is required, is the document properly endorsed? ❑

Glossary

THE FOLLOWING TERMS are excerpted from the *Dictionary of International Trade*, also by Edward G. Hinkelman and published by World Trade Press.

ACCEPTED DRAFT A bill of exchange accepted by the drawee (acceptor) by signing it (acceptance) on its face. In doing so, the drawee commits to pay the bill upon presentation at maturity.

ACCEPTING BANK A bank that by signing a time draft accepts responsibility to pay when the draft becomes due. In this case, the bank is the drawee (party asked to pay the draft) but only becomes the acceptor (party accepting responsibility to pay) upon acceptance (signing the draft). See ACCEPTANCE; BILL OF EXCHANGE.

ACCEPTOR The party that signs a draft or obligation, thereby agreeing to pay the stated sum at maturity. See ACCEPTANCE; BILL OF EXCHANGE.

ADVICE (banking/letters of credit) The forwarding of a letter of credit, or an amendment to a letter of credit to the seller, or beneficiary of the credit, by the advising bank (typically the seller's bank).
The term "advice" connotes several types of forms used in the banking field. Generally speaking, an advice is a form of letter that relates or acknowledges a certain activity or result with regard to a relations with a bank. Examples include credit advice, debit advice, advice of payment, and advice of execution. In commercial transactions, information on a business transaction such as shipment of goods.

ADVISING BANK The bank (also referred to as the seller's or exporter's bank) that receives a letter of credit or amendment to a letter of credit from the issuing bank (the buyer's bank) and forwards it to the beneficiary (exporter/seller) of the credit.

AFTER DATE A notation used on financial instruments (such as drafts or bills of exchange) to fix the maturity date as a fixed number of days past the date of drawing of the draft. For example, if a draft stipulates "60 days after date," it means that the draft is due (payable) 60 days after the date it was drawn. This has the effect of fixing the date of maturity of the draft independently of the date of acceptance of the draft. See ACCEPTANCE; BILL OF EXCHANGE.

AFTER SIGHT A notation on a draft that indicates that payment is due a fixed number of days after the draft has been presented to the drawee. For example, "30 days after sight" means that the drawee has 30 days from the date of presentation of the draft to make payment. See BILL OF EXCHANGE.

AIR WAYBILL (also airbill) (shipping) A shipping document used by airlines for air freight. It is a contract for carriage that includes conditions of carriage including such items as limits of liability and claims procedures. The air waybill also contains shipping instructions to airlines, a description of the commodity, and applicable transportation charges. Air waybills are used by many truckers as through documents for coordinated air/truck service.
Air waybills are not negotiable. The airline industry has adopted a standard formatted air waybill that accommodates both domestic and international traffic. The standard document was designed to enhance the application of modern computerized systems to air freight processing for both the carrier and the shipper. See BILL OF LADING; NEGOTIABLE.

AMENDMENT (law/general) An addition, deletion or change in a legal document. (banking/letters of credit) A change in the terms and conditions of a letter of credit (e.g., extension of the letter of credit's validity period, shipping deadline, etc.), usually to meet the needs of the seller. The seller requests an amendment and if the buyer agrees, the buyer instructs the bank (the issuing bank) to issue the amendment. The issuing bank informs the seller's bank (the advising bank) who then notifies the seller of the amendment. In the case of irrevocable letters of credit, amendments may only be made with the agreement of all parties to the transaction.

ARRIVAL NOTICE (shipping) A notice furnished to the consignee and shipping broker alerting them to the projected arrival of freight and its availability for pickup.

ASSIGNMENT (law/shipping/banking) The transfer of rights, title, interest, and benefits of a contract or financial instrument to a third party.
(banking/letters of credit) The beneficiary of a letter of credit is entitled to assign all claims to all or any part of the proceeds to a third party. Usually the beneficiary informs the issuing or advising bank that the claims or partial claims under the letter of credit were assigned and asks the bank to advise the assignee (third party) that it has acknowledged the assignment. The validity of the assignment is not dependent on bank approval. In contrast, the transfer requires the agreement of the nominated bank. An assignment is possible regardless of whether the letter of credit is transferable.

AT SIGHT (banking) A financial instrument that is payable upon presentation or demand. A bill of exchange may be made payable, for example, at sight or after sight, which (respectively) means it is payable upon presentation or demand or within a particular period after demand is made. See BILL OF EXCHANGE.

AUTHENTICATION See CERTIFICA-TION.

AVAILABILITY (banking/letters of credit) In letters of credit, refers to the availability of documents in exchange for payment of the amount stated in the letter of credit. Availability options are: (1) By sight payment: payment on receipt of the documents by the issuing bank or the bank nominated in the letter of credit. (2) By deferred payment: payment after a period specified in the letter of credit, often calculated as number of days after the date of presentation of the documents or after the shipping date. (3) By acceptance: acceptance of a draft (to be presented together with other documents) by the issuing bank or by the bank nominated in the letter of credit,

and the payment thereof at maturity. (4) By negotiation: meaning the giving of value by the nominated bank to the beneficiary for the documents presented, subject to receipt of cover from the issuing bank.

BANK ACCEPTANCE (banking) A bill of exchange drawn on or accepted by a bank to pay specific bills for one of its customers when the bill becomes due. Depending on the bank's creditworthiness, the acceptance becomes a financial instrument that can be discounted for immediate payment. See BILL OF EXCHANGE.

BANK DRAFT (banking) A check drawn by one bank against funds deposited to its account in another bank.

BEARER (general) The person in possession. (banking/finance/law/shipping) A person who possesses a bearer document and who is entitled to payment of funds or transfer of title to property on presentation of the document to the payee or transferor. A buyer, for example, who presents bearer documents of title (such as a bill of lading) to a shipper that transported the goods is entitled to receive the shipment. A seller who presents to a bank a negotiable instrument, such as a check, that is payable to the bearer is entitled to payment of the funds. See BEARER DOCUMENT; ENDORSEMENT.

BEARER DOCUMENT (banking/finance/law/shipping) A negotiable instrument, commercial paper, document of title, or security that is issued payable or transferable on demand to the individual who holds the instrument, or one that is endorsed in blank. A bearer document authorizes the payment of funds or the transfer of property to the bearer when the bearer presents the document to the person, such as a bank or a shipper, that is holding the funds or property. See BLANK ENDORSEMENT, BEARER; ENDORSEMENT.

BENEFICIARY (banking/letter of credit) The individual or company in whose favor a letter of credit is opened.
(insurance) The person or legal entity named to receive the proceeds or benefits of an insurance policy.

BILL OF EXCHANGE (banking) An unconditional order in writing, signed by a person (drawer) such as a buyer, and addressed to another person (drawee), typically a bank, ordering the drawee to pay a stated sum of money to yet another person (payee), often a seller, on demand or at a fixed or determinable future time. The most common versions of a bill of exchange are: (1) A draft, wherein the drawer instructs the drawee to pay a certain amount to a named person, usually in payment for the transfer of goods or services. Sight drafts are payable when presented. Time drafts (also called usance drafts) are payable at a future fixed (specific) date or determinable (30, 60, 90 days etc.) date. Time drafts are used as a financing tool (as with Documents against Acceptance, D/A terms) to give the buyer time to pay for the purchase. (2) A promissory note, wherein the issuer promises to pay a certain amount.

BILL OF LADING (shipping) A document issued by a carrier to a shipper, signed by the captain, agent, or owner of a vessel, furnishing written evidence regarding receipt of the goods (cargo), the conditions on which transportation is made (contract of carriage), and the engagement to deliver goods at the prescribed port of destination to the lawful holder of the bill of lading. A bill of lading is, therefore, both a receipt for merchandise and a contract to deliver it as freight.

BLANK ENDORSEMENT (law/banking/shipping) The signature or endorsement of a person or firm on any negotiable instrument (such as a check, draft, or bill of lading), usually on the reverse of the document, without designating another person to whom the endorsement is made. The document therefore becomes bearer paper. In shipping, for example, the holder of a blank endorsed bill of lading can take possession of the shipment. See ENDORSEMENT; BEARER DOCUMENT.

CERTIFICATE OF ANALYSIS A document issued by a recognized organization or governmental authority confirming the quality and composition of goods listed in the certificate. Certificates of analysis are often required by authorities in importing countries for animal and plant products for consumption and for pharmaceuticals.

CERTIFICATE OF INSPECTION A document certifying that merchandise (such as perishable goods) was in good condition at the time of inspection, usually immediately prior to shipment. Pre-shipment inspection is a requirement for importation of goods into many developing countries. Often referred to as a certificate of analysis.

CERTIFICATE OF ORIGIN (customs) A document attesting to the country of origin of goods. A certificate of origin is often required by the customs authorities of a country as part of the entry process. Such certificates are usually obtained through an official or quasiofficial organization in the country of origin such as a consular office or local chamber of commerce. A certificate of origin may be required even though the commercial invoice contains the information.

CERTIFICATE OF WEIGHT (shipping) A document stating the weight of a shipment.

CERTIFICATION (LEGALIZATION or AUTHENTICATION) Official certification of the authenticity of signatures or documents in connection with documents such as certificates of origin, commercial invoices, etc. by chambers of commerce, consulates, and similar authorities.

CLAUSED BILL OF LADING (shipping) Notations on bills of lading that specify deficient condition(s) of the goods and/or the packaging.

CLEAN BILL OF LADING (shipping) A bill of lading receipted by the carrier for goods received in "apparent good order and condition," without damages or other irregularities, and without the notation "Shippers Load and Count."

CLEAN COLLECTION (banking) A collection in which the demand for payment (such as a draft) is presented without additional documents. See BILL OF EXCHANGE.

CLEAN DRAFT (banking) A sight or time draft that has no other documents attached to it. This is to be distinguished from documentary draft. See BILL OF EXCHANGE.

CLEAN LETTER OF CREDIT (banking) A letter of credit against which the beneficiary of the credit may draw a bill of exchange without presentation of documents.

CLEAN ON BOARD BILL OF LADING (shipping) A document evidencing cargo laden aboard a vessel with no exceptions as to cargo condition or quantity.

C O L L E C T I O N (general) The presentation for payment of an obligation and the payment thereof.

(banking) The receipt of money for presentation of a draft or check for payment at the bank on which it was drawn or presentation of any item for deposit at the place at which it is payable.

C O M B I N E D   B I L L   O F   L A D I N G (shipping) A bill of lading covering a shipment of goods by more than one mode of transportation.

C O M B I N E D   T R A N S P O R T (shipping) Consignment (shipment) sent by means of various modes of transport, such as by rail and by ocean.

C O M B I N E D   T R A N S P O R T   B I L L   O F   L A D I N G (shipping) A bill of lading covering a shipment of goods by more than one mode of transportation.

C O M M E R C I A L   I N V O I C E (general) A document identifying the seller and buyer of goods or services, identifying numbers such as invoice number, date, shipping date, mode of transport, delivery and payment terms, and a complete listing and description of the goods or services being sold including quantities, prices, and discounts. (customs) A commercial invoice is often used by governments to determine the transaction value of goods to assess of customs duties and to prepare consular documentation. Governments using the commercial invoice to control imports often specify its form, content, number of copies, language to be used, and other characteristics.

C O N F I R M E D   L E T T E R   O F   C R E D I T A letter of credit that contains a guarantee on the part of both the issuing and advising banks of payment to the seller so long as the terms and conditions of the letter of credit are satisfied.

C O N S I G N E E (shipping) The person or firm named in a freight contract to whom goods have been shipped or turned over for care.

C O N S O L I D A T O R ' S   B I L L   O F   L A D I N G (shipping) A bill of lading issued by a consolidating freight forwarder to a shipper.

C O N S U L A R   I N V O I C E (customs) An invoice covering a shipment of goods certified (usually in triplicate) by the consul of the country for which the merchandise is

destined. This invoice is used by customs officials of the country of entry to verify the value, quantity, country of origin, and nature of the merchandise imported. See C O M M E R C I A L   I N V O I C E .

D I S C R E P A N C I E S (banking/letters of credit) The noncompliance of documents with the terms and conditions of a letter of credit. Information (or missing information or missing documents/papers, etc.) in the documents submitted under a letter of credit, that: (1) is not consistent with its terms and conditions; (2) is inconsistent with other documents submitted; (3) does not meet the requirements of the Uniform Customs and Practice for Documentary Credits (UCPDC).

D O C U M E N T A R Y   C O L L E C T I O N A method of effecting payment whereby the exporter/seller ships goods to the buyer, but instructs a bank to collect a certain sum from the importer/buyer in exchange for the transfer of title, shipping, and other documentation enabling the importer/buyer to take possession of the goods.

D O C U M E N T A R Y   L E T T E R   O F   C R E D I T See L E T T E R   O F   C R E D I T .

D O C U M E N T A T I O N (general) All or any of the financial and commercial documents relating to a transaction. Documents in an international trade transaction may include: commercial invoice, consular invoice, customs invoice, certificate of origin, bill of lading, inspection certificates, bills of exchange and others.

(customs) The documents required by the customs authority of a country to effect entry of merchandise into the country.

(shipping) The function of receiving, matching, reviewing, and preparing all the paperwork necessary to effect the shipment of cargo. This includes bills of lading, dock receipts, export declarations, manifests, etc.

D R A F T See B I L L   O F   E X C H A N G E .

E L E C T R O N I C   D A T A   I N T E R C H A N G E (E D I) The electronic exchange of data (especially documents) between computers using telecommunications. EDI refers to different data systems and standards.

E N D O R S E M E N T (banking/law) (In UK, indorsement) The act of a person who is the holder of a negotiable instrument in signing his or her name on the back of that instrument, thereby transferring title or ownership. An endorsement may be made in favor of another individual or legal entity, resulting in a transfer of the property to that other individual or legal entity.

(1) A *blank endorsement* is the writing of only the endorser's name on the negotiable instrument without designating another person to whom the endorsement is made, and with the implied understanding that the instrument is payable to the bearer.

(2) A *collection endorsement* is one that restricts payment of the endorsed instrument to purposes of deposit or collection.

(3) A *conditional endorsement* is one that limits the time at which the instrument can be paid or further transferred or that requires the occurrence of an event before the instrument is payable.

(4) A *restrictive endorsement* is one that directs a specific payment of the instrument, such as for deposit or collection only, and that precludes any other transfer.

FINANCIAL INSTRUMENT (banking/ finance) A document that has monetary value or is evidence of a financial transaction. Examples include: checks, bonds, stock certificates, bills of exchange, promissory notes, and bills of lading.

HOUSE AIR WAYBILL (HAWB) (shipping) A bill of lading issued by a freight forwarder for consolidated air freight shipments. In documentary letter of credit transactions HAWBs are treated exactly the same as conventional air waybills, provided they indicate that the issuer itself assumes the liability as carrier or is acting as the agent of a named carrier, or if the credit expressly permits the acceptance of a HAWB. See AIR WAYBILL; BILL OF LADING.

INCOTERMS 2000 A codification of international rules for the uniform interpretation of common contract clauses in export/import transactions. "INCOTERMS" is an acronym for INternational COmmercial TERMS. Developed and issued by the International Chamber of Commerce (ICC) in Paris. The version which is currently valid is Publication No. 560 from 2000. The thirteen Incoterms 2000 are:

(1) Ex Works (EXW), (...named place)

(2) Free Carrier (FCA), (...named place)

(3) Free Alongside Ship (FAS), (...named port of shipment)

(4) Free On Board (FOB), (...named port of shipment)

(5) Cost and Freight (CFR), (...named port of destination)

(6) Cost, Insurance and Freight (CIF), (...named port of destination)

(7) Carriage Paid To (CPT), (...named port of destination)

(8) Carriage and Insurance Paid To (CIP), (...named port of destination)

(9) Delivered At Frontier (DAF), (...named place)

(10) Delivered Ex Ship (DES), (...named port of destination)

(11) Delivered Ex Quay (DEQ), (...named port of destination)

(12) Delivered Duty Unpaid (DDU), (...named port of destination)

(13) Delivered Duty Paid (DDP), (...named port of destination)

For a comprehensive and illustrated guide to Incoterms 2000 see the *Dictionary of International Trade, 4th Edition*, also by World Trade Press. For a copy of ICC publication No. 560 contact ICC Publishing, Inc., 156 Fifth Avenue, New York, NY 10010 USA; Tel: (212) 206-1150; Fax: (212) 633-6025 or the International Chamber of Commerce (ICC), 38, Cours Albert 1er, 75008 Paris, France; Tel: [33] (1) 49-53-28-28; Fax: [33] (1) 49-53-29-42.

INSPECTION CERTIFICATE A document confirming that goods have been inspected for conformity to a set of industry, customer, government, or carrier specifications. Inspection certificates are generally obtained from independent, neutral testing organizations.

INSURANCE CERTIFICATE (insurance) A document indicating the type and amount of insurance coverage in force on a particular shipment. Used to assure the consignee that insurance is provided to cover potential loss of, or damage to, the cargo while in transit. See "Special Documents" on page 100.

INSURANCE POLICY (insurance) Broadly, the entire written contract of insurance. More specifically, the basic written or printed document, as well as the coverage forms and endorsement added to it.

INVOICE A document identifying the seller

and buyer of goods or services, identifying numbers such as invoice number, date, shipping date, mode of transport, delivery and payment terms, and a complete listing and description of the goods or services being sold including quantities, prices, and discounts. See COMMERCIAL INVOICE.

IRREVOCABLE LETTER OF CREDIT (banking) A letter of credit that cannot be amended or canceled without prior mutual consent of all parties to the credit. Such a letter of credit guarantees payment by the bank to the exporter/seller (beneficiary) provided the beneficiary complies with all stipulated conditions. This credit cannot be changed or canceled without the consent of both the buyer and the seller.

ISSUANCE DATE OF THE DOCUMENTS (shipping) Unless otherwise stipulated in a transport document, the date of issuance is deemed to be the date of shipment or loading on board of the goods.

ISSUING BANK The buyer's bank that opens a letter of credit at the request of the buyer, in favor of the beneficiary (exporter/seller). Also called the buyer's bank or the opening bank. See also ADVISING BANK; NEGOTIATING BANK.

LETTER OF CREDIT (banking) A document issued by a bank stating its commitment to pay someone (supplier/exporter/seller) a stated amount of money on behalf of a buyer (importer) so long as the seller meets the specific terms and conditions of the credit. Letters of credit are more formally called documentary letters of credit because the banks handling the transaction deal in documents as opposed to goods. See "Documentary Letters of Credit" on page 81.

NEGOTIABLE BILL OF LADING (shipping) A bill of lading transferable by endorsement. There are three possibilities: (1) to XY & Co. or their order; (2) to the order of XY & Co.; and (3) to order, without the name of the party. In the latter case the bill remains to the order of the shipper until he endorses it.
These types of bills of lading are usually endorsed on the reverse. The opposite of a negotiable bill of lading is the straight bill of lading See BILL OF LADING; EN-DORSEMENT.

NEGOTIABLE INSTRUMENT (law/banking/shipping) A written document (instrument) that can be transferred merely by endorsement (signing) or delivery. Checks, bills of exchange, bills of lading, and warehouse receipts (if marked negotiable), and promissory notes are examples of negotiable instruments.
(USA) The Uniform Negotiable Instruments Act states: "An instrument, to be negotiable, must conform to the following requirements: (1) it must be in writing and signed by the maker or drawer; (2) it must contain an unconditional promise or order to pay a certain sum in money; (3) it must be payable on demand, or at a fixed or determinable future time; (4) it must be payable to order or to bearer; and (5) where the instrument is addressed to a drawee, he must be named or otherwise indicated therein with reasonable certainty."

NEGOTIATION (banking) (1) The action by which a negotiable instrument is circulated (bought and sold) from one holder to another. (2) In letter of credit transactions, the examination of the seller's documentation by the bank to determine if they comply with the terms and conditions of the credit.

NON-NEGOTIABLE (law/banking) Not transferable from one person to another. Usually refers to the transferability of a title document (e.g., non-negotiable bill of lading). Possession of a non-negotiable title document alone does not entitle the holder to receive the goods named therein (e.g., non-negotiable sea waybill, air waybill, forwarder's receipt, etc.). See NEGOTIABLE; NEGOTIABLE INSTRUMENT.

OCEAN BILL OF LADING A receipt for cargo and a contract for transportation between a shipper and the ocean carrier. It may also be used as an instrument of ownership (negotiable bill of lading) that can be bought, sold, or traded while the goods are in transit. To be used in this manner, it must be a negotiable "order" bill of lading.

ORIGINAL DOCUMENTS (banking/letters of credit) Unless otherwise stated in the letter of credit, the requirement for an original document may also be satisfied by the presentation of documents produced or appearing to have been produced: (1)

reprographically, (2) by automated or computerized systems, or (3) as carbon copies, and marked as "originals" and where necessary appearing to be signed.

PACKING LIST A document prepared by the shipper listing the kinds and quantities of merchandise in a particular shipment. A copy is usually sent to the consignee to assist in checking the shipment when received. Also referred to as a bill of parcels.

PHYTOSANITARY INSPECTION CERTIFICATE A certificate, issued by the government authority of an exporting nation to satisfy import regulations of foreign countries, indicating that an export shipment has been inspected and is free from harmful pests and plant diseases.

PRO FORMA INVOICE An invoice provided by a supplier prior to a sale or shipment of merchandise, informing the buyer of the kinds and quantities of goods to be sent, their value, and important specifications (weight, size, and similar characteristics). A pro forma invoice is used: (1) as a preliminary invoice together with a quotation; (2) for customs purposes in connection with shipments of samples, advertising material, etc.

RAIL WAYBILL (shipping) Freight document that indicates goods have been received for shipment by rail. A duplicate is given to the shipper as a receipt for acceptance of the goods (also called duplicate waybill). See BILL OF LADING.

REMITTANCE (banking) Funds forwarded from one person to another as payment for bought items or services purchased.

REVOCABLE LETTER OF CREDIT (banking) A letter of credit which can be canceled or altered by the drawee (buyer) after it has been issued by the drawee's bank. Due to the low level of security of this type of credit, they are extremely rare in practice.

SEA WAYBILL (shipping) A non-negotiable transport document for carriage of goods by sea. The sea waybill indicates the "on board" loading of the goods and can be used in cases where no ocean bill of lading, (i.e., no document of title) is required. For receipt of the goods, presentation of the sea waybill by the consignee named therein is not required, which

can speed up processing at the port of destination.

SHIPMENT Except as otherwise provided, cargo tendered by one shipper, on one bill of lading, from one point of departure, for one consignee, to one destination, at one time, via a single port of discharge.

SIGHT DRAFT (banking) A financial instrument payable upon presentation or demand. A bill of exchange may be made payable, for example, at sight or after sight, which means it is payable upon presentation or demand, or within a particular period after demand is made. See BILL OF EXCHANGE.

STRAIGHT BILL OF LADING (shipping) A non-negotiable bill of lading that designates a consignee who is to receive the goods and that obligates the carrier to deliver the goods to that consignee only. A straight bill of lading cannot be transferred by endorsement. See BILL OF LADING.

SWIFT (banking) An acronym for Society for Worldwide Interbank Funds Transfer.

TENOR (banking) The maturity date of a financial instrument. Usually 30, 60, 90 days, etc.

TRANSFERABLE LETTER OF CREDIT (banking) A letter of credit where the beneficiary specified in the credit has the option of instructing his bank to transfer the credit fully or in part to another beneficiary. This credit allows the supplier to transfer all or part of the proceeds of the letter of credit to a second beneficiary, usually the ultimate supplier of the goods.

VALIDITY The time period for which a letter of credit is valid. After receiving notice of a letter of credit opened in his/her behalf, the exporter/seller/beneficiary must meet all the requirements of the credit within the period of validity. See LETTER OF CREDIT.

WAYBILL (shipping) A document prepared by a transportation line at the point of a shipment, showing the point of origin, destination, route, consignor, consignee, description of shipment, and amount charged for the transportation service, and forwarded with the shipment, or direct by mail, to the agent at the transfer point or waybill destination. See BILL OF LADING; AIR WAYBILL; OCEAN BILL OF LADING.

CHAPTER 14

Resources

On-Line Resources

http://www.aeilogistics.com This is a fee-based worldwide document resource guide developed by one of the world's largest logistics/freight-forwarding firms.

http://www.trade.gov/td/tic/ U.S. government managed website provides documentation and trade information for many countries. Search by country, subject, or trade agreement.

http://exportsource.gc.ca/dindex2_e.html Canadian managed website contains detailed information for a number of countries.

http://www.fsis.usda.gov/OFO/export/explib.htm#cr_alpha This U.S. Dept. of Agriculture website is an invaluable resource providing a great deal of country by country information.

http://www.austrade.gov.au/GettingReadyToExport/ Click on the Steps for Successful Exporting and then look under the 2nd step. Directed toward Australians.

http://mkaccdb.eu.int/ The European Union has useful information on its Market Access Database website. Some functions are limited if you are view from outside of the EU.

Books

Training Handbook on Export Documentation. Geneva: International Trade Center, 1994.

Brand, Ronald A. (ed.) *Fundamentals of International Business Transactions: Documents.* Dordrecht, Netherlands: Kluwer Law International, 2000.

Cheng, Chia-Jiu, *Basic Documents on International Trade Law Third Revised Edition.* Dordrecht, Netherlands: Kluwer Law International, 1998.

Johnson, Thomas E. *Export/Import Procedures and Documentation.* New York: Amacom, 1997.

Export Documentation Handbook. New York: Dun & Bradstreet International, 1977.

Hinkelman, Edward G. *Dictionary of International Trade, 4th Edition.* Novato, CA USA: World Trade Press, 2000.

Forms Software

Unz & Co.; 700 Central Avenue; New Providence, NJ 07974-1139 USA; Tel: (800) 631-3098; Fax: (908) 665-7866; E-mail: unzco@unzco.com; www.unzco.com

Shipping Solutions; PO Box 22267; Eagan, MN 55122 USA; Tel: (651) 905-1727; Fax: (651) 905-1827; E-mail: info@intermart-inc.com; www.shipsolutions.com

Smart Zone/Foreign-Trade Zone; 2062 Oldshell Road; Mobile, Alabama 36607; Tel: (334) 471-6725; Fax: (334) 471-6727; E-mail: SmartZone@ftzsoftware.com; www.ftzsoftware.com

Organizations

Trade Documentation Center; UNCTAD/WTO; Palais des Nations; 1211 Geneva 10; Switzerland; Tel: [41] (22) 730-0231; Fax: [41] (22) 730-0802; E-mail: tdc@intracen.org; www.intracen.org/tdc/welcome.htm